Also by Linda Bird Francke

Ground Zero: The Gender Wars in the Military
Growing Up Divorced
The Ambivalence of Abortion

ON THE ROAD
WITH FRANCIS OF ASSISI

Random House · New York

*To Kate
Merry Christmas
Patti
200x*

ON THE ROAD
WITH FRANCIS OF ASSISI

A Timeless Journey Through Umbria and Tuscany, and Beyond

LINDA BIRD FRANCKE

For Oona
And all the places we will travel together

CONTENTS

INTRODUCTION

I have wanted to write a book about St. Francis and St. Clare since my husband and I first went to Assisi some twelve years ago to see the Giottos. It was St. Francis's basilica at one end of Assisi, and St. Clare's pink and white basilica at the other end that captivated me, along with the story I heard there from a Franciscan sister that Francis had died in Clare's arms. That turned out to be historically incorrect, but no matter. I was hooked.

Other book projects intervened, and it was not until 2002 that I could return to Francis and Clare. A search of Amazon.com, however, revealed so many books about Assisi's saints that I was discouraged. My agent, Lynn Nesbit, suggested a travelogue format, which, though a great idea, essentially eliminated Clare, who entered a convent at eighteen—and never came out.

Francis, by contrast, crisscrossed Italy for twenty years, preaching peace and repentance in hill towns and valleys and withdrawing to the solitude of mountaintop hermitages, an astonishing number of which exist to this day. We followed him virtually everywhere he went, using his medieval biographies as our guidebooks and telling his story through the places we visited.

Several of those books were written by his contemporaries and fellow friars, the most immediate being Brother Thomas of Celano, whose official biography of Francis was completed in 1229, just three years after Francis died, and expanded in 1246. We also drew from other contemporary, thirteenth-century biographies, including *The Legend of the Three Companions, The Life of St. Francis of Assisi* by St. Bonaventure, and the fourteenth-century epic *The Little Flowers of St. Francis.*

Our journey with Francis was a glorious one, taking us to lakes and forests and twelfth-century churches and hermitages we never would have gone to without him. The art was unparalleled, the scenery spectacular, and the food, delicious.

Like Francis's, our adventure started in Assisi. I hope you will come along with us.

LINDA BIRD FRANCKE
Sagaponack, N.Y.
March 2005

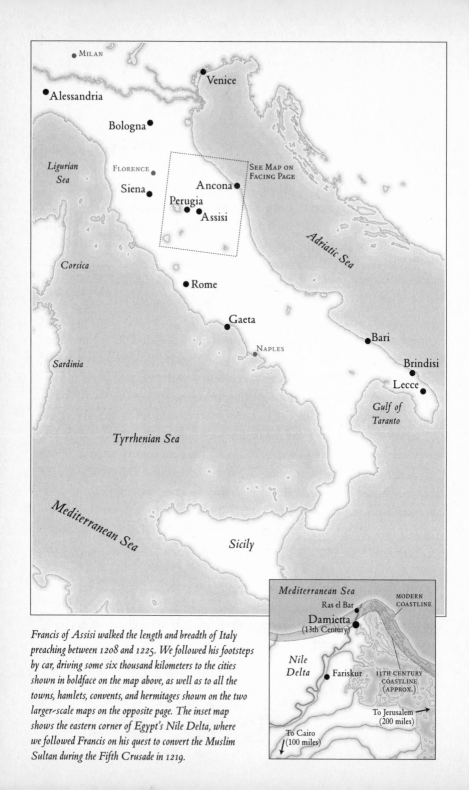

Francis of Assisi walked the length and breadth of Italy preaching between 1208 and 1225. We followed his footsteps by car, driving some six thousand kilometers to the cities shown in boldface on the map above, as well as to all the towns, hamlets, convents, and hermitages shown on the two larger-scale maps on the opposite page. The inset map shows the eastern corner of Egypt's Nile Delta, where we followed Francis on his quest to convert the Muslim Sultan during the Fifth Crusade in 1219.

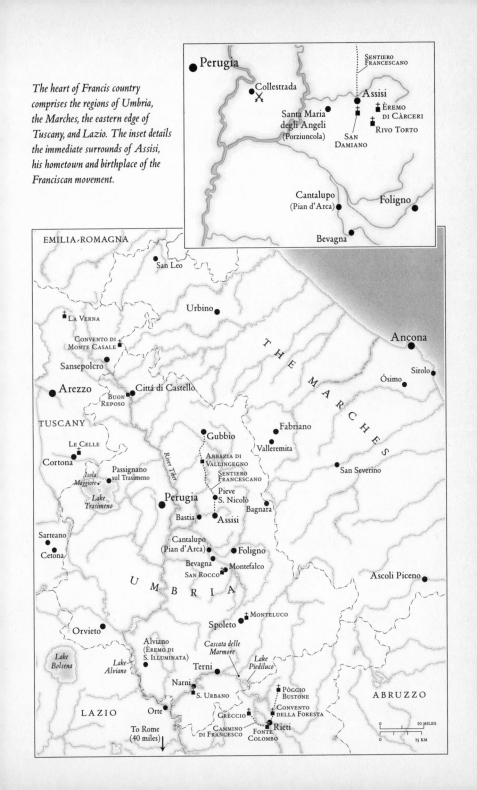

The heart of Francis country comprises the regions of Umbria, the Marches, the eastern edge of Tuscany, and Lazio. The inset details the immediate surrounds of Assisi, his hometown and birthplace of the Franciscan movement.

Inset:

Perugia
Collestrada
Assisi
Santa Maria degli Angeli (Porziuncola)
ÈREMO DI CÀRCERI
SAN DAMIANO
RIVO TORTO
SENTIERO FRANCESCANO
Cantalupo (Pian d'Arca)
Foligno
Bevagna

Main map:

EMILIA-ROMAGNA

San Leo

Urbino

La Verna

CONVENTO DI MONTE CASALE

Sansepolcro

THE MARCHES

Ancona

Arezzo
BUON REPOSO
Città di Castello

Sìrolo
Òsimo

TUSCANY

Fabriano
Gubbio
Valleremita
ABBAZIA DI VALLINGEGNO
SENTIERO FRANCESCANO
San Severino

Le Celle
Cortona

River Tiber

Passignano sul Trasimeno
Isola Maggiore
Lake Trasimeno

Pieve S. Nicolò
Bagnara

Perugia
Bastia
Assisi

Sarteano
Cetona

Cantalupo (Pian d'Arca)
Foligno
Bevagna
SAN ROCCO
Montefalco

Ascoli Piceno

UMBRIA

Orvieto

Spoleto
MONTELUCO

Lake Bolsena

Alviano (EREMO DI S. ILLUMINATA)
Lake Alviano

Cascata delle Marmore
Terni
Lake Piediluco

Narni
S. URBANO
PÒGGIO BUSTONE
CONVENTO DELLA FORESTA

Orte
GRÉCCIO
FONTE COLOMBO
Rieti

ABRUZZO

LAZIO

To Rome (40 miles)

CAMMINO DI FRANCESCO

10 MILES

15 KM

ON THE ROAD
WITH FRANCIS OF ASSISI

I *Mozart Among the Giottos*

ASSISI, *where Francis and Clare are born and Francis spends his indulgent youth*

Assisi looks like an enchanted kingdom from the roads crisscrossing the Spoleto Valley. The small, medieval hill town hovers on the side of Mount Subasio, not so high as to seem inaccessible and not so low as to seem commonplace. The massive thirteenth-century Basilica of St. Francis rises above the city walls at the western end of the town and is visible from miles away, a luminous, milky beige by day, dramatically lit by night. The thirteenth-century Basilica of St. Clare lies farther down the hill, at the other end of Assisi, a smaller but no less imposing building whose striped façade of Subasio stone is pink and white.

The approach to Assisi is tantalizing. The road climbs and curves, bringing us closer to the town's walls, then circling us away. Up and up, then around, until we think that we must have missed Assisi altogether, that it was a fantasy after all, and then, finally, parking lots, one after another, filled with the jarring reality of cars and multinational tour buses.

My husband, Harvey, and I are just two of the close to five million people who visit Assisi each year. Most are clergy and pilgrims from all over the world who come to pray in the birthplace of Assisi's endearing—and enduring—native saints: Francis, Italy's patron saint and the founder of three ongoing Franciscan orders; and

Clare, Francis's spiritual companion and the first and sainted member of his Order of Poor Ladies. The combination makes Assisi second only to Rome as an Italian pilgrimage destination.

Almost as many visitors are tourists who come just to see the extraordinary early Renaissance frescoes in the Basilica of St. Francis by the leading artists of the time—the Sienese painters Simone Martini and Pietro Lorenzetti; the Florentine Cimabue, whose portrait of a stark, suffering St. Francis in the lower basilica is the world's most familiar, and accurate, image of the saint; and, of course, the incomparable early-fourteenth-century Florentine artist Giotto.

Giotto's twenty-eight larger-than-life frescoes of the life and legend of St. Francis in the upper church of his basilica are the most popular and perhaps the best-known narrative fresco cycle in the world. The familiar story marches around the walls: Francis, naked, confronting his father; Francis, preaching to the birds; Francis, expelling the devil from Arezzo; Clare bidding farewell to Francis after his death. On and on. One memorable evening my husband and I go to the basilica for a free, standing-room-only performance of the Mozart Requiem conducted by a Franciscan friar during which, unbelievably, I end up perching on a box of programs directly under Giotto's famous depiction of Francis receiving the stigmata.

Clare's basilica used to be just as brilliantly frescoed, but no more. A stern German bishop had the frescoes obliterated in the seventeenth century to protect the Franciscan nuns cloistered there from any contamination by visiting tourists. The austere interior walls of Clare's basilica still bear fragments of the frescoes, but they are all that remain, in the words of one Franciscan historian, "of a decoration that was once as abundant as that of San Francesco."

Frescoes aside, there is an overriding and alluring presence of Francis and Clare throughout the cobbled hill town. Both saints were born here, Francis in 1181 and Clare in 1193. And both are buried here, in their respective basilicas.

I spend time in both their crypts, sitting in a pew and listening to the muffled and unceasing sound of the rubber-soled shoes of tourists and pilgrims alike on the stone floors. Few of those moving quietly around Francis's stone sarcophagus know the dramatic events that overtook his remains after his death in 1226. His body was first kept in his parish church of San Giorgio, some say sitting up and visible to all, his eyes open and staring, his stigmata wounds prominently displayed.

Whether that is true or not, what is undeniable is that four years after his death and two years after he was officially canonized as a saint, his body was transferred under heavy guard to his semiconstructed basilica on what had been known in Assisi as the Hill of Hell, where criminals were executed, which was quickly renamed the Hill of Paradise.

The fear was so great that his body might be stolen for its limitless value as a source of relics by the marauding, rival hill town of Perugia, or simply by thieves, that his coffin was hidden, tunneled somewhere deep in the rock below the basilica, and the access to it sealed. His body would lie in that secret spot for the next six hundred years, until it was discovered in 1818.

Few of the people gathered in front of Clare's crystal coffin, looking somewhat uneasily at her realistic effigy clothed in a brown habit and a black cowl and displayed with darkened face, hands, and bare feet, are aware that her body, too, was kept at San Giorgio after her death in 1253, twenty-seven years after Francis died; that she, too, would be transferred, five years after her canonization in 1255, to her new pink and white basilica built on the foundations of San Giorgio. Clare, too, would lie hidden until her body was discovered in 1850 and placed some years later in the crypt.

I have always been fascinated by the relics and artifacts people leave behind after their deaths, like the army of terra-cotta warriors chosen by Emperor Qin Shi Huang in China, or the rather gruesome slice of a seventeenth-century callus I saw enshrined in a church in Guatemala from the remains of Pedro Hermano, a Franciscan friar so devout that he walked only on his knees. The relics left behind by the saints of Assisi are an odd lot as well, and understandably spare, in that Francis and Clare chose to own nothing in life. What relics there are, however, are bookmarks to their lives.

On a prior visit to Assisi, I had breezed through Francis's relics displayed in the lower church of his basilica, having no idea of their significance. On this visit, having immersed myself in his legend, I find them fascinating.

There is a letter Francis wrote in his own hand, one of only two in existence, giving his blessing to Brother Leo, one of his first and most faithful friars. Leo was so moved by the gift that he carried the increasingly fragile blessing next to his heart until he died, forty years later.

Francis's quest to convert the Muslim "Saracens" in the Holy Land, or be martyred trying, is represented by a silver-and-ivory horn given to him in 1219 by the sultan of Egypt. In what turned out to be a futile gesture, the horn was ceremoniously shown to Tariq Aziz, Iraq's deputy prime minister and a Chaldean Christian, as an icon of peace by the Franciscan leadership in February 2003, when he made a high-profile visit to Assisi during the countdown to the Iraq war.

Another treasured relic is the framed Franciscan Rule of Life, dated November 29, 1223, which Francis dictated to Brother Leo at a hermitage in the Rieti Valley and which still governs the Franciscan Order today. Also displayed are some linen cloths and a tunic, which by themselves seem forgettable but which actually represent one of the more curious aspects of Francis's life.

The linens were brought to Francis on his deathbed by a young widow, Lady Jacopa di Settesoli, with whom he often stayed in Rome and whom he had asked to see one last time before he died. (Her spontaneous arrival in Assisi without having received his message is considered a miracle.) Lady Jacopa is said by all his early biographers to have been "highly pious," so pious that Francis gave her the honorary title "Brother" Jacopa. As proof of her treasured role in his life, she is buried near him in his basilica, along with four of his early friars, Leo, Angelo, Masseo, and Clare's cousin Rufino.

Then there are his clothes—a patched, coarse gray habit, a pair of his tattered leather sandals, a piece of leather that is said to have covered the wound in his side from the stigmata. That seems a stretch. Could they really have been worn by him over eight hundred years ago? But perhaps I am being too rational instead of losing myself in the legend.

Still, I feel the same way looking at relics in the Cappelli di Santa Chiara in Clare's basilica. Another patched, uneven habit belonging to St. Francis and a tunic and cape that look far too big for the man Celano describes as of "medium height, closer to shortness." Then there is a white, full-length gown identified as belonging to Clare, but its proportions are grotesquely big, which she couldn't have been. She is described by Celano, who knew her and wrote her biography as well, as a "lovely young girl" in her early years, and there would have been little opportunity for her to gain weight in her later years. Clare fasted three full days a week until Francis ordered her not to, and then she ate little more than crusts of bread. As for the relic of her blond curls displayed in a glass box . . .

The religious relics are more convincing, among them a *breviàrio* or prayer book used by St. Francis and the *grata di S. Chiara*, a filigree iron screen with a central opening through which Clare and her cloistered "sisters" discreetly received communion from a male priest. Upstairs, in the glassed-in Chapel of the Blessed Sacrament, are the most important relics of all: another and undeniably authentic book of the Gospels used by Francis with an inscription by Brother Leo; and the original, six-foot-tall, colorfully painted Byzantine crucifix that, legend holds, spoke to Francis in the little ruined church of San Damiano in 1205 and started him on his life's mission.

I leave the relics, feeling rather guilty at having any uncharitable thoughts. I have grown very fond of Clare and Francis in the course of my research, and looking at some of their personal artifacts, especially their old clothes, makes me feel like a voyeur rummaging, uninvited, through their closets.

I don't have a clear, physical impression of Clare, but I do of Francis. To Celano's everlasting credit, he provides a detailed portrait of Francis in his biography of the saint. Beyond his short stature, which a later examination of his bones would pinpoint at only five foot three, three inches shorter than the average medieval Italian man, Francis had a "cheerful countenance," a "round" head, a face "a bit long," a forehead that was "smooth and low," "black" eyes, hair, and a beard, "not bushy." His eyebrows were "straight," his nose "symmetrical, thin and straight," his ears "upright, but small," his temples "smooth," his lips "small and thin," his teeth "set close together, even, and white."

Celano goes on to describe this appealing-sounding man as having a "slender" neck, "straight" shoulders, "short" arms, "slender" hands, "long" fingers, "extended" fingernails, "thin" legs, and "small" feet. "His skin was very delicate, his flesh very spare," Celano ends.

As we move on to see the other vestiges of Francis and Clare dotted around Assisi, it is extraordinary to think that we are walking on the same streets they did and seeing at least a few of the same medieval structures they did. The first-century Temple of Minerva in Assisi's central Piazza del Comune, for example, is clearly visible in one of Giotto's frescoes in Francis's basilica. Now a secular Franciscan church, the pagan temple in their time was used as the local jail.

Not surprisingly, some visitors to Assisi, and not only the many pilgrims and religious groups, feel a deeply spiritual presence on these streets. One friend of mine spent a month here after being treated for cancer and returned home in a newly serene state of mind. Another friend, a Muslim diplomat, told me he had experienced a spiritual awakening in Assisi second only to one he had felt during a pilgrimage to Mecca.

But another aspect of Assisi is undeniably commercial. As uncomfortable a reality as it might be, Francis, and to a lesser extent Clare, is a profitable industry for Assisi. The only one, in fact. Besides the many restaurants and hotels supported by visitors to Assisi, shops all over town sell multisized replicas of the San Damiano cross, religious medals with Francis's likeness on them, and his signature tau cross carved out of olive wood, which many visitors wear on leather cords around their necks.

Pottery shops sell ashtrays and plates with scenes from Francis's life on them, and at least one bakery sells "Pane di San Francesco," a local bread laced with the *limoncello* liqueur so popular in Italy. One shop even sells Umbrian wine with replicas of the saints by Simone Martini on the label—St. Francis on the red wine, St. Clare on the white.

The Francis we have come to know as a saint would have been disgusted by the money changing hands in his name. The Francis we know less well as a young man, however, would have welcomed the exchange and perhaps even profited from it.

Francis was born into an emerging merchant class to a mother who is thought to have been French and a successful Assisi fabric merchant, Pietro di Bernadone. Pietro amassed a sizable fortune bringing home embroidered silks and velvets and damasks from France, fashioning them into stylish clothes in his workshop, and selling them to the nobles and affluent burghers of Assisi. Consumerism was taking hold in the late twelfth century, a trend that marked the accumulation of fancy clothes and dress for status, rather than simpler clothes for warmth and practicality. Pietro added more to his coffers by investing in land around Assisi, amassing so many farms, orchards, meadows, and forests that it is believed he was one of the hill town's larger landowners.

No one is absolutely sure where the Bernadone family lived in Assisi. Some historians believe they lived in a house known as the T.O.R. Casa Paterna near the Piazza del Comune. Others believe the family home was on the Vicolo Sup. San Antonio, also near the Piazza del Comune. The choice of that location is supported by the presence of a tiny, charming shrine with fading frescoes that has been called the Oratorio di San Francesco Piccolino since the thirteenth century and that, with unsubtle religious symbolism, bears a placard in Latin stating Francis was born here—in a stable.

The most generally recognized location of the Bernadone home, however, and the one marked on tourist maps, is under the seventeenth-century Chiesa Nuova, just south of the Piazza del Comune. With some excitement we walk the short distance to the house from the oratorio but find its semiexcavated remains quite dull. There is archaeological value in the subterranean section of the ancient cobbled street on which the house fronted and the presumed remains of Pietro Bernadone's shop where Francis worked for his father selling cloth. But we don't sense any presence there of Francis.

More interesting is the suggestion of a *porta del morto,* or "door of the dead," in the house's old vaulted brick-and-stone exterior wall. One of Assisi's intriguing medieval trademarks, the small and elevated *porta del morto* is thought to have been opened only to transfer dead bodies outside, but it probably also had a more practical use, as a security measure. Most houses in Assisi had two entrances—one on the street level, which opened into the stable or whatever business the family was in, the other, higher, leading into the living quarters and reached by wooden steps that were taken up at night for safety. Quite a few houses in Assisi still have a *porta del morto,* though the "doors" have long since been either cobbled over or glassed in as windows.

The only hint of Francis we find at the house he presumably lived in for the first twenty years or so of his life with at least one younger brother, Angelo, is the iron-barred *carceri* or cell displayed inside the Chiesa Nuova at ground level. It was in this "dark cellar," according to the *Legend of the Three Companions,* that Pietro locked up his rebellious son for days on end to dissuade him from his spiritual conversion. But I'm getting ahead of the story.

Pietro was away on one of his months-long buying trips to France when Francis was born. Francis's mother, Lady Pica (whether she really was a noble "Lady" or even French has never been determined), took her son to be christened at either Santa Maria Maggiore, the first cathedral in Assisi, or the "new" cathedral, dedicated to San Rufino, Assisi's patron saint, which was then under construction.

I would like to think that Francis was baptized in the charming eleventh-century Santa Maria Maggiore, adjacent to the Bishop's Palace on the equally charming, small, tree-lined Piazza del Vescovado. The old cathedral's simple stone Romanesque façade, with its one rose window, and the faded frescoes in its barrel-vaulted nave seem much more in keeping with the simplicity of Francis than the cavernous San Rufino, Assisi's current cathedral, which took another hundred years to complete.

Redone in the sixteenth century, San Rufino's Gothic interior seems quite cheerless by comparison with the warmth of Santa Maria Maggiore. But whether Francis was baptized there or not, San Rufino would play a major role in the legend of Francis and Clare. A splendid pair of sculpted stone lions guard the doors to the cathedral, and during his conversion, Francis is said to have stood on top of the lions to preach to the incredulous people in the cathedral's piazza. His makeshift pulpit would have been clearly visible from the house Clare grew up in, and perhaps the adolescent Clare first saw him from a window and was stirred by his message of peace and love—unlike the people who initially jeered at him and thought this son of Assisi had gone mad.

Francis was certainly in San Rufino in later years. He would preach often in the cathedral, and he undoubtedly entered San Rufino, as we do, through a door in its original and splendid twelfth-century stone façade. He may also have walked on the cathedral's original, uneven stone floor, a portion of which is visible beneath protective glass.

But what tips the scales toward San Rufino as the site of Francis's baptism is that just inside the entry, on the right, is the marble baptism font at which Francis was baptized, as was Clare eleven years later. Lady Pica had her son baptized Giovanni or John, after John the Baptist, but the name was short-lived. Pietro evidently did not want his son named after a desert saint, and when he returned from France, he changed his son's name to the more businesslike Francesco or Francis, which means "the Frenchman."

Francis, by all accounts, was a wild and spoiled youth who cut quite a figure in Assisi. An indulged member of the nouveau riche, Francis always had a purse full of money, which he lavished on food and drink with his friends, and on stylish clothes for himself. According to the *Legend of the Three Companions,* "He would use only the finest materials and sometimes his vanity took an eccentric turn, and then he would insist on the richest cloth and the commonest being sewn together in the same garment."

Needless to say, there are no marked sites in Assisi that record the ne'er-do-well youth of Francis, save for the streets themselves, which he prowled late into the night with his friends, singing and carrying on and undoubtedly wenching in the spirit of the times. He wasn't just part of the pack; he led it. "He was the admiration of all and strove to outdo the rest in the pomp of vainglory, in jokes, in strange doings, in idle and useless talk, in song, in soft and flowing garments," writes Thomas of Celano. Francis agreed. In his Testament, written in the Bishop's Palace in Assisi shortly before he died, he refers to the first twenty-five years of his life as a time "while I was in sin."

Francis received his rudimentary schooling in reading and writing Latin at the church of San Giorgio, over which the Basilica of St. Clare was constructed, just a few streets from his family home. Little remains of the old church except, perhaps, the back wall of the basilica's glassed-in Chapel of the Blessed Sacrament.

Francis was definitely not a Latin scholar. There are missteps in the two surviving letters in his own hand, which evidently made him sympathetic to the errors made by the better-educated friars who took his dictation. "And what is no less to be admired," writes Celano, "when he had caused some letters of greeting or admonition to be written, he would not allow even a single letter or syllable to be deleted, even though they had often been placed there superfluously or in error."

He did, however, speak fluent French, then the universal language of commerce. He also sang in French, and well. All his early biographers praise his voice—"strong, sweet, clear, and sonorous," says Celano. There were limitless songs, both bawdy and chivalric, for him to choose from. It was the time of the French troubadours, who traveled all over Italy, enter-taining the nobility (the *majores*) in their castles and the common folk (the *minores*) at tournaments and religious festivals, of which there were no fewer than 150 a year in Assisi. The troubadours sang the stories of brave knights and heroic deeds, passing on the legends of Charlemagne and Roland and the legendary court of King Arthur; his bravest knight, Lancelot; and Lancelot's forbidden love, King Arthur's wife, Guinevere. A whole class of Italian *jongleurs* emerged to interpret the French into an argot of Franco-Italian, and everyone on the streets, including Francis, learned the stories of heroism, sacrifice, and courtly love.

Standing in the Piazza del Comune, it is easy to imagine the trouba-dours and *jongleurs* captivating the medieval crowds, who had no other source of entertainment. In the busy but peaceful piazza, it is harder to imagine the violence and bloodshed that marked twelfth-century Assisi.

Francis grew up in a time of civil foment and bloody confrontations be-tween feuding families, rival hill towns, peasants and nobles, and most par-ticularly, Church and State. The State was not the Italy we know but the Holy Roman Empire, which kept a tight grip on most of the region, in-cluding the prosperous but increasingly rebellious Assisi. Assisi had been captured by the emperor Frederick Barbarossa in 1160, twenty years before Francis was born, and its people had chafed under the imperial yoke ever since. Assisians wanted their independence and had risen up against the imperial forces in 1174 but had been defeated. It was only a matter of time before the people would try again.

Looming above the piazza at the top of the hill town is the Rocca Maggiore, the restored twelfth-century military fortress from which the German forces of the emperor, supported by most of Assisi's nobility, kept one
eye on Assisi, the other on the road from Assisi's always threatening archri-
val, the Papal town of Perugia, fifteen miles to the west. All the while the
frustration and fury of Assisi's middle-class citizens continued to fester, directed not only at the emperor's forces in the Rocca but at Assisi's feudal
lords, who levied taxes and tariffs on the merchants like Pietro Bernadone
while giving the growing burgher class few political rights.

Francis was seventeen when the people rose again in 1198, and though
there is no record of his having taken part in the ransacking of the garrison,
few of his biographers doubt that he and his friends were eager partici-
pants. It was a bloody moment in Assisi's history. The townspeople
slaughtered the imperial forces, tore down the fortress stone by stone, then
turned their wrath on the nobility. Some feudals threw in their lot with the
newly formed independent commune of Assisi, but others did not.

In the ensuing class warfare, which lasted for two years, many of the nobility were massacred and their estates sacked. The more prudent feudals
fled to nearby Perugia; they included the noble Offreduccio family with
their six-year-old daughter, Clare, who left just before their house next to
the Cathedral of San Rufino was razed. The canny Bernadone bought up
as much of the nobles' deserted land as he could, presumably at bargain
prices.

We leave the main piazza to clamber up to La Rocca after fortifying
ourselves with cappuccino at a sunny outdoor trattoria. Standing on the
fourteenth-century reconstruction of the fortress, we can see what a brilliant vantage point it had been for the imperial forces—every building and
church in Assisi is clearly visible. So is the road to Perugia and, in the distance, the nobility's temporary sanctuary itself. Also visible are the surviving crenellated gates or *pòrte* through the twelfth-century city walls that the
victorious Assisians quickly built after the siege of La Rocca with the
stones from the dismantled fortress. All of Francis's biographers agree that
he must have learned the art of stonemasonry by helping to construct those
walls, a skill he would rely on during his conversion.

We retrace our steps to join the swarms of tourists and pilgrims milling about the fountain in the sun-warmed piazza in front of the Basilica of St. Clare. It is late on a mid-October afternoon, and the smell of roasting chestnuts gives a pungent flavor to the crystal-clear air. A newspaper kiosk is doing brisk business in multinational journals and magazines on one edge of the piazza, while on another, a brightly painted van pumps out the Toreadors' Theme from *Carmen*. Drawn by the music, children cluster around the van to covet an eclectic offering of toys laid out on the ground—a rooster with a peacock tail, an old Barbie wearing an Italian flag as a miniskirt, a replica of the milk-heavy wolf who nursed Romulus and Remus.

It is a beautiful afternoon. The sun turns Assisi's stone and stucco houses, with their enviable balconies and roof gardens, into impossibly warm shades of tan and ocher—"a beige tweed city," I write in my notes. In contrast, the view beyond the city walls and across the Spoleto Valley is a mélange of color—the rich green of fall crops, the dark brown corduroy of tilled fields, the pink and purple hills on the far side of the valley as a backdrop. Just an arm's length away, over the piazza's marble-columned balustrade, groves of ancient olive trees begin their steep, stepped descent toward the valley, and white butterflies flit among the ripening fruit.

Francis could easily have stood on that very spot eight hundred years ago, looking out over that same valley. Assisi was much smaller in his day, and San Giorgio lay outside the city walls, but the elevation would have been the same. Francis would have seen many more trees back then; the valley floor was thick with oak forests and wetland marshes, which have since been drained. But on a day as clear as ours, he might have seen Perugia—with no realization as a schoolboy of what was to come.

Three years after the citizens of Assisi waged their war of independence against feudalism and the empire—and risked excommunication by Pope Innocent III for not turning the city over to Papal protection—Perugia declared war on Assisi. The displaced nobles of Assisi who had fled to Perugia wanted not only vengeance but compensation for their losses, which the commune of Assisi refused to honor. The furious nobles persuaded Perugia, a longtime rival of Assisi, to teach the hill town's upstarts a lesson. So Francis, then twenty-one, and his friends prepared for the glorious victory they would inflict on Perugia, their heads filled no doubt with the glories of heroism and bravery in battle that had been sung to them by the troubadours and the *jongleurs.*

What a sight it must have been when the church bells in Assisi sounded the call to arms in November 1202 and the commune's citizens mustered in front of San Rufino to march against Perugia. One of Francis's modern biographers, Julien Green, imagines the scene. The cathedral's piazza was ablaze with the flags of each quarter of the town that would lead the column to war. Behind them would come the infantry, armed with swords, pikes, and crossbows; then the men on horseback encircling a wagon drawn by white oxen, draped in Assisi's flag and bearing a traveling altar complete with a crucifix, lighted candles, and priests saying mass.

Francis, though not an aristocrat, rode through the city gates with the noble knights because his family was rich enough to own a horse. He no doubt was wearing some sort of splendid battle dress, underscoring his early biographers' observation that he often dressed better than his social position "warranted." The fanfare of trumpets that sent Assisi's army on its way must have been thrilling to young Francis, who thought his heraldic battlefield fantasies were about to fulfilled. They weren't.

We drive the fifteen minutes from Assisi to the hill above the ancient village of Collestrada on the border between the two warring hill towns, a journey that took the men of Assisi four hours. The battlefield on which the armies met is now a shopping mall, with no hint of the carnage that took place there. Already tired, Assisi's men were no match for the furious forces from Perugia, who had only to sweep down from their town and cross the Tiber River at Ponte San Giovanni. The sons of Assisi were quickly overwhelmed. Then slaughtered. The displaced nobles in Perugia rode down the Assisians fleeing for cover throughout the valley and the woods and hacked them to death.

Ironically, it was Francis's pretension that saved his life. The Perugians spared the nobles and took them prisoner for the ransom they would fetch. Francis, mistakenly identified as a noble by the clothes he wore, his manners, and especially the fact he had a horse, was spared as well. That meant money in the bank to the Perugians and a year of hell for Francis.

We follow him from the industrial town of Ponte San Giovanni to Pe rugia, where he would spend the next twelve months or so in a dungeon somewhere under the town, without light, without sanitation, without adequate food or clean water, without a change of clothes in the cold of winter and the heat of summer.

He almost died.

2 *Lost in Perugia*

THE HILLTOP CITY *where Francis is imprisoned* · ASSISI, *where he returns, very ill, and goes back to his frivolous ways*

Perugia sprawls across Umbria's high hills, a red‑roofed city with a modern population of 150,000, more than six times the current population of the commune of Assisi. Whatever possessed the sons of Assisi to think they could defeat this muscular stronghold, assuming the skewed population ratio was roughly the same in their time, is beyond me. Even now Perugia is quite forbidding in its inaccessibility, and getting there is not half the fun for us—or certainly for Francis. He was undoubtedly marched up the hills and paraded through the cobbled streets with the other captured Assisians, jeered at and stoned by Perugia's citizens. We escape any such humiliation, but after maneuvering all the hairpin turns up the hillside, we can't find a place to park.

It is the afternoon rush hour; the first parking lot we come to, just inside the city walls, is full, and the Italians' natural penchant for driving uncomfortably fast strains our resolve to press on. Instead of reentering the narrow speedway to look for another lot, we take the path of least resistance and follow a convoy of local cars into the hill town itself. Our high‑fives of self‑congratulation when we find a parking place on the street turn into a grueling forced march, up and down the steep streets, then up and around and down and up again until we achieve the city's historic, and at first unwelcoming, medieval center.

Virtually all the Italians we encounter in our geographic search for St. Francis are extremely helpful, giving us advice and driving directions, a few even leading us to tricky destinations in their own cars. In one extraordinary gesture, the young owners of the upscale pasta takeout in the tiny village near our rented villa invite us to their home for a five-course dinner and to listen to their recording of *Francesco,* a musical about Francis that they have seen four times in Assisi.

An exception is the woman behind the commune desk in Perugia at the massive medieval Palazzo dei Priori, Perugia's equivalent of a city hall. We are trying to locate the dungeon Francis was locked in, if it still exists. We fail. "I don't know where it was," the woman says with a shrug. "Perhaps it was right under this building." When I ask her if she could refer me to anyone with more knowledge of Francis and medieval Perugia, she shakes her head. "There is nothing about St. Francis in Perugia," she says. "Go to Assisi." "What about the church of San Francesco al Prato?" I persist, pointing to the thirteenth-century church marked on the map she'd given me. "It's closed," she says.

We have better luck on a return trip to Perugia with a professional local guide named Inger. The dismissive woman in the commune office had been right about the closing of the church of San Francesco. The church had suffered water damage, Inger tells us, and is being renovated for use as a concert hall. I imagine that would please the young Francis, the troubadour, though in later life he would decry any music that did not contribute to the worship of God.

As to the medieval dungeon where Francis spent such a miserable year, Inger knows just where it is. We set out at a brisk pace across the windy, high plateau Perugia sits on and along the Piazza Matteotti to the very edge of a sheer cliff into which a five-story building has been built. Inger points at the bottom floor, and resisting an attack of vertigo, I lean over to look straight down at the site where, according to Inger, Francis was imprisoned.

How bleak it must have been, if Inger is correct—close to being buried alive. I imagine the dampness, the darkness, the airlessness. There is some thought that the prisoners were chained to the walls in the dungeons that were subsequently used to store salt. I am relieved when we turn away from our vantage point and my overwrought imagination begins to fade.

· · ·

Perugia, understandably, would never be a favorite venue of Francis, though he would return here often to preach. Several of his miracles were centered in and around Perugia—a mute restored to speech, a cripple restored to physical health. But he persisted in calling it Babylon, and with good reason. The belligerent city not only regularly attacked and pillaged its neighbors but was a den of internal intrigue. Medieval Perugia was known for its deadly poisons, its murders and mutilations, its ritual war of stones, in which teams of men heaved rocks at each other until enough were dead or wounded to signal the game was over.

Such savagery is hard to imagine as we leave Inger and stroll around Perugia's beautiful main square, the Piazza IV Novembre, watching its ocher palazzos turn burnt orange in the late afternoon sun. Instead of preparing to slaughter each other, the Perugians we see are preparing for their annual, weeklong Eurochocolate festival, which draws chocolate lovers from all over the world and showcases the city's own Perugina chocolates.

The people in the cobbled streets seem very friendly toward each other, unlike their warring medieval predecessors. At one sorry point, recorded in Franciscan annals as the "Curse of Perugia," the animosity within the city grew so venomous that it interrupted Francis's sleep, fifteen miles away in Assisi. A vision of the pending carnage of an all-out civil war between knights and citizens, nobles and peasants came to Francis in a dream and led him quickly to Perugia to preach peace. It was not a welcome message.

I could imagine Francis standing on the steps of Perugia's duomo, which also fronts on the Piazza IV Novembre, being heckled by the bloodthirsty knights who, Celano writes, "interfered with his words." The slight friar in the tattered brown habit held his ground against the knights, warning them time and again not to "attack your neighbors with arms, kill and plunder them." The knights evidently did not heed his warning that "wrath will teach you, for kindness has not," because shortly thereafter, Perugia descended into civil strife with "unrestrained fury and slaughter," just as Francis had envisioned.

But then again, little was sacred to medieval Perugians, including the Pope. One particularly gruesome incident would occur in July 1216, when Pope Innocent III died suddenly of an embolism in Perugia while on a countrywide tour raising recruits for the Fifth Crusade. Pending the funeral rites, his body was locked for safekeeping in the cathedral, where it quickly began to rot in the heat. Upon hearing of the Pope's death, Francis hurried to Perugia, to discover not only that the body was decaying but that thieves had broken in and stripped the body of all its clothes and Papal trappings.

My husband and I enter the duomo with some trepidation—two other Popes, one of whom was poisoned to death, are buried there—but its vast, Baroque space seems benign. Mass is being said in a side chapel, and we linger, listening to the music of the liturgy. The cathedral has been rebuilt since the time of Francis, so there is no physical remnant of him there, but there is a great deal of Franciscan history.

Soon after Pope Innocent III died—and rotted—there, Francis was propelled by another dream to return to the duomo to meet with the new Pope, Honorius III. In this dream, which Francis had at the Porziuncola, his tiny chapel near Assisi, Jesus instructed him to ask the new Pope for a favor that would please God and bring salvation for humankind. Honorius was startled and his college of cardinals highly resistant when Francis asked the extraordinary favor: the Papal pardon of sin and remission of punishment to every single person who came to confess at the Porziuncola. Such a Papal indulgence was the carrot the Church offered to those who went off on the Crusades to slay the heathens, and its persuasive value would be severely diminished if redemption were available locally. But Francis persisted and the Pope finally relented, albeit with a restriction. Instead of the indulgence being granted to penitents every day, as Francis asked, it would be limited to one day a year, August 2. Francis returned home in ecstasy, saying, "I shall send them all to Paradise." Who knows whether he succeeded, but the Porziuncola Indulgence started bringing thousands of penitents to Assisi on August 2; one chronicle in 1582 numbered them at over one hundred thousand.

We leave Perugia for the comfortable villa we have rented just north of of the town, so different from the dungeon where Francis spent that miserable year while his father negotiated for his release. Yet Francis's biographers claim he remained cheerful throughout his incarceration, to the point where, Celano writes, "His grieving companions resented his happiness and considered him insane and mad." Francis's answer to their derision was to ascribe his joy to his conviction that someday he would be "venerated as a saint throughout the whole world," a boastful prophecy that surely only confirmed their opinion that he was "insane and mad." And perhaps he was.

The Francis who returned to Assisi at the age of twenty-two was not the naïve young man who had ridden gaily to war the year before. He was sick, very sick, most certainly with malaria and some say bone tuberculosis. He was more or less bedridden for a year, suffering debilitating fevers. When he finally began to get around with the help of a cane, he was a changed man. He would remain frail for the rest of his life and need constant care.

His ordeal in Perugia had diminished everything about Francis, including his sense of joy. During his recovery, Celano writes, "he went outside one day and began to look about at the surrounding landscape with great interest. But the beauty of the fields, the pleasantness of the vineyards, and whatever else was beautiful to look upon, could stir in him no delight. He wondered therefore at the sudden change that had come over him, and those who took delight in such things he considered very foolish."

Celano's sentiment about Francis's joylessness rings true, but his last clause smacks of revisionist biography, for Francis himself continued to be foolish. He did not know how else to live. When Assisi's displaced nobles began to return from Perugia in 1205, the price of Assisi's defeat being the commune's capitulation to the nobles' demands for compensation, Francis went back to singing and carousing and indulging his friends.

He did become more charitable, however. In a scene commemorated by Giotto in Assisi, Celano writes that, at some point after Francis was "freed from his chains" in Perugia, he encountered an unfortunate knight in the road "who was poor and well nigh naked." Francis, who had always idolized knights, "was moved by pity" and gave the knight the "costly garments he was wearing." Francis made the gesture "for Christ's sake," according to Celano, which may very well be true, but then again, Francis may have been identifying with the knight because of the good fortune that had suddenly come his way.

An unknown noble from Assisi, possibly one of his fellow prisoners from Perugia, invited Francis to ride with him to Apulia in southern Italy to join Pope Innocent III's forces against the imperial troops backed by the princes of Germany. The issue at hand was really a custody fight over guardianship of young Frederick II, son and heir of the late Emperor Henry VI, whose widow had entrusted the child's education to the Pope instead of to the imperial court. The bloody struggle between Church and State over Frederick had been going on for almost seven years by the time Francis learned of the nobles' impending mission. "Upon hearing this," writes Celano, "Francis, who was flighty and not a little rash, arranged to go with him."

It would be a very expensive endeavor. To be a knight required a full suit of custom armor, a chain-link protective blanket and trappings for his horse, a well-turned-out squire to ride with him. Then there were the weapons—a lance, a sculpted sword, assorted daggers—and an out-of-armor wardrobe that would be suitable for a man of noble status. It is thought that Pietro Bernadone had to sell several of his properties to outfit his son properly, but it must have seemed worth it for the higher social standing that having a knight in the family would bring the Bernadones.

The twenty-four-year-old Francis must have been ecstatic in the winter of 1205 as armorers all over Assisi hammered out his battle dress. Glory and honor were within his reach. He even had a reassuring dream about his future as a Papal warrior, which "raised his spirits with a vision of the heights of glory," Celano writes. In the dream, his father's house was filled with "the trappings of war, namely saddles, shields, lances and other things," rather than the more customary "piles of cloth to be sold." All these arms would "belong to him and his soldiers," a voice told Francis in the dream. The interpretation seemed as simple then as it does now. "When he awoke, he arose in the morning with a glad heart, and considering the vision an omen of great success, he felt sure that his journey to Apulia would come out well."

It did not.

3   *The Missing Letter in Spoleto*

THE GOLDEN CITY *where Francis gives up becoming a knight ·* MONTELUCO, *the hermitage he founds near Spoleto just because it is so beautiful · the* CARCERI, *the cave near Assisi where he prays for guidance*

Spoleto rises out of the Umbrian hills like a golden beacon, its bell towers and churches gleaming against the blue sky. Twenty-four miles south of Assisi and a day's ride by horse, Spoleto is known today for its classical music summer festival and the frescoes of the fifteenth-century artist Fra Lippo Lippi in the apse of the cathedral. In 1205, according to Francis's biographers, it was the town where he had to abandon his quest for knighthood.

It was spring when Francis and his traveling companion set out from Assisi on what might very well have been a hot day. His new armor must have felt heavier and heavier as they rode along, as must his shield. It is not known whether they stopped to rest at one of the towns along the way or rode straight through to Spoleto, where they were to spend the night. In any event, by the time they reached Spoleto that night, Francis was sick again with a high fever.

In his delirium, he had a dream that began to change his life course. A voice spoke to him, according to Celano, asking him who could do better for him, the servant or the Lord. "The Lord," Francis replied. Then why, the voice continued, was he looking for the servant instead of the Lord? "Lord, what do you want me to do?" Francis asked. "Go back to the place of your birth for through me your vision will have spiritual fulfillment," the voice said.

Many biographers have wondered about the "voice" in that dream. Some think it must, of course, have been the voice of God preparing Francis for his more honorable role to come. Others think the voice might have been that of Francis himself, half delirious, realizing he could not continue his journey. Still others wonder if the "voice" Francis heard was that of his traveling companion, presumably a lord, who knew Francis would not be up to the journey and could be a liability. In any event, the dream remains a critical juncture in his legend, and his illness, at least, was real. His bout with the recurring chills and fever of malaria kept him in Spoleto for some time while his companion, presumably, rode on without him.

We follow Francis from Assisi to Spoleto, not only because Spoleto is so pivotal to his legend but also because the high hill town houses a unique Franciscan treasure: a letter Francis wrote in his own hand to Brother Leo. I had seen the only other surviving handwritten document of his, also to Leo, in the lower church in Assisi, but there is something exciting about seeing this second document in a location outside the Franciscan-rich collections in Assisi.

We arrive in Spoleto at noon and, with great anticipation, walk up the long, gently curving Via Filitteria to the Cathedral of Santa Maria Assunta, where the letter is displayed in the Reliquary Chapel. The Rough Guide notes that the duomo is closed between 1:00 P.M. and 3:00, but as anyone who has been to Italy knows, Italians have their own interpretation of time, and when we reach the astonishingly beautiful twelfth-century cathedral, we find it has closed an hour early and will be *chiuso* until 4:00.

But no matter. Downtime is a gift in Italy, and we spend some of it over a delicious lunch of local sausage, artichokes, and homemade pasta, and while away the rest walking around the graceful, fan-shaped piazza in front of the cathedral, dodging the local children playing soccer, and wondering who all the men carrying bright orange tote bags and milling around the piazza might be. (They turn out to be obstetricians gathered for a convention.)

We are the first into the cathedral when the small, very round priest arrives with an ancient iron key ring the size of a bicycle tire to unlock the door. The cathedral, I quickly discover, is not a model of high technology. Each very dark chapel requires a twenty-five-cent euro coin in a light box to shed temporary electric light on its treasures, including an unfinished fresco by a teenage Pinturicchio. Nervously clutching my coin, I enter the Reliquary Chapel and position myself in front of the case on the wall that holds the letter. But when the light comes on, albeit fleetingly, I can't believe my eyes. The case is empty.

I rush after the priest to ask about the letter and deduce from his torrent of Italian, arm waving, and finger pointing that the letter is somewhere up the steps at the top of the piazza, in the Museo Diocesano. It takes us another half an hour to find the little yellow sign near an arch on the Via Aurelio Saffi that leads us to Sant'Eufemia, Spoleto's revered twelfth-century church, and the museum's central courtyard.

I am so intent on finding the letter that I barely glance at what surely are treasures in the museum's five rooms, and suddenly, there is the letter, displayed in a glass case rimmed in silver and mounted on red marble. Turns out that the document is on loan from the cathedral for a monthlong Umbria-wide exhibition of Franciscan artifacts.

It is an extraordinary feeling to see once again Francis's actual handwriting, especially so well displayed and lit. Francis wrote the letter, in Latin, toward the end of his life, when his eyesight was failing, which accounts for the painfully shaky script and the irregular lines. But it is a remarkable and tender document written to Brother Leo during a troubled period in Leo's life.

Brother Leo, [wish] your Brother Francis health and peace. I speak to you, my son, as a mother. I place all the words which we spoke on the road in this phrase, briefly, and [as] advice. And afterwards, if it is necessary for you to come to me for counsel, I say this to you: In whatever way it seems best to you to please the Lord God and to follow His footprints and His poverty, do this with the blessing of God and my obedience. And if you believe it necessary for the well-being of your soul, or to find comfort, and you wish to come to me, Leo, come!

Historians differ on where Francis was when he wrote this letter. All agree, however, that Francis was at one of the many mountaintop hermitages to which he would often withdraw to pray and meditate, one of which, on the sacred mountain of Monteluco, is just five miles from Spoleto. And utterly charming.

To even begin to understand Francis of Assisi, it is critical to leave the museums and cathedrals and the hill towns to go, as he did, to the hermitages. After his conversion, he would divide his time between preaching in the towns and retreating to the mountaintops, where he fasted and prayed in isolation and often talked directly with God. "The world was tasteless to him who was fed with heavenly sweetness, and the delights he found in God made him too delicate for the gross concerns of man," writes Celano. "He always sought a hidden place where he could adapt not only his soul but also all his members to God."

The hermitage Francis would found in 1218 on top of the 2,650-foot-high Monteluco is well worth the hairpin turns and narrowing road that lead us above the clouds and the smoke from fires farmers in the valley have set to burn off the rubble on their fall fields. We make one false stop, at what looks like an ancient convent but turns out to be a pizza restaurant adjoining the twelfth-century church of San Giuliano. The restaurant is not yet open for dinner, but an obliging waitress brings us espressos, which we sip gratefully in front of a television set tuned in to *Milionario,* the Italian version of *Who Wants to Be a Millionaire.*

The "hidden" hermitage, when we finally achieve the mountain's level summit, turns out to be inside a Franciscan convent tucked into the sheer face of the far side of the mountain, with a view of the Spoleto Valley normally reserved for those flying in small planes. Hardly a ruin, the fifteenth-century convent that grew up around the primitive hermitage looks newly restored, with a shiny carved wooden door leading into a beautiful cobbled courtyard bordered on one side by a small one-story, tile-roofed building.

Big ceramic pots of grasses and geraniums dot the courtyard and beyond, through an open door, a small and graceful cloister with a central—and miraculous—well. Local legend holds that Francis, in search of water, drew a spring of fresh water from a rock. Adding to this magical scene is a young Franciscan friar chatting with a young woman at the doorway of the convent. "Buona sera," they welcome us as we step through the door into a corridor and follow a sign that reads "1218 Primitivo Convento." It turns out to be as close to Francis as we ever get.

This quintessential Franciscan hermitage consists of seven crude and tiny wooden cells, each barely five feet long and wide, that Francis and his friars built along the edge of the mountain next to a twelfth-century chapel dedicated to St. Catherine of Alexandria. The cells are not gussied up, as are so many of the Franciscan sites in Assisi, but are as simple and stark as the life Francis set out to live. It is easy to imagine him here, stooping slightly to enter the four-foot-high door, sleeping on the wooden plank that remains in one of the cells, looking out the small casement window to nothing but sky. How much farther from the "world," as Francis called it, could he get?

He is just as present in the "Sacred Grove" outside the convent, where we follow a path through a stand of giant ilex whose roots radiate above-ground, some high enough to sit on, for at least thirty feet. The ancient Romans decreed the mountain a holy place because of these trees and limited their cutting to one day a year. A replica of the third-century B.C. order carved in stone just inside the entrance to the Sacred Grove (the original is in the Archaeological Museum in Spoleto) warns in archaic Latin that anyone disobeying the order must pay a fine and sacrifice an ox to Jove.

Francis would have approved of the Roman sentiment to protect the trees, though he would also have championed the protection of "Brother" Ox. I feel much closer to Francis in this natural sanctuary of peace and beauty, as I would in all the hermitages we visit, than I do in the hill towns, including Spoleto and even Assisi. The old towns, though beautifully preserved for the most part, are up-to-date communities where the residents watch television, park their cars, talk on their cell phones. It is easier to picture Francis in the more ageless surroundings of nature, praying without interruption or distraction and walking with his friars under the canopy of the trees.

The sound of guitar music drifting out of the convent lures us back into the courtyard. A friar named Angelo is on his way to the 6:00 P.M. Dominus prayers and invites us to accompany him. Regretfully, we decline. The sun is setting in brilliant streaks of burnt orange, and we have to navigate back down the narrow, winding mountain road to Spoleto. But we can't help lingering outside the window of the little building as the friars inside begin to sing a chant—"Alleluia . . . alleluia"—the same chant Francis and his friars might have intoned here more than eight centuries ago.

Francis was not feeling as harmonious when he was well enough to re⁄ turn to Assisi from Spoleto in the spring of 1205. Gone was his dream of becoming a knight, and he had, as yet, no other dream to replace it. He ev⁄ idently sold his armor en route and arrived home, most probably, in humil⁄ iation. Celano does not record Pietro Bernadone's reaction to his son returning without the glory and status of knighthood—and without the armor he had paid so dearly for. The assumption has to be that Pietro was furious at his son, who presumably pocketed at least some of the money for the armor, because soon after he arrived home Francis was back out on the street with a full purse, entertaining his friends.

Francis was such a soft touch it seems inevitable that, soon after he re⁄ turned from Spoleto, his friends chose him to be "king" of Assisi's revels, a traditional summerlong debauch of eating, drinking, and carousing— which Francis bankrolled. "He was chosen by them to be their leader, for since they had often experienced his liberality, they knew without a doubt that he would pay the expenses for them all," Celano writes. It was out of the "obligations of courtesy," Celano claims, that Francis hosted one final "sumptuous banquet, doubled the dainty foods; filled to vomiting with these things, they defiled the streets with drunken singing."

But something happened to Francis that early summer night that began his conversion and made that feast his last. According to all his biogra⁄ phers, he was struck dumb and unable to move, remaining rooted on the street while his friends went on. They came back for him when they real⁄ ized he was missing and interpreted his trancelike state as a fit of lovesick⁄ ness. "Francis, do you wish to get married?" his friends teased him. Jolted back to consciousness, Francis gave the reply that is central to his legend. "I shall take a more noble and more beautiful spouse than you have ever known," he told them, according to Celano. "She will surpass all others in beauty and will excel all others in wisdom."

Francis's vision of his coming betrothal to "Lady Poverty" is commem⁄orated at a festival every year in Assisi during the week following the first Tuesday in May. Eight hundred years ago it marked the moment when he began his conversion from sinner to saint.

Mount Subasio rises steeply above Assisi, its oak, pine, and ilex forests laced with caves and streams and hiking trails. Two and a half miles up a very steep pilgrim footpath from Assisi's Porta Cappuccini, or by car on the Via Santuario delle Carceri, is the Eremo delle Carceri, one of the ear⁄liest Franciscan hermitages and a refuge, for hundreds of years before that, for hermits and priests fleeing persecution from eastern Europe.

Francis was not fleeing persecution from anyone when he first sought out this lovely, serene spot, but confronting himself. The *carceri,* or prison, is be⁄lieved to be the location of the cave he secretly frequented with an unidenti⁄fied friend after seeing the vision of Lady Poverty that night on the streets of Assisi.

The beginning of Francis's conversion from playboy to penitent "in a certain grotto near the city," according to Celano, was a slow, painful process. Francis spent long hours on his knees praying to God to hear again the voice that had instructed him to return to Assisi to await the vi⁄sion that promised him "spiritual fulfillment"—but there was only silence and Francis's considerable guilt. "He repented that he had sinned so griev⁄ously and had offended the eyes of God's majesty," writes Celano, "and neither the past evils nor those present gave him any delight."

But Francis was still of this "world," and not yet fully confident that he would be able to resist the temptations of the flesh. According to the *Leg⁄end of the Three Companions,* the devil took advantage of his uncertainty by tempting him with a horrible image. There was, in Assisi, a "humpbacked and deformed woman and the Devil recalled her to Francis's mind with the threat, that unless he turned from the good he had embarked on, he would free her from her deformity and cast it upon him."

That image, and other "inopportune ideas," plagued Francis in the cave and "greatly worried and distressed him." The struggle within himself ev⁄idently took a considerable toll. He couldn't rest, and he often wept for hours. "Consequently, when he came out again to his companion, he was so exhausted with the strain, that one person seemed to have entered, and another to have come out," notes Celano.

There are no devils at the *carceri* during our visits. On one occasion we meet a small group of elderly nuns from Germany, clambering with some difficulty up and down the narrow, slippery paths to the caves marked by the names of Francis's first followers—Brothers Leo, Rufino, Silvester, and Masseo—and to the now enclosed grotto overlooking a gorge where Francis prayed and slept. *"Grüss Gott,"* each nun greets us. *"Grüss Gott."*

Along Leo's path we also we meet up with a group of Franciscan academicians from America, some forty of them, who are touring Umbria's Franciscan sites under the auspices of www.franciscanpilgrimages.com. Their leader, Father John, is explaining the significance of a curious bronze sculpture grouping of three life-size friars looking up at the sky.

Some of the early Franciscans were scientists, he explains, and among the first to study nature. One of the bronze friars looks heavenward trying to identify the North Star. Another is measuring the distance between the stars with his hand. The third is lying on his back on the ground, smiling, with his hands under his head. "That's St. Francis," Father John says, "just looking up at all the stars and having a delightful time."

Legends abound along the shaded paths of the *carceri*—the well in the courtyard, which Francis successfully coaxed to fill with water, the riverbed he would empty after a storm because the sound of the rushing water interfered with his prayers, the tree supposedly from the time of Francis that still clings to the side of the precipitous ravine with the aid of metal stakes and guy wires. Birds evidently gathered regularly in the tree to sing to Francis and just as regularly fell silent at his polite request when he wanted absolute quiet to pray.

We retrace our steps to the courtyard to a tiny chapel with a smoke-blackened ceiling the early friars built in a cave. Along the way we run into a Swiss family wearing sturdy hiking boots and carrying walking staffs. They have just come down a very steep path marked "Sister Moon," a clearing high in the woods from which the early friars observed the skies, and they are breaking out protein bars to fuel them on the equally steep footpath back to Assisi.

. . .

We leave the *carceri* with some reluctance, unlike Francis, who must have been relieved to distance himself from his early travails with his conscience in the cave. He was making headway, and "his heart was aglow with divine fire," notes the *Legend of the Three Companions,* but he still had not heard any instructions from the "voice" of Spoleto. Instead, he began to redirect his life on his own. "He was already a benefactor of the poor, but from this time onwards he resolved never to refuse alms to anyone who begged in God's name, but rather to give more willingly and abundantly than ever before."

His preoccupation with the poor spilled over into his home life. His mother, Lady Pica, who is described by all the early chroniclers as deeply religious, was far more sympathetic to Francis's new charity than was his father. Famine was rampant around Assisi following the devastation of the countryside's crops by a storm, and the number of hungry and starving had increased dramatically. When Pietro Bernadone was away, as he frequently was, Lady Pica went along with Francis's request to bake extra loaves of bread for the beggars who came to the door. And she presumably supported or at least turned a blind eye to his new habit of giving away his clothes to the poor when he found himself with no money. "He would give his belt or buckle, or if he had not even these, he would find a hiding place and, taking off his shirt, give it to the beggar for love of God," reports the *Legend of the Three Companions.*

Seeing the change in her son and the "new ardor which was taking possession of him and filling him with repentance for his past grave sins," Lady Pica, perhaps, was the one who urged Francis to go on pilgrimage to Rome in that same life-altering year of 1205. It was a long trip, some 120 miles, and it is not known whether he walked or rode on horseback. But no matter. The important part of the legend is what happened to Francis when he got there.

4 *The Old Rome*

ROME, *where Francis identifies with the beggars* · SAN DAMIANO, *where he finally hears a message from the Lord* · FOLIGNO, *where he acts on that message—with dramatic results*

St. Peter's Basilica looms ever larger from the Via della Conciliazione, the grandiose, column-lined boulevard Mussolini built to the Vatican in the 1930s by razing a medieval neighborhood. We hike across the basilica's vast and familiar Piazza San Pietro, where thousands of empty white plastic chairs await the faithful for the Pope's weekly blessing. One hundred and forty sculpted saints march around the top of Bernini's graceful colonnade rimming the sixteenth-century piazza, and I am warmed to see Francis among them. ✎ If the scope of St. Peter's is meant to humble mere mortals, it succeeds. Two-story-high marble sculptures of Jesus and his disciples look down on the piazza from the basilica's imposing façade, while huge marble replicas of St. Peter and St. Paul flank the broad marble steps leading up to the basilica. The separation is appropriate given that the two saints had a falling-out in the earliest years of Christianity and rarely spoke to each other again. ✎ For centuries St. Peter's was the largest church in Christendom, until it was eclipsed in 1990 by Our Lady of Peace in Yamoussoukro, the capital of the Ivory Coast. But no matter. It is to St. Peter's in Rome that Catholic pilgrims, including Francis, have always journeyed from all over the world.

. . .

Francis was furious when he entered the basilica in 1205. Here he was in the very heart of the Catholic Church, yet the offerings left at the altar by other pilgrims were paltry in comparison with the stature of the saint they were supposedly honoring. Save Christ himself, and possibly the Virgin Mary, no other Christian was as venerated as Peter. Christ himself had changed the disciple's name from Simon the Fisherman to Peter the Rock, and the Church considered Peter the first Pope, from whom all the subsequent Popes descended.

Moreover, Peter, like Christ, had accepted, even sought out, his martyrdom. He and other Christians had been wrongly accused and subsequently persecuted by Emperor Nero for having caused the fire that engulfed Rome in A.D. 64. Legend has it that Peter had escaped Nero's jail in Rome and was on his way out of town to safety when he met a man on the Via Appia and asked him the famous question *"Quo vadis?"* When the man replied that he had come to be crucified for a second time, Peter realized he was speaking to Christ and immediately turned around to go back to Rome—and his certain death.

That such a man should be so poorly served at his own grave caused Francis to all but empty his purse at the altar. "Astounded when he came to the altar of the prince of the apostles that the offerings of those who came there were so meager, he threw down a handful of coins at that place, thus indicating that he whom God honored above the rest should be honored by all in a special way," writes Celano.

The sacred basilica Francis was visiting, the "old" St. Peter's, was built by Constantine, the first Christian-convert emperor, at the beginning of the fourth century over the necropolis where the martyred Peter had been buried. The "new" and current St. Peter's would be built on the same site thirteen centuries later. Tradition holds that both the Papal altar in today's St. Peter's, framed by Bernini's hundred-foot-tall canopy of bronze (stolen and melted down from the Pantheon's portico), and the more modest altar in the "old" St. Peter's were sited directly over Peter's grave. It is intriguing to think some of the coins from Francis's purse may be among the assortment found during a subterranean search for Peter's remains; early pilgrims to the old St. Peter's evidently dropped coins directly into the grave through a grille in the marble slab covering it.

Having made his dramatic offering to St. Peter, Francis left the basilica as he had entered it—through an enclosed garden known as Paradise. But the atrium hardly fit the definition of Paradise, filled as it was with beggars and the poorest of the poor pleading for a coin or two. Francis surely gave the poor what coins he had left, but the gesture was suddenly not enough for him.

Instead he stopped among the beggars and committed one of the famous acts of his ongoing conversion—he swapped his fancy clothes with a beggar for his rags and found they suited him. "He put off his fine garments out of love of poverty, clothed himself with the garments of a certain poor man, and joyfully sat among the poor in the vestibule before the church of St. Peter," writes Celano.

This, presumably, was the first time Francis had actually cross-dressed with the poor. His biographers all make note of his increasing sense of charity toward the least fortunate and the various articles of clothing he had spontaneously taken off and given to others. But there is no indication that he had ever given away all his clothes and donned beggars' rags in return—though he wanted to.

Celano postulates that Francis had resisted the temptation because he was worried about what people in Assisi would think of his already strange behavior and waited to experiment until he was out of town. "Many times he would have done a similar thing had he not been held back by shame before those who knew him," Celano writes.

Safely away in Rome, Francis did not stop with the clothes exchange. He joined the beggars outside St. Peter's and started begging for alms himself—in French. Though Francis certainly could have afforded to buy himself a good meal, he settled down with his new friends to share their scraps of food. "Considering himself one of them," notes Celano, "he ate eagerly with them." Celano does not record how the beggars must have felt having this seemingly crazy man enter their midst, don their rags, and eat their stale crusts with relish, but Francis probably felt the first stirrings of the pleasure, and ultimate freedom, of doing without. He was still playing a role, however. He wasn't a true *poverello*—yet.

. . .

Francis came closer on the way home to Assisi, where he confronted his greatest nightmare, as in a different sense do we. Ours occurs on the ancient Via Flaminia, the Roman road linking Rome with the Adriatic coast, as it passes through the southern industrial city of Terni. We have every intention of stopping in this modern bus and train hub to find the little twelfth-century church of San Cristoforo, where Francis preached in his later years, and the stone he stood on outside the bishop's residence. But we are foiled by a soccer game.

The rush-hour traffic inside Terni is gridlocked by the large police contingent double- and triple-parked along the streets to oversee the regional soccer game about to take place in the city's stadium. Our nightmare begins when a convoy of police cars, lights flashing and sirens screaming, tries to force a busload of players through our car into the stadium parking lot. It is compounded when yet another flashing, screaming police car suddenly roars out of the parking lot and fetches up half an inch from my side of our car. We can't move forward or back, despite the sirens and flashing lights. When we finally manage to extricate ourselves from Terni, vowing never to return, I try to dispel my negative feelings about the city by reminding myself it is the birthplace of St. Valentine.

Francis met his nightmare farther along that same road when he came face-to-face with a leper. Of all the diseases for which there was no cure at the time, leprosy was the most vile, mutilating, and feared. It was believed to be highly contagious, so that anyone with skin ulcers, suppurating sores either from leprosy or from other skin diseases like St. Anthony's fire from eating contaminated grains, was forcibly quarantined for forty days in leprosariums, or *lazzaretti,* before being allowed into any of the walled cities.

Assisi had several such leprosariums nearby, places of such horror to Francis that, like most of his fellow citizens, he went far out of his way to avoid them. His fear of lepers was so strong, according to the *Legend of the Three Companions,* that "if, by chance, he happened to pass anywhere near their dwellings or to see one of the lepers, even though he was moved to give them alms through some intermediate person, he would nevertheless turn his face away and hold his nose."

It is not surprising, then, that the story of Francis and the leper he en-

countered on the road just outside Assisi became one of the legendary turning points of his conversion. In one of the agonizing sessions in the cave
outside Assisi during which he'd pleaded with God to tell him what do,
God had evidently given him an answer in the form of a riddle: "O Francis, if you want to know my will, you must hate and despise all that which
hitherto your body has loved and desired to possess," recounts the *Legend of
the Three Companions.* "Once you begin to do this, all that formerly seemed
sweet and pleasant to you will become bitter and unbearable; and instead,
the things that formerly made you shudder will bring you great sweetness
and content."

So, coming face-to-face with the leper, the source of his greatest shudder, really put it to Francis. He knew what he wanted to do, but this time,
remembering God's admonition, he did not flee from the shrouded, stink-
ing, rattle-shaking miserable or turn his face or hold his nose. "Though the
leper caused him no small disgust and horror," records Celano, "nevertheless, lest like a transgressor of a commandment he should break his given
word, he got off the horse and prepared to kiss the leper."

Celano then adds a mystical dimension to the encounter, writing that
when Francis remounted his horse and looked back at the leper, "though
the plain lay open and clear on all sides, and there were no obstacles about,
he could not see the leper anywhere." Whatever the truth of this story, the
historical reality is that for the rest of his life Francis would seek out leprosariums and lavish attention on their wretched inmates with such intimacy that it is widely believed he eventually caught the disease. "He
washed all the filth off them and even cleaned out the pus of their sores,"
writes Celano.

Francis evidently saw lepers as a gift sent to him by God as a test of his
humility. In his Testament, written shortly before he died, Francis said:
"When I was yet in sin, it seemed too bitter for me to see lepers, and the
Lord led me among them and I showed mercy to them." His ongoing dedication to lepers would play a central role not only in his life but also in the
lives of others who wanted to join his order. "When postulants presented
themselves, whether nobles or commoners, they were forewarned that
among other things they would have to serve the lepers and live in their
hospitals," records the *Legend of Perugia.*

We drive the short distance from Assisi to the site of one of those hospitals, San Salvatore della Parte, now a rather elegant, privately owned building called the Casa Gualdi. It sits near a crossroads on the old and well-traveled Via Francesca, the Road of the French, so named because it was the trade and pilgrimage route between Assisi, Rome, and France. But aside from a plaque on the building identifying it as a historic Franciscan site, there is nothing to suggest the suffering of the medieval lepers who were confined there, or the role lepers played in changing Francis's life. "Strengthened by God's grace, he was enabled to obey the command and to love what he had hated and to abhor what he had hitherto wrongly loved," notes the *Legend of the Three Companions.*

It was the next directive from on high, however, in this same year of 1205, that started the sequence of events that would scandalize Assisi and catapult Francis along the road to sainthood. This one took place in a small, half-ruined, twelfth-century church named San Damiano, less than a mile from Assisi, tended by an old, itinerant priest. It was not the priest who transformed Francis the day he wandered into San Damiano, but the twelfth-century Byzantine cross, painted by a Syrian monk, that hung over the altar. In one of the most critical moments in Francis's life, re-created by Giotto in Assisi's basilica, the crucified Jesus depicted on the cross spoke to Francis, some say even bowed to him, and repeated three times: "Francis, go, repair my house, which as you see, is falling completely to ruin."

Francis must have been ecstatic finally to get the clear order promised him in the dream he had had months before, and he took the order literally. Rebuild this crumbling church. So that was what he was meant to do. But how? The reconstruction would take money, more money than he had. Where would he get it? Of course! His father's shop. "After fortifying himself with the sign of the holy cross, he arose, and when his horse was made ready, he mounted it," writes Celano. "Taking with him scarlet cloth to sell, he quickly came to a city called Foligno."

Foligno surprises us. The once-thriving medieval market town nine miles east of Assisi (and strategically located at the crossroads of the ancient Via Flaminia and a secondary but equally vital trade road connecting the town to Spello, Perugia, and Assisi) is so universally trashed in our guidebooks as a dreary industrial, agricultural, and transportation center that we dread going there. But we find the valley city surprisingly inviting. It is a relief to be walking on flat pavement after our stiff climbs around the hill towns and a welcome change to be on wide, pedestrian-only streets and not dodging cars.

Our goal in Foligno is to find the medieval marketplace where Francis sold the "scarlet" cloth he had taken from his father's shop and the horse he had taken from his father's stable. It takes awhile. The obvious starting point is Foligno's unexpectedly charming main Piazza della Repubblica with its funky twelfth-century duomo, whose carved façade boasts a pagan panoply of animals and signs of the zodiac. We step inside the church to hear a small group of worshipers singing harmoniously in a side chapel, but we see no sign of Francis.

The Piazza San Domenico, at the far end of the old town down a flag-lined shopping street and past a Benetton, seems more promising. The piazza is big enough for a marketplace; it is shaded by oak trees and close to an ancient city gate. It also has an unexpected treasure: the sunken, low, pink and white stone church of Santa Maria Infraportas, which bears a startling plaque identifying it as the "Mother Church of Foligno, established in 58 A.D." This church, too, is said to have pagan origins and to be the venue of a conversion sermon delivered to local animists by none other than St. Peter.

Surely Francis visited this little Romanesque church, with its recycled columns supporting the sunken portico. At the risk of sounding other-worldly, we feel him there. What we neither feel nor find, however, is any indication that this is the piazza where he sold his father's cloth and horse.

We retrace our steps to the Piazza della Repubblica and find consolation in an elegant *pasticceria* along the Via Garibaldi. The unassuming doorway opens into a cheerfully lit ancient stone vault with modern yellow and burgundy fleurs-de-lis frescoed on its ceiling and arches, and glass cases displaying irresistible tarts and pastries. Regulars are gathering for their nightly card game, and while we drink our caffè latte we watch them share the news of the day with some degree of envy. Our appreciation of Foligno is heightened further by the *pasticceria*'s manager, who gives us a parting present from the overflowing shelves of chocolates wrapped in gleaming gold, blue, red, and green wrappers.

And then, of course, we see it. In the Piazza della Repubblica. Over a candy store. A plaque, fifteen feet off the ground, identifying the piazza we'd started from two hours before as the site of Francis's signature transaction. Though we feel somewhat like chumps, we are also grateful. If we'd seen the plaque right away, we would not have explored the old town and seen the hauntingly old Santa Maria Infraportas and discovered the *pasticceria* that so typifies the serendipitous wonders of Italy.

We leave Foligno in a cheerful mood, as presumably did Francis until he returned to San Damiano, on foot, with all the money he had made to repair it—and the priest refused to accept it. The priest was all too aware of Francis's high-living reputation and interpreted the humble conversion he was professing as mockery. "It seemed to him that Francis, just the day before was living outrageously among his relatives and acquaintances and exalting his stupidity above others," Celano writes. Francis somehow managed to persuade the priest at least to let him stay at the church, but the priest left the bag of money, untouched, in a windowsill "out of fear of Francis's parents." He was right to be afraid of Francis's parents. And so, with good reason, was Francis.

Freud could have written volumes about the father-son relationship in the ensuing struggle between Pietro and Francis Bernadone. And it began as soon as his father found out that Francis not only had sold the family's fabric and horse but also had moved into the priest's house at San Damiano. "Calling together his friends and neighbors, he [Pietro] hurried off to find him [Francis]," records the *Legend of the Three Companions*. But Francis was nowhere to be found. "When he [Francis] heard of the threats of his pursuers, foreseeing their arrival, he hid from his father's anger by creeping into a secret cave which he had prepared as a refuge."

Francis hid from his father in that "secret cave" for a month. Someone, no one knows who (I think it was his mother), brought him food while he "prayed continually with many tears that the Lord would deliver him from such persecution." And the Lord did, after a fashion. The Francis who voluntarily emerged at last from the cave was a changed man, "glowing with inner radiance . . . ready to face the insults and blows of his persecutors." And he got them.

One can only imagine the reaction on the streets of Assisi when Francis returned "light-heartedly" from his month underground, dressed in rags, pale, emaciated—and smiling. "When his friends and relatives saw him, they covered him with insults, calling him a fool and a madman, and hurling stones and mud at him." Not surprisingly, and perhaps accurately, they thought "he must be out of his mind." His father certainly did.

Pietro Bernadone shoved his way through the crowd stoning his son, but instead of protecting him, he "sprang on his son like a wolf on a lamb; and, his face furious, his eyes glaring, he seized him with many blows and dragged him home." The excavated cell still visible in the designated remains of the Bernadone house in Assisi became a torture chamber for Francis. "For many days, his father used threats and blows to bend his son's will, to drag him back from the path of good he had chosen, and to force him to return to the vanities of the world," notes the *Legend of the Three Companions*. He failed.

Francis held fast, in the age-old Christian tradition of enduring physical trials and overcoming temptations. When his father was called away on business, his mother tried to reason with him in a more gentle manner, but Francis rebuffed her entreaties as well. And then she did what any caring mother would do: "When she saw that his mind was irrevocably made up and that nothing would move him from his good resolution, she was filled with tender pity, and, breaking his bonds, she set him free."

But Pietro was not through with his son. Soon after he returned to Assisi, and roundly beat his wife for freeing Francis, he went to the local civil authority and formally charged his son with robbery. "When the authorities saw how enraged Pietro was, they sent a messenger to summon Francis," continues the *Legend of the Three Companions*. But Francis had inherited his father's shrewdness and summarily rejected the civil complaint, claiming that he was "the servant only of God and therefore no longer owed obedience to the civil authorities."

The stalemate must have been a relief to the city fathers, who wanted nothing to do with the domestic dispute, but it did nothing to appease Pietro. Instead he went to the bishop of Assisi and "repeated his accusation." In turn, Bishop Guido, who is described in the *Legend of the Three Companions* as "a wise and prudent man," summoned Francis to answer his father's indictment. Francis agreed to "willingly appear before the Lord Bishop who is the father and lord of souls." And the stage was set for the final and most dramatic confrontation between father and son—and Assisi's most famous scandal.

5 *Showdown in Assisi*

ASSISI, *where Francis repudiates his father and is reborn* · THE SAN VERECONDO MONASTERY, *where he nearly dies* · GUBBIO, *where he is saved* · ASSISI, *where he returns to rebuilding San Damiano*

Assisi's small, tree-lined Piazza del Vescovado is a study of serenity on a fall afternoon. The leaves dapple the sunlight onto the central fountain and the quiet cobblestones in front of Santa Maria Maggiore, Assisi's first cathedral; next to it is the bishop's age-old and renovated residence. Surprisingly, neither the simple old Romanesque church, with its recessed brick vault and fragments of frescoes, nor the bishop's unassuming walled residence merits much of a mention in the guidebooks to Assisi, though both are central to the legend of Francis. Perhaps it is because there are no tourist trattorias in the piazza and most of it is given up to parking spaces. The only other people we see are young French backpackers looking for an inexpensive room in a lovely old Franciscan residence run by nuns across from Santa Maria Maggiore. It is full.

Vescovado was hardly a study of serenity in the spring of 1206, when Francis and Pietro Bernadone finally squared off there—for good. Some historians set the father-son confrontation in the Piazza del Comune, others in the piazza fronting San Rufino, but the majority point to little Vescovado. The showdown took place in and around the bishop's residence, which was in the same location in 1206 as is the current residence today.

So this is where we have come to reenact in our imaginations the drama of epic proportions.

Picture Pietro, the father and accuser, glowering with accumulated rage at the loss of his money and fury at his stubborn, undeserving son. Imagine Francis, the crazy son and thief, arriving at the bishop's residence smiling and laughing, joyfully obeying the bishop's commands while ignoring those of his father. Imagine the crowd of gossipy Assisians gathered to witness the living soap opera of the Bernadone family. Some say that even young Clare was among the crowd that spring day, which, though a tantalizing possibility, seems doubtful, given her youth and her family's high position.

The hearing before Bishop Guido started uneventfully enough. There was no disputing the fact that Francis had taken and sold his father's cloth and his horse without permission, that he had tried to give the money to the priest at San Damiano as a restoration fund, that his father wanted his son to give the money back. And that was just what Bishop Guido told Francis to do. "Your father is highly incensed and greatly scandalized by your conduct," the bishop admonished Francis according to the *Legend of the Three Companions.* "If therefore you wish to serve God, you must first of all return him his money, which may indeed have been dishonestly acquired."

Francis was quick to obey—and to add a flourish of his own. "My Lord Bishop, not only will I gladly give back the money which is my father's, but also my clothes," he said. And with that, Francis briefly repaired into the bishop's residence, took off all his clothes, laid the sack of money on top of them, and reappeared in the piazza in front of the bishop, his father, and the good folk of Assisi, stark naked.

Standing there in the buff (or wearing a hair shirt, by some accounts), Francis then proceeded to sever all ties with his father in what has to be one of the greatest renunciation scenes of all time. Addressing the gawking and surely tittering crowd, Francis called out: "Listen all of you, and mark my words. Hitherto I have called Pietro Bernadone my father. But because I am resolved to serve God, I return to him the money on account of which he was so perturbed, and also the clothes I wore which are his; and from now on I will say 'Our Father who art in heaven,' and not Father Pietro di Bernadone."

What a devastating moment for Pietro. His son renouncing him as a father. For all of Assisi to see and hear. The son he had fed and clothed, the son he had ransomed from prison in Perugia, the son he had outfitted in vain as a knight, trained in his shop, maybe even loved. This same ungrateful son now telling him in front of his neighbors and customers that he, Pietro, was no longer his father. And doing it naked.

Pietro presumably did not dwell on the symbolism of his son's nudity, whether it was Francis's emulation of Christ on the cross or his more literal return to his first birth, marking the beginning of his second. All Pietro saw was red. "His father rose up burning with grief and anger," the *Three Companions* continues, gathered up the clothes and the bag of money, pushed his way through the hooting crowd, and went home.

The mood of the crowd evidently shifted with Pietro's abrupt departure. Suddenly it was he who became the object of collective scorn, for taking away his son's clothes and leaving him standing there, shivering and naked, in the piazza. Francis's biographers, whose sources were presumably not present at what they call "the spectacle," claim that the same crowd which had jeered Francis minutes before—and would again—was moved to tears of "piety" by his predicament. It would fall to Bishop Guido to calm the crowd and end the "spectacle" by stepping forward and enveloping Francis in his mantle.

This act, too, was given spiritual meaning. With Francis's rejection of his earthly father and his embrace of an adopted heavenly father, it could only follow that the bishop would interpret the "spectacle" as "prompted by divine counsel," and not human theater. From that moment, Francis's biographers universally agree, the bishop of Assisi "became his helper, exhorting, encouraging, loving and embracing him with the depths of his charity."

Standing in the Piazza del Vescovado, I try to figure out just where the dramatic confrontation took place. In front of the old cathedral? Around the fountain? Then, on the wall of the bishop's residence, I see a handwritten sign, *"Aperto"* (Open), for the Libreria Fonteviva inside the courtyard. We follow it to what turns out to be a spiritual bookstore. "Do you know where Francis renounced his father?" I ask the woman behind the desk and am stunned when she replies matter-of-factly: "In the next room, the Sala del Trono. Come. I'll show you." And with that, she unlocks the door and turns on the light in what looks like a conference room, fitted out with long tables, chairs, microphones—and a velvet throne for the bishop. "Right here?" I say incredulously. "Right here," she replies, explaining that the piazza had been larger in Francis's time and the room had been built over it.

I am dumbfounded, standing on the exact spot where Francis had stood over eight hundred years ago and handed over his worldly goods to his father to start a new life. A huge painting of the scene covers the far wall of the Throne Room, which is hardly surprising. That same renunciation scene has been re-created not only by Giotto in the basilica but by every other artist and filmmaker attempting to document Francis's life. But there I am, physically, at the heart of the family saga, which suddenly feels very real.

What Francis did next is a matter of chronological choice. Determining exactly what he did and when and where he did it has proven impossible in many instances for modern historians because his medieval biographers were less interested in following a time line than they were in storytelling. The *Legend of the Three Companions* has Francis returning immediately to his work restoring San Damiano; Thomas of Celano, in his *First Life of St. Francis,* reports that he left Assisi in the direction of Gubbio, some say still naked, others say dressed in a simple workman's tunic and mantle donated by the bishop's gardener. We choose Celano and set off to follow Francis the thirty miles or so north to the hill town of Gubbio, though he had a much more difficult time getting there than we do.

Thieves jumped Francis in a forest en route, while he was "singing praises to the Lord in French." What the robbers hoped to glean from the bare-legged, tunic-clad man spouting French is questionable, but attack him they did, and "savagely." When they demanded to know who he was and he replied, "I am the herald of the great King!" they beat the mad little fellow, took his cloak, and tossed his body into a snow-filled ditch. "Lie there, you stupid herald of God," the thieves reportedly said to him before retreating back into the forest to await a more lucrative target. Unperturbed by the attack, young Francis managed to climb out of the snowy ditch, and "exhilarated and with great joy," he set off again, singing loud praises to the Lord. But his travails were not over.

To the everlasting chagrin of the monks at San Verecondo, a Benedictine monastery Francis came upon five miles south of Gubbio, little charity was given him. Though he was obviously in need of food and clothing and perhaps even medical attention, the monks gave him none and instead put him to work as a scullery boy in the kitchen. (One local legend even has him being held prisoner by the princes of Gubbio in a nearby castle, though I can't imagine why.) When later Francis's reputation as a man of God spread far and wide, the prior of the monastery begged his forgiveness and tried to make up for his harsh treatment. According to a late-thirteenth-century text written by one of San Verecondo's monks, the monastery would "graciously" host Francis "quite often" over the years and supply food and apple wine for a subsequent gathering of his followers. But such was not the treatment he received in 1206.

Unbelievably, San Verecondo is still there, just off the road to Gubbio. The first view of the old monastery, since renamed the Abbazia di Vallingegno, is so splendid that we pull off the road into a convenient photo opportunity site one hundred yards or so from the driveway. Who could resist the image of such a picture-perfect hilltop bell tower, church, and cloister buildings nestled in a grove of cypresses?

We drive the short distance to the renovated *abbazia* to discover that its up-to-date hospitality is now available to everyone. Owned by a family in Gubbio and leased to a young couple from Rome, the old monastery is now an *agriturismo* inn and working farm with a website—www.ab baziadivallingegno.it. Francis could have e-mailed ahead to book any one of six apartments for seventy euro a day, take riding lessons, and survey from the swimming pool the beautiful country he'd just walked through.

It is a beautiful, sunny morning, and we chat with a touring German family at the picnic table outside their rooms. In such a serene setting, it is hard to imagine the rather vicious miracle Francis had gone on to perform at San Verecondo. Recounted by all his early biographers, it involves a lamb born at the monastery during one of his visits, and the lamb's imme-

diate demise from the "ravenous bite" of a "cruel sow." Francis was so incensed at the pig for killing "brother lamb, innocent animal," Jesus being
known as the Lamb of God or *Agnus Dei,* that he put a curse on her. The
pig was dead within three days. To further avenge the lamb, the monks
threw the sow's body into a ditch at the monastery, where it "dried up like
a board" and did not become "food for any hungry creature." So much for
Sister Sow.

Francis was far more charitable, in another San Verecondo legend, toward a killer wolf. There are many wolf stories, but the first emanated from
that same monk's medieval text. This quite benign version has a sick and
frail Francis riding a donkey at twilight along the road to the monastery
and being entreated not to proceed by local farmers because of the "ferocious wolves" in the area. Francis replied that he did not fear "Brother
Wolf" because neither he nor his Brother Donkey had done any harm to
him, and they completed their journey to San Verecondo intact.

That same route from Assisi to what is now the Abbazia di
Vallingegno may still be in existence today. A network of seven footpaths
linking Assisi to the old monastery and beyond, to Gubbio, was opened
for the millennium in 2000. Some pilgrims followed all or part of the
thirty-mile Sentiero Francescano della Pace on foot, others on horseback.

I walk the second leg, a beautiful three-mile track downhill from Pieve
San Nicolo, a hamlet on a hill four miles north of Assisi, to the tiny two-
building locality of Il Pioppi. It was on this leg, which winds through
high fields of wild broom and then very steeply down through a forest, that
Francis is thought by some historians to have been jumped by the thieves
and to have sought refuge at the nearby abbey of Santa Maria Assunta.
Others mark the site of the attack near Caprignone, a hill and ditch much
nearer to Vallingegno, along the fifth leg of the Sentiero Francescano.
Early Franciscans built a monastery and a still-standing church on the top
of Caprignone hill to memorialize the event, which would seem to indicate
that this was the crime scene.

Sitting at the picnic table at the Abbazia di Vallingegno and looking
out over the valley all the way to Mount Subasio, I wished I had walked
farther in Francis's footsteps along the Sentiero Francescano. I feel somewhat better when, later, an Italian friend who had walked the entire peace

trail told me she had gotten hopelessly lost on the section leading to the old abbey.

She was better off, however, than was Francis during his first, mean stay with the Benedictines at the monastery. "No mercy was shown to him," Celano says flatly. Half starved and half naked—he had only a peasant shirt, according to Celano, and "wanted only to be fed at least some soup"—Francis was in desperate straits. He soon left the monastery, "not moved by anger but forced by necessity," and found his way to Gubbio.

There can be no more beautiful road in Italy than the approach to Gubbio. Up, up from the valley, curving through rough plowed fields, olive groves, then down and up again, through vineyards with neat rows of grapevines tied on triangular wooden frames. Finally, the walled, medieval city appears, tucked into Mount Ingino on the western rim of the already snowcapped Apennines.

It is the fall truffle season in Gubbio, made clear in the parking lot near the church of San Francesco della Pace by a billboard advertising a two-month-long market and exhibition of *tartufi bianchi,* white truffles. The church is *chiuso* until the late afternoon, so we follow the promise of fresh truffles to Fabiani, a restaurant near the church on the Piazza Quaranta Martiri (so named for the forty "martyrs" of Gubbio shot by the Nazis in 1944), where the truffles, however delicious, are not *bianco* but *negro,* black. White or black, I feel a pang of guilt indulging in the local delicacy, remembering the hunger with which the half-starved Francis arrived here.

Good fortune reportedly came his way from a merchant family named Spadalonga, who gave Francis the first charity he'd received since he left Assisi—and perhaps even saved his life. Francis had befriended one of the Spadalonga sons, thought to be Federico, but nobody knows where or why. There is conjecture that they were imprisoned together in Perugia, that Federico was the unidentified friend who had accompanied Francis on his secret lamentations in the cave near Assisi, that Francis and young Spadalonga had met in a merchants' guild.

In any event, Federico's act of charity was to give Francis a tunic and cloak to wear, replacing the inadequate rags that had obviously suffered on his perilous trip from Assisi. Presumably the family also gave him food and shelter, not only on that visit but on so many subsequent visits that the thirteenth-century church of San Francesco della Pace, the church we are waiting to enter, incorporated the Spadalongas' home and warehouse, then outside the walls of Gubbio. The room Francis slept in is preserved just off the church's sacristy in what is called the Chapel of Peace.

The massive church, when it opens in the late afternoon, tells the story of the cloak giving over and over—in a stained glass window, in a bronze relief, in the inscription on a stone wall leading to the Chapel of Peace: *"Qui presso il fondaco degli Spadalonga Francesco d'Assisi, evangelista della pace, e del bene trove asilo e conforto al principio della sua conversione.—1206."* A rounded arch, presumably representing the doorway to the Spadalonga house, frames the entrance to the simple chapel, along with an old bell and rope that offers an irresistible invitation to pull.

For all the pride Gubbio takes in the legend of the Spadalongas' charity, the city is more popularly known for another legend—Francis and the wolf. Indeed, the miracle of Francis and the wolf, presumably a different wolf from the one terrorizing farmers near the Abbazia di Vallingegno, almost defines Gubbio. There is a huge bronze sculpture of Francis with the wolf in the garden just outside the church and another near the Porta Romana gate into the city. The Rough Guide lists San Francesco e il Lupo (wolf) and the Taverna del Lupo as two of the city's most popular restaurants. The saint and the wolf appear on souvenir ceramic tiles and mugs and wall hangings in shops all over Gubbio. Everyone loves the miracle of Francis and the wolf.

The Gubbio legend began when a wolf, described on one of the sculptures as *"un grandissimo lupo, terribile et feroce,"* was terrorizing Gubbians by killing livestock and farmers alike. The good people were scared to go outside the city walls until Francis arrived on a visit—and decided to confront the wolf himself. The people begged him not to, but off he went toward the forest and soon encountered the *grandissimo lupo* slouching toward him, teeth bared. And the miracle begins.

Francis stopped the wolf in midstride, according to *Little Flowers of St. Francis,* by making the sign of the cross. He then ordered "Brother Wolf" to come to him, which the wolf summarily did and meekly "lay down at the Saint's feet as though it had become a lamb." After scolding the wolf for committing "horrible crimes," Francis proceeded to negotiate peace with the beast. Would he promise to stop his killing spree if the people of Gubbio promised to give him food every day? The wolf nodded his head, then placed his paw in Francis's hand to cement the pledge. Francis and the wolf, now walking beside him "like a very gentle lamb," returned to the marketplace, where a huge crowd had gathered.

After delivering a sermon from a rock—now enshrined in the church of San Francesco—Francis exacted a promise from the people of Gubbio to "feed the wolf regularly." They evidently did. "It went from door to door for food. It hurt no one and no one hurt it," recounts the *Little Flowers of St. Francis.* The Gubbians were even sorry when the wolf died two years later and erected a shrine over its burial site on the Via Globo. In a startling validation of the legend, an excavation of the shrine in the late nineteenth century is said to have revealed the skeleton of a wolf, with its *feroce* teeth and skull intact.

So powerful was the legend of the wolf among early Franciscans that in 1213 the bishop of Assisi persuaded the Benedictines to give Francis and his friars La Vittorina, a tiny church just outside the current city walls, where the taming of the wolf took place. We have a rather difficult time finding the church in the confluence of roads looping around it, but we manage, guided by a modern bronze sculpture of a barefoot, tattered Francis being licked in the face by the adoring wolf. We clearly are not the only ones to have sought out the legendary shrine: Stuffed in Francis's sculpted bronze hand is a bouquet of fresh red roses.

I want to digress for a moment here to explain why I am including so many of Francis's miracles and in such detail. Some of his modern biographers downplay or even exclude the many miracles attributed to him. They are more concerned with Francis's spiritual development and the rapid growth of the Franciscan movement. That, of course, is understandable and entirely relevant, but I think diminishing the miracles misses an instructive and charming dimension of the Franciscan legend. Obviously, there's no way to prove the miracles, which if taken literally often seem silly.

One has to suspend disbelief and not only give in to the mysticism that laced medieval times but factor in a political aspect as well.

Francis's medieval biographers, all of whom were Franciscan friars, were determined to present him as a messenger of God on earth and thus armed him with all sorts of otherworldly powers. They were also determined to confirm and maintain his status as a saint, which gives even more credence to their emphasis on miracles. That they were successful goes without saying, but their body of evidence seems far less relevant and even embarrassing today to some modern Franciscan friars.

"Yes, that *supposedly* happened here," says Padre Tonino, a friar we meet at the Franciscan church in Alessandria, Lombardy. We have gone miles out of our way to the attractive, quite modern city because eight centuries ago Celano had recorded a charming miracle there, performed on Francis's behalf, after a dinner party.

The legend holds that Francis's host in Alessandria, where he had come to preach, was so thrilled to have Francis at his table that he ordered the ultimate delicacy—a seven-year-old capon—to be served for the meal. A wicked man, posing as a beggar, came to the door during dinner and received as alms a piece of the capon from Francis. But he did not eat it. Instead, the next day, hoping to expose the humble Francis as a closet hedonist, the wicked man (described as a "son of Belial" by Celano) waved the incriminating capon to a crowd gathered to hear Francis preach so the people could "see what kind of man this Francis is." But his scheme backfired when the capon in his hand turned miraculously into an everyday fish.

It was that documented story of Francis in Alessandria that had brought us to the city, but to Father Tonino, as to many other friars we talk to all over Italy, it is the spiritual legacy of Francis and the very real work they are doing now that identifies their faith, not medieval capons turning into fish.

Father Tonino, for example, an attractive man of fifty with close-cropped hair and cheerful brown eyes, was a missionary in Zaire until his mission was burned, rebuilt, and then bombed. He now feeds upward of thirty poor people a night in Alessandria with the help of volunteers and five resident friars. The cloister of his quite modern church is not reserved for contemplative prayer but has been turned into a miniature soccer field for local children. And a sunny, new meeting room, next to the church's massive library under reconstruction, sports a colorful painting by a group of ten-year-olds, which includes not only St. Francis asleep in St. Clare's arms but also a portrait of the Italian author and native Alessandrian Umberto Eco.

Like the people he serves, Father Tonino lives very much in the here and now. "Excuse me, I must go to work now," he says as a young man enters the church and steps into the confessional.

I understand the impatience and even embarrassment of today's friars toward the miracles, but I think they are instructive. They are filled with the mystery and often the superstitions of the medieval age—seven-year-old capons, for example, were believed to have precious stones in their entrails, while eight-year-old capons were reserved for a king. The miracles also speak to the very real fears and dangers of the time: predatory wild animals, life-snuffing diseases, crippling injuries, poverty, drought, floods, famine, and violence, always violence. Because medieval doctors had very little ability to cure anything, injury or illness, people naturally turned to the healing powers of the godly—and hoped for a miracle.

One of my favorites, also recorded by Celano, occurred in Gubbio. A woman whose hands were "so crippled that she could do no work at all with them" hurried to Francis during one of his visits to the town and begged him to touch them. "Moved to pity," he did so, and presto, her hands were cured. What makes this miracle so beguiling is that she did not fall on her knees to praise God or instantly become a Franciscan convert but instead ran home to make a cheese cake for Francis "with her own hands."

Francis must have recovered his physical strength in Gubbio, thanks to the generosity of the Spadalonga family. And he did not waver from his search for spiritual strength. The brigands who set upon him in the forest and the Benedictine monks who did not succor him merely reinforced his conviction in his new calling. In the spirit of "the things that formerly made you shudder will bring you great sweetness and content," he spent his time taking care of the lepers at a nearby leprosarium before setting out again for Assisi.

Francis left the lepers in Gubbio in the summer of 1206 to return to

restoring the little ruined church of San Damiano. He still took the mission from Christ to rebuild his church literally. Collecting stones for the
project was in order, but Francis soon realized it would take many more
stones than he could glean from the surrounding land. So he decided, for
the first time, to beg.

"Whoever gives me a stone will get a reward from the Lord," he evidently called out to the citizens of Assisi. "Whoever gives me two stones
will get two rewards." And so on. When that did not work, he would
break into song, singing the praises of the Lord, in French.

One can only imagine the stupefaction of the Assisians who for years
had heard Francis singing heroic ballads and love songs and now found
him singing to the Lord and dressed in a hermit's tunic on the back of
which he had etched a cross with a brick. Perhaps the stones he started lug-
ging back to San Damiano were given to him out of pity or just to get rid
of him, but he eventually had enough to start rebuilding the church.

It was hard work, too hard for Francis. He had never been a particularly
strong person, and he had never really recovered his health from his imprisonment in Perugia. The old priest at San Damiano was worried about
him and started giving Francis larger portions and choicer selections of
whatever food he had, but Francis soon caught on to the priest's sacrifice.
And another moment in the legend was solidified: Francis decided to go
door to door in Assisi and beg for his food.

Assisians were well used to beggars, but to have young Francis
Bernadone, the party animal who had always lavished money on food and
drink for his friends, come to the door with a begging bowl was beyond
comprehension. Some of them must have filled his bowl, because Francis
did not starve to death, but the quality of what they gave him was questionable if not insulting. "When he saw his bowl full of all kinds of scraps, he
was struck with horror," writes Celano, "but mindful of God and con-
quering himself, he ate the food with joy of spirit."

A particularly awkward transaction took place when Francis, who had
also taken to begging for oil to light San Damiano's lamps, arrived at one
house to discover his former fellow revelers partying inside. In one of the
more human moments recorded by his biographers, Francis was struck
with "bashfulness and retraced his steps." He then "rebuked" himself and,

after passing "judgment on himself," returned to the scene of his humiliation and successfully begged for the oil "in a kind of spiritual intoxica-
tion."

His father and brother were evidently embarrassed beyond measure by
Francis's antics. And understandably so. The snickering in Assisi about
the fancy man-about-town transformed into a tattered, French-spouting
beggar for God must have been mortifying. There is no further mention of
Francis's mother in the early biographies, but his brother, Angelo, merits
at least one venomous story. Seeing Francis shivering with cold one day
and struggling to carry a load of stones, Angelo turned to a friend and said,
"Tell Francis to sell you a pennysworth of sweat," to which Francis cheerfully and predictably replied, "Indeed, I will sell my sweat more dearly to
my Lord."

Pietro di Bernadone remains the same, particularly unpleasant, charac-
ter in the early biographies. Every time the status-seeking merchant saw his
former son on the streets of Assisi, according to Celano, he "would lash
out at him with curses." To protect himself from his father, who must still
have frightened him, Francis persuaded a local outcast, with whom he
shared his alms, to stand in for his father. Every time Pietro di Bernadone
cursed him, Francis would ask—and receive—a paternal blessing from
the ragged father figure.

But it was the restoration of San Damiano that Francis cared about the
most. And slowly, with the masonry skills he had presumably learned as a
teenager from building the defensive walls around Assisi, he finished. It
was the spring of 1208, almost exactly two years after he stripped naked
outside the bishop's residence and traded in Pietro di Bernadone for a heavenly father.

His biographers claim that others helped Francis rebuild San Damiano, drawn perhaps by his joy and good humor, not to mention his melo-
dious singing voice. And perhaps that is true. Or perhaps they were drawn
by his grandiose and quite outrageous prophecy, delivered loudly in
French, of course, that San Damiano was no mere church but would
someday be a monastery, as Celano puts it, for "the holy virgins of Christ."
In other words—for women.

6 *Clare's "Prison"*

Father Antonio is struggling to maintain his composure. The attractive, young, English-speaking friar is in charge of San Damiano, and his cell phone never stops ringing. There's a tour bus about to arrive and a group of nuns from Africa and cars pulling into the parking lot and people arriving by foot along the walkway from Assisi. And there are Harvey and me, with our cameras and notebooks.

⚞ He sincerely wants to show us around San Damiano, and in between arrivals he hurries us along the covered entrance portico. "San Damiano was once a hospital for lepers, and because of that, no one ever came here," he says, telling us a bit of information, albeit somewhat breathlessly, that we did not know before.

⚞ What we do know is that Francis's prophecy for San Damiano came true. In 1212, four years after he finished the restoration, Francis installed Clare, his most recent and illustrious convert, in San Damiano, with the consent of the bishop of Assisi. We'll get to the details of that story later, but it was here, inside San Damiano's small cluster of old stone buildings, that Clare would be cloistered for an incredible forty-one years.

⚞ We hurtle along behind Father Antonio through the door leading toward the sisters' dormitory. Some fifty women would join Clare at San Damiano in the

Franciscan Order of Poor Ladies, the second order founded by Francis; among them were the daughters and sisters of Assisi's noble families and Clare's own mother and sister. They filled their days caring for the sick, growing their own vegetables and grains, doing chores around the convent, and engaging in contemplation and prayer, eight times a day. They ate very little, being in a state of constant fast, except for Christmas Day, when they were allowed two meals.

Conversation was forbidden in the dormitory, in the church, and during meals. Even the act of confession to a priest was tempered. "And they shall take care not to introduce other talk unless it pertains to the confession and the salvation of souls," Clare wrote in her Rule for the Poor Ladies. The ensuing devotional silence was so profound that an early biographer of Francis and Clare claimed that several sisters had difficulty remembering "how to form words as they should."

We are moving so fast in Father Antonio's wake that it is difficult to contemplate what it must have been like to be a cloistered Poor Lady. But then again, it probably would have been just as difficult had our pace been more leisurely. Father Antonio leads us through the morgue or *sepolcreto,* where the early sisters, including Clare's mother, Ortolana, and her sister, Agnes, were buried until their remains were moved to Clare's basilica in Assisi. We look into the adjoining sisters' choir, with its primitive, pitted wooden stalls and a fifteenth-century frescoed wall that had unfortunately replaced the grille, now in St. Clare's basilica, through which the sisters, ever chaste, heard mass and received communion from a male priest. It was through that grille that Clare and the other Poor Ladies are thought to have viewed Francis's body for the last time as it was being carried to Assisi by his friars. That final farewell, which Giotto portrayed with artistic license as being outside San Damiano, is part of his fresco cycle in St. Francis's basilica in Assisi.

The full impact of Clare's life within the walls becomes depressingly clear when we follow Father Antonio up a flight of old stairs, past her tiny, walled *giardinetto,* or garden, and into her dormitory. It was here, on the stone floor of the austere rectangular room and under a wood-beamed roof, that Clare lived with her sisters. The only sources of light are two small windows, which frame what must have been a tantalizing view of the spires of Assisi. There doesn't appear to be any source of heat until Father Antonio tells us that there had been a fireplace but it had to be covered over "because of the tourists."

This one, bleak room was for years Clare's only world. "She had arthritis and had difficulty with the stairs," Father Antonio explains. Here Clare lived, ate, slept, sewed and embroidered altar cloths for poor churches (an example of which is among the relics in her basilica in Assisi), and as abbess, ministered to the other Poor Ladies, later known as Poor Clares. She prayed in the small adjoining oratorio. The grille still there in the chapel floor provided access for communion to be passed up to her from below, Father Antonio tells us, and some say it was through this grille, not the one downstairs, that she looked at the dead body of Francis.

Clare's life, too, was documented by Thomas of Celano, in *The Life of St. Clare Virgin,* begun in 1255, soon after her canonization. Numerous other books have been written about her, some in English or in English translations, including a comic book for children we bought in Assisi titled *Clare of Assisi, The Little Flowers of Saint Clare* by the contemporary Italian author Piero Bargellini and a narrative written by the prodigious Franciscan author and friar Murray Bodo titled *Clare: A Light in the Garden.*

All of Clare's biographers stress her devotion to "Blessed Francis" and her ardent embrace of poverty, but Celano supplies excruciating details. Clare reportedly went barefoot year-round on those cold, stone floors and during Lent fasted completely three days a week and lived on bread and water alone the other days. Francis and the bishop of Assisi intervened when they were alerted to her self-imposed food deprivation and ordered Clare "not to let a day go by without eating at least an ounce and a half of bread."

She "mortified" her body in penance, according to Celano, by wearing a hair shirt, and not just any hair shirt; Clare chose secretly to wear the skin of a pig with the bristle side inward under her already patched and inadequate clothing. As if that weren't excruciating enough, she is said to have alternated the bristly pig hide with "a stiff hair shirt woven with horsehair with knots all over it," which she cinched tightly to her body with rough cords. A comfortable bed was out of the question. Clare slept on vine branches with her head on a piece of wood until her health began to give out. She moved to a mat on the floor with straw for a pillow until finally, at Francis's order during the onset of her "prolonged illness" with arthritis at the age of thirty-one, she began sleeping on a bag stuffed with straw.

And she cried, a lot, for Christ's suffering, though it's hard to believe it didn't include her own. Celano writes about the "rivers of tears" bursting from her eyes after the last prayer of the night, setting off similar tears among the other women in the dormitory. Clare's weeping even brought the devil to her one night in the form of a dark child. "Don't weep so much or you'll go blind," the devil-child said to her, to which Clare replied, "Anyone who shall see God will not be blinded." The devil-child tried another tack. "Don't cry so much or your brain will dissolve and run down your nostrils and then your nose will be crooked." But Clare drove him off for good by retorting, "No crookedness is suffered by those who serve the Lord."

Clare performed a multitude of miracles at San Damiano, several of which had to do with food. At one point, when the larder was almost bare, she multiplied a single loaf of bread into enough to amply feed both the fifty Poor Ladies and the friars assigned to look after them. Another time, during a visit by Pope Innocent IV, crosses miraculously appeared on loaves of bread after Clare blessed them.

Others of Clare's miracles at San Damiano would change the course of history. The best known is her stand against the mercenary army of Saracens and Tartars raised by Emperor Frederick II against Rome. In the ongoing battle between Church and State, the emperor unleashed his forces on the Christian towns of the Spoleto Valley. On a Friday in September 1240, the mercenary hordes arrived at the gates of San Damiano, scaled the walls, and streamed into the cloister. The Poor Ladies, quite naturally, were terrified, but the bedridden Clare saved the day. Ordering her sisters to carry her to the front door of the convent, or into the refectory as some claim, she prostrated herself in prayer before the ciborium, the box that held the bread for communion, and called on Jesus to save San Damiano and Assisi. He evidently answered her call. The marauders inexplicably withdrew from San Damiano as quickly as they had entered, and Assisi, though damaged, was not overrun.

But it is a miraculous event that occurred toward the end of her life that lives on to this day. Clare was very ill and unable to attend a Christmas ser/ vice being celebrated in the church of St. Francis five miles away in Assisi, yet she both heard the music and the prayers and saw the crèche of Jesus. That miracle would move Pope Pius XII, in 1958, to bestow the title of Patron Saint of Television on Clare for having seen the first live broadcast on the thirteenth/century wall of her cell. As a reminder, the late ABC News anchor, Peter Jennings, kept a statue of St. Clare on his desk.

For all of Clare's poor health, she would outlive Francis by twenty/seven years. Her final illness culminated in a personal victory. For years she had been pleading with the various cardinals and Popes in Rome to approve the Privilege of Poverty that she and her order resolutely followed, but one after another had refused. The sticking point was her absolute refusal for the order, or any sister within the order, to own any property, an unheard/of concept then for nuns or sisters. The Popes felt that women of the Church should be financially protected and, like the Benedictines, at least own communal property so they would not have to depend completely on alms for food and housing.

But Clare was determined, especially after Francis died and some of his friars began to bend his strict rules against owning property in order to live more comfortably. In defiance, she wrote her own Rule of Life as a legacy for her order; it states emphatically that no sister can receive or have "pos/ session or ownership either of themselves or through an intermediary, or even anything that might reasonably be called property." The only excep/ tion she allowed was the land "as necessity" around a convent for the sis/ ters' "proper seclusion" and its cultivated use as a garden "for the needs of the sisters."

As Clare lay dying, one church official after another came from Rome to visit her, including Pope Innocent IV—twice. Her influence had spread far beyond the walls of San Damiano. By then some 150 convents were associated with the Poor Ladies, not only in Italy but in France, Spain, Poland, Slovakia, Moravia, and the most famous, Prague, estab/ lished by Princess Agnes, daughter of the king of Bohemia. (Agnes of Prague forswore marriage to the Emperor Frederick II as well as to King Henry III of England to become a Poor Clare. And Isabelle, sister of

Louis IX of France, founded her own Poor Clare convent at Longchamp rather than marry Frederick II's son.) But Clare still did not have what she wanted most. Though one cardinal had approved her Rule, she wanted the ultimate guarantee: a Papal bull on parchment with all its attendant seals and ribbons ensuring the right of her sisters everywhere to live in extreme, communal poverty.

In his book *The Little Flowers of St. Clare,* Piero Bargellini paints a moving portrait of Clare's yearning for the Papal guarantee on her deathbed: "For this reason, she gazed lovingly at the hands of the Cardinals and Bishops who came to visit her; then, not seeing this roll of parchment with the leaden bull, the seal hanging from it, she would sigh again, turn her head away, close her eyes and repeat her silent prayer." She entreated Francis's original companions who visited her to pray "that she would not die before that Papal Bull arrived at San Damiano."

She succeeded—but just. On August 10, 1253, the sealed bull arrived, just one day after the Pope had signed it in Assisi. It reads, in part: "No one is permitted to destroy this page of our confirmation or to oppose it recklessly. If anyone shall have presumed to attempt this, let him know that he will incur the wrath of Almighty God and of his holy Apostles, Peter and Paul."

Clare died the next day, at the age of sixty. The spot is roped off on the stone floor at the end of the dormitory, lit by two naked lightbulbs, and identified by a wooden cross on the wall and the inevitable fresh flowers.

It is with some relief, on my part anyway, that we leave Clare's dormitory and follow Father Antonio down a passage to the courtyard outside. He apologizes that he cannot show us the sisters' second-floor infirmary; the small building, formerly the residence of San Damiano's priest, had been structurally damaged in the 1997 earthquake and is closed to visitors. So is the ground-floor refectory where the Poor Ladies ate their meager meals in silence, listening to the Bible. Clearly visible through the open door, however, are the smoke-blackened walls and frescoes, the jumbled stone floor, and the sisters' original dark, heavy wood tables and benches. The scene is so authentic that we fully expect to see Clare take her place under the wooden cross that marked the abbess's place. Further enhancing the medieval mood is the sound of psalms being sung quite beautifully by a group of German pilgrims at San Damiano's entrance.

Father Antonio has to leave us in the courtyard to hurry back to his post, and we thank him profusely for his time. "Please take these as a gift," he says, thrusting several prayer and history cards of San Damiano into our hands. "God bless you."

I am happy to linger in front of the refectory, with all its memories of Clare. What an extraordinary woman she was. Though her legend may very well have been exaggerated, she was a person of steadfast determina-tion and dedication. When she heard of the martyrdom of five Franciscan friars in Morocco in 1220, she chafed at being unable to go to the Muslim country herself to emulate their sacrifice. She stood up to Popes and cardi-nals, looked after her sisters, and not only embraced what I would consider a horrible cloistered life but shared her passion for it with other Poor Clares.

"What you do, may you always do and never abandon," she wrote to Agnes of Prague, whom she addressed as the "daughter of the King of Kings," in 1235. "But with swift pace, light step and unswerving feet, so that even your steps stir up no dust, go forward securely, joyfully and swiftly, on the path of prudent happiness."

Clare was also very human. Mindful perhaps of her own extreme penance, which would advance her ill health and leave her an invalid for almost thirty years, she cautioned Agnes in a later letter about the rules for fasting and abstinence. "But our flesh is not bronze nor is our strength that of stone," she wrote in 1238. "No, we are frail and inclined to every bodily weakness! I beg you, therefore, dearly beloved, to refrain wisely and pru-dently from an indiscreet and impossible austerity in the fasting that I know you have undertaken. And I beg you . . . to offer to the Lord your reasonable service and your sacrifice always seasoned with salt."

I am reluctant to leave San Damiano. Though its historical emphasis is on Francis and the replica of the talking cross that hangs over the altar in the convent's old, smoke-blackened church, the soul of San Damiano is Clare. In 2003 there were twenty thousand members of the Poor Clares worldwide, either cloistered as she was or working with the needy in their communities. The Poor Clares have a multitude of websites, including www.poorclares.org for the sisters in Canton, Ohio, where they still live by her hard-fought Rule.

But there wouldn't, of course, have been a Clare at all without Francis. It was his stunning influence and ascetic way of life that had influenced her and so many others in the Middle Ages. I struggle to comprehend how one man could cause so many to give away all their earthly possessions to the poor, often over the furious objections of their would-have-been heirs, and enter, with joy, into lives of abject deprivation. But thousands did.

I wander into the little church at San Damiano that had started the whole sequence of events and study the replica of the original cross. It is huge, some six feet high and four feet wide, and painted on cloth in bright, cheerful colors. The Christ is not the traditional Christ in agony, with blood dripping from the crown of thorns on his head and the wounds in his hands, feet, and side, but a peaceful Christ, whose wounds don't seem to hurt. The San Damiano Christ is not dead but alive. His eyes are open, his arms outstretched in rebirth. There are the requisite details depicting the story of his death, resurrection, and ascension into heaven, and the usual cast of characters—the Virgin Mary, John, Mary Magdalene, the Roman soldiers who crucified him, and others—but it is the Christ figure that dominates. He is strong, even healthy looking, and bathed in light.

Sitting quietly there in the church, I can see how that figure transfixed Francis. The San Damiano cross does not speak out loud to me, of course, as it did to Francis, but as much as the icon projects sadness and loss, it also speaks of hope. That must have been a powerful message in the Middle Ages, when there was so much despair and uncertainty.

In my reverie about the cross, I almost miss the windowsill to the right of the entrance where Francis hurled the sack of money to restore San Damiano after the priest refused to accept it. Amazingly, the *fenestra del dinaro* is still there, framed by two fourteenth-century commemorative frescoes, one showing Francis being dragged away from San Damiano by his furious father in front of the terrified priest, the other depicting Francis praying before the cross.

That San Damiano remains so authentic is due largely to the faith—and charity—of one British family. Lord Ripon, a British statesman, former viceroy of India and dedicated convert to Catholicism, bought San Damiano some 150 years ago, just as the secular government of Camillo Cavour was poised to nationalize it and expel its friars. By buying San Damiano and holding it in his name, Lord Ripon was able to give use of his private property to the Franciscans, who were not, of course, allowed to own any property themselves. Lord Ripon also restored the convent at his expense, an extraordinary act recorded in Latin on a wall outside the convent.

The ownership of San Damiano was passed down through the family until 1983, when its then heir returned San Damiano officially to the Franciscans—but with conditions. The Franciscans were enjoined to keep the medieval convent of Francis and Clare unchanged forever and to preserve its spiritual purpose by welcoming worshipers to prayers with the friars in the old church and limiting tourist hours.

The result is the jewel of Assisi's shrines to Francis and Clare. Set in terraced olive groves, rimmed with cypresses, and nestled on the slope of Mount Subasio, little San Damiano speaks more of the saints it honors than any of the other, more tarted-up Franciscan sites around Assisi, especially Santa Maria degli Angeli, or the Porziuncola, the second church Francis restored—which is virtually unrecognizable.

7 *Peace March in Santa Maria degli Angeli*

The tiny Porziuncola *inside Santa Maria degli Angeli, where Francis finds a spiritual home and the Franciscan movement is born*

The Patriarchal Basilica de Santa Maria degli Angeli looms over the valley at the foot of Mount Subasio, just a mile and a half from Assisi. The basilica's enormous size and neo-Baroque architecture, with all its attendant swirls and curls (not to mention the recorded organ music broadcast outdoors over loudspeakers), prompts adjectives like "kitsch" or "grotesque." Even the official Assisi tourist map describes the basilica as "grandiose," while the less politic Rough Guide declares it a "majestically uninspiring pile."

Steeped as we are in the message of poverty and simplicity that Francis both preached and lived, we find it almost impossible to comprehend how such an overblown edifice could have been built to shelter the little Porziuncola, the second, and most important, church Francis restored. The domed basilica is visible for miles by day and is just as prominent at night: the three-story-high gilded bronze replica of the Virgin Mary on its façade is crowned with a halo of bright electric lightbulbs.

Inside this architectural sand castle run amok is a replica of the tiny, decrepit chapel Francis chanced on in the forest soon after restoring San Damiano. He was captivated by what Celano describes as a "church of the

Blessed Virgin Mother of God that had been built in ancient times, but was now deserted and cared for by no one." Francis set to rebuilding the church, which measured just ten feet by twenty-three feet and was nicknamed the Porziuncola either for the "little piece" of land it sat on owned by the local Benedictines or, as others suggest, for the "little piece" of stone from the site of the Virgin Mary's assumption into heaven brought back there by pilgrims from the Holy Land.

Whatever the source of the Porziuncola's nickname, the derelict church and its spiritual aura resonated with Francis. Not only did he revere the Virgin Mary but while he was restoring "her" church, he was visited often by the angels inherent in the church's formal name. The combination led to his decision to live at the Porziuncola. "He decided to stay there permanently out of reverence for the angels and love for the Mother of Christ," writes St. Bonaventure. "He loved this spot more than any other in the world."

Eight hundred years later, no other church, including his own basilica in Assisi, is so closely associated with Francis and his legend. It was at the Porziuncola that Franciscanism took hold; that Francis welcomed the runaway Clare; that Francis lived for eighteen years with his friars; that in 1219 his order gathered, some five thousand strong; that Francis resigned as head of the order in 1220, and that, six years later, he died.

The humble church where it all began quickly became an international shrine. To accommodate the crowds, a huge basilica was erected over the tiny chapel in the sixteenth and seventeenth centuries, rebuilt after an earthquake in the nineteenth century, and restored again after the earthquake of 1997. A town quickly grew around the basilica, both named Santa Maria degli Angeli, and the old forests were felled and replaced with grids of paved streets. Hotels, restaurants, and coffee bars followed, as did shops and street bazaars featuring sweatshirts with the logo "Assisi."

Nonetheless, the power of that original, simple chapel extended worldwide, including America. A Franciscan friar exploring California in 1769 named a river, in Spanish, Nuestra Señora de los Angeles de la Porciuncula, and the settlement established later along its bank came to be known as El Pueblo de Nuestra Señora la Reina de los Angeles de Porciuncula, or the Town of Our Lady the Queen of Angels of the Little Por- tion. The name of that settlement would, in time, be shortened to Los An- geles.

The town of Santa Maria degli Angeli is a madhouse during one of our visits there in the fall of 2004. The streets are being overrun by Italians, waving placards and banners and flags and marching in a *Manifestazióne di pace.* It is that once-a-year day when more than one hundred thousand Ital- ians march for peace from Perugia to Assisi via Santa Maria degli Angeli, and we find ourselves, accidentally, among them. It seems entirely fitting that Francis, a medieval monument for peace, would have brought all these people to the town named after his little church and on to his hometown in the midst of the war with Iraq. *"Pace,"* the tie-dyed banners read. Peace.

Francis would have loved the foot-weary peace pilgrims sprawled on their backpacks in the gigantic piazza in front of the equally gigantic church. But he would have been stunned to see what had happened to his simple little church, which used to stand along a narrow path in the woods below Assisi.

The Porziuncola now sits on acres of marble floor inside the triple-nave basilica, dwarfed by massive columns and the basilica's sky-scraping dome. It looks more like a gaily painted doll's house than the simple home of the Franciscan Order. The only authentic feeling of Francis is in the chapel's rough stone interior and the excavated fragments of the original church under the altar. The fourteenth-century frescoes depicting scenes from his life help somewhat, but I can't avoid the sensation I am in some sort of theme park named Francis World.

Still, the chapel evokes deep feelings among many of its visitors. On this crazy day of the peace march in 2004, people stand patiently in snaking lines to move quietly through it; a nun finds a seat inside the chapel to say her prayers and, an hour later, is still there. On a quieter day the year be- fore, we had seen a group of young Franciscan sisters leaving the chapel, some in tears. They had celebrated mass inside the Porziuncola, led by a Franciscan priest, and were obviously deeply moved.

So I fight my critical self and move on across the marble floor from the Porziuncola to the Cappella del Transito or Chapel of the Transitus, a replica of the friars' infirmary where Francis died. A huge nineteenth-century painting on the chapel's exterior wall shows Francis in the midst of his friars being welcomed into heaven by angels and broadcasts the chapel's significance, though it would have been more poignant if the "infirmary" had been made of wood and thatch, not brick.

Far more touching, inside the chapel is a simply beautiful white-enameled terra-cotta sculpture of Francis by the fifteenth-century genius Andrea Della Robbia. The barefoot figure holding a gold cross positively glows, and the gentle expression on his face fits comfortably my mental image of Francis. The seeming confusion about the date of his death—October 4, 1226, on the outside of the chapel, October 3 on the inside—is explained by a passing friar. Dusk, not midnight, marked the beginning of a new day in the Middle Ages, and Francis died at night.

Many of the legends about Francis took place at the Porziuncola, and we follow the sign to the Cappella delle Rose or Chapel of the Roses. Along the way is a glassed-in garden that sets the scene for one of Francis's most human moments. Distracted one night in his prayers by feelings of earthly yearning—that is, lust—Francis threw himself into a thicket of brambles. Miraculously, the briars did not pierce his flesh but instead were transformed into a bush of thornless roses. The still-thornless roses in the current garden, supposedly descendants of the benign medieval bushes, still bloom every May, followed by the immediate shedding of their leaves, seemingly stained with blood.

The re-created garden is a welcome relief from the basilica's massive marble interior. Goldfish swim in a fountain. White pigeons and doves feast on birdseed around a garden sculpture of Francis holding a basket for alms. A second garden sculpture of him, this one with a lamb, suggests another legend at the Porziuncola. Francis was given a lamb as a gift, and wanting to keep it, he instructed the lamb to praise God and not to bother the other friars. The lamb evidently took his instructions to heart. Not only did it go regularly into the church, kneel at the altar, and bleat its praises to the Virgin Mary but it took communion equally piously as well.

The garden honors another charming animal legend in a little niche in the wall. This one involves a cricket in a fig tree outside Francis's cell that he tamed. "Come, Sister Cricket," Francis would say, according to the

Legend of Perugia. "Sing, Sister Cricket." The cricket sat on Francis's finger and serenaded him an hour a day for eight days, until he gave it permission to leave. "Blessed Francis found so much joy in creatures for love of the Creator that the Lord tamed the wild beasts to console the body and soul of his servant," explains the *Legend of Perugia.*

The sunken, thirteenth-century Chapel of the Roses is farther down the corridor from the thornless rose garden. Constructed originally by St. Bonaventure around Francis's favorite cell and enlarged by St. Bernardino of Siena in the fifteenth century, it is said to have been a place Francis passed entire nights in prayer. It was presumably from this now subterranean grotto that Francis tamed Sister Cricket and that his straying thoughts prompted his plunge into the nearby brambles. A sixteenth-century fresco of the Miracle of the Roses adorns the chapel wall, along with frescoes of Francis with his first companions and the granting of the indulgence at the Porziuncola.

I'm on my hands and knees peering through a grate into the underground chapel when the narrow corridor is suddenly filled with singing. I pull myself to my feet to hear the beautiful voices of a visiting choir of Russian Orthodox women, standing right behind me, singing a Laud in close harmony. They have come a long way to celebrate the spirit of Francis here, and once again I am reminded of the impact he continues to have on the spiritual lives of so many.

I am struck further by an Italian couple we meet in the basilica's courtyard who had driven two and a half hours from Brescia to march in the peace demonstration. The man's name is Francesco, he tells us. His father named him after the saint because he was born prematurely and had to spend the first two months of his life in an oxygen-rich incubator. There was fear that he might be blind as a result, and his father had come to Assisi every day to pray for him. "I'm now a heart surgeon," Francesco says proudly, then asks my husband to take a picture of him and his wife holding a *"Pace"* banner in front of a statue of his namesake and patron saint.

Standing there in the courtyard, I realize I envy the people flocking to Santa Maria degli Angeli—like the Russian Orthodox choir and the nun praying for hours in the Porziuncola, and our new friend Francesco—who are not at all put off by the contradictions of the basilica but can see beyond it to embrace the spirit of Francis. And there are many, many like them, of every faith and national origin.

The basilica's bookstore is a blueprint of Francis's global appeal. There are aisles and aisles of books about Francis and some about Clare, in Italian, English, French, German, Dutch, Russian, Japanese, Chinese, Serbian, Croatian, Spanish, and Portuguese. This multitude of languages is mirrored in the basilica's gift shop. The souvenir bins, observed by security cameras, offer tau and San Damiano crosses in every size, crucifixes, pictures of Francis, multilingual videos and copies of the Canticle to Brother Sun, on and on, all of which customers can buy in the language of their choice, the selections being posted by each cash register. Even confession is global. Each confessional booth inside the basilica has the padre's language abilities posted outside: Italian-English, Italian-French-German, and so on.

However grandiose and contrived Santa Maria degli Angeli may seem, there is no doubt that the basilica is central to the religious legacy of Francis. While Francis is buried in Assisi, his basilica there is really more an unparalleled Renaissance art gallery than it is his spiritual heart. He was never physically at the basilica in Assisi, after all, but he was certainly at the Porziuncola, the tiny chapel in the woods near Assisi, where on a winter morning in 1208, his life changed forever.

8 *Francis Gets His Marching Orders*

THE PORZIUNCOLA, *where Francis receives his calling* · ASSISI, *where he converts his first companions* · RIVO TORTO, *where he teaches his friars to follow his vision*

Francis was praying in the little Porziuncola on the Feast of St. Matthias, and a priest from the Benedictine convent higher up on the mountain had come to say mass for him. The priest chose to read the Mass of the Apostles, which contains the Mission of Christ to His Disciples. Francis, who still thought he was fulfilling Jesus' command from the cross at San Damiano by rebuilding San Damiano and the Porziuncola, suddenly saw the bigger picture.

After the mass, which had been in Latin, Francis asked the priest to explain more fully Jesus' instructions, presumably in his own Umbrian dialect. The priest summed up Jesus' orders to his apostles from St. Matthew's Gospel: They were to preach as they went, spreading the message that the Kingdom of God was at hand. They were not to take anything with them on their journey—no gold or silver or copper or a bag or two tunics or shoes or a staff. They should trust in God to supply their needs and wish peace on any house that was worthy.

The impact on Francis was immediate. Taking the message of the Gospels to be his own, new instructions, and embracing them with "inconceivable joy," St. Bonaventure writes, Francis "cast off the shoes from his feet, laid aside the staff which he bore, and throwing away his purse and all that he possessed, he clad himself in a single tunic and, instead of the belt which he wore, he girded himself with a cord."

Barefoot, wearing a "poor and mean tunic," which Francis designed with the arms extended to look like a cross, he set out from the Porziun-cola to Assisi on his new mission to preach penance and redemption. But his was an uplifting message, not one of fire and brimstone. "God give you peace and well-being," he would say to every startled bystander he passed, a salutation that no one in that violent time had presumably heard before and that today is reproduced on flags and ceramic tiles and key chains all over Assisi, both in Latin—*Pax et Bonum*—and in Italian—*Pace e Bene.*

At first the people of Assisi regarded this latest version of Francis with skepticism and, often, scorn. But there was something about the fervor with which he spoke, the joy he apparently felt in his poverty, the care he had taken of the lepers that made the people wonder whether he really was some sort of prophet. And he was always cheerful, smiling and singing and preaching to whomever would listen to him.

Slowly Francis began to make an impression on those who were willing to suspend disbelief and at least consider that he had honestly converted to a life of poverty and spiritual service. The priest at his parish church of San Giorgio, where Francis had received his rudimentary schooling, even in-vited him to preach there. Celano writes that Francis began by "wishing peace to the congregation, speaking without affectation but with such en-thusiasm that all were carried away by his words."

That may very well be an exaggeration, but there is no doubt he was having an impact. What set Francis apart from the clergy of the time is that he delivered his simple, direct message in the language of the people, not in Latin. He also faced the people, unlike the priests, whose practice was to turn their backs to the congregation. And he soon began to win his first supporters.

We are standing in front of the house just off the Via San Gregorio in Assisi where Francis received his first convert. The inscription in the stone arch over the front door identifies the house as having belonged to Assisi's rich and well-born Bernardo di Quintavalle, a law graduate from the University of Bologna, and it was in this house, during a long night in 1208, that Bernardo tested Francis's devotional authenticity.

Bernardo, who had known Francis as a flamboyant youth, had watched him labor to restore the churches, care for the lepers, and live happily in poverty. Intrigued, he often invited his friend to spend the night in his house. Legend has it that Bernardo once feigned sleep so as to observe Francis, and after seeing him "praying all night long, sleeping rarely, prais, ing God and the glorious Virgin, His Mother," concluded that Francis "truly is from God" and decided to join him.

The legend immediately continues back in the Piazza del Comune, at what is now the post office but in 1208 was the church of San Nicolo. Francis was puzzled at first about what he was supposed to do with Bernardo. "After the Lord gave me brothers, no one showed me what I had to do," he would write in his Testament. So Bernardo and Francis, accom, panied by Peter of Catania, a canon at San Rufino who would become an, other early convert, went to San Nicolo to seek guidance on what God expected them to do. According to the *Legend of the Three Companions,* Francis randomly opened the book of the Gospels to find this passage from Matthew: "If you wish to be perfect, go, sell what you have, and give it to the poor, and you shall have treasure in heaven." Wanting "a threefold con, firmation of the words," Francis opened the book of the Gospels two more times. "Take nothing for your journey," he read from Luke. And again from Matthew: "If any man will come after me, let him deny himself."

These three passages became the absolute Rules for what would become the Franciscan Order of the Friars Minor. On April 16, 1208, Bernardo gave away all his possessions and money to the poor, followed by Peter, who had far less wealth, and the two men went to live with Francis at the Porziuncola. "Having sold everything, these two took the habit of poverty which blessed Francis had already adopted," the *Legend of the Three Com, panions* continues, "and from then on, he and they lived according to the precept of the holy Gospel as the Lord had shown them."

Within a week, eighteen,year,old Egidio, or Giles, of Assisi also joined them. Others would follow over the next year or so, among them a monk nicknamed Philip the Tall; Rufino, Clare's cousin from Assisi; Masseo, a lay brother who would be buried with Francis; Leo, a priest in Assisi; Silvester, another priest from Assisi; Juniper, a lay follower from Assisi; and Angelo Tancredi, the first knight to join Francis, from the city of Rieti.

There was only one bad apple among the early brothers, a man from Assisi named Giovanni di Capella. According to the *Little Flowers of St. Francis,* Francis had to scold Brother Giovanni several times for abusing his strict rule of poverty. Giovanni would break ranks several years later to found a new but unapproved order of lepers. He later hung himself after contracting leprosy.

At some point the early brothers moved temporarily to a farm shed near Assisi known as Rivo Torto. The few years they spent there are well documented in the early biographies. "Blessed Francis betook himself with the rest of his brothers to a place near Assisi called Rivo Torto," Celano writes. "In that place there was a certain abandoned hovel." The shed at Rivo Torto, which became known as the Sacred Hovel, may not have the ongoing historical weight of San Damiano and the Porziuncola, but it is an important part of the legend—and another re-created shrine on the Francis trail around Assisi.

Like the little Porziuncola encased within the basilica of Santa Maria degli Angeli, the Sacred Hovel is encased inside the church of Santa Maria di Rivotorto, three miles below Assisi. The big stone sanctuary is not half so massive or ornate as that of Santa Maria degli Angeli, but still, the nineteenth-century building makes quite a presence in the town that has grown up around it, also named Rivo Torto. A modern, life-size, and quite graphic sculpture of Francis washing a leper with rotted fingers stands near the entrance to the church. Another sculpture in the entrance courtyard is more cheerful, depicting birds flocking to Francis while children dance around him.

A large contingent of nuns is praying inside the church on the afternoon we are there. One of them, Sister Dorothy from Zambia, explains that she and her sisters from all over the world are attending a weeklong meeting in Assisi. I eye the one-page history of Rivotorto in English she is holding, and she presses it into my hands. "God bless you," she says.

Inside the sanctuary, the centerpiece is the tiny, stone-block replica of the

Sacred Hovel where Francis and his companions lived in extreme discomfort. "The place was so cramped that they could hardly sit or lie down to sleep," records the *Legend of the Three Companions*. Francis evidently wrote the names of the individual friars on the beams in the hut "so that each one, when he wished to sit or pray, should know his own place, and that no unnecessary noise due to the close quarters should disturb the brothers' quiet of mind."

Standing in Rivo Torto's two impossibly small, lowceilinged rooms and imagining them filled with men makes me feel as if I am in a medieval submarine—without a mess room. "Very often for lack of bread their only food was turnips, for which, in their poverty, they begged here and there," the *Legend of the Three Companions* continues. The communal austerity finally caused one companion to break down.

"I'm dying," a very hungry brother is said to have cried out in the middle of a night. According to the *Legend of Perugia,* a thoughtful Francis ordered a meal made not only for him but for all the other brothers, so that the starving one would not "blush from eating alone." And he gave the brothers a lecture on fasting very much like the advice Clare gave to St. Agnes of Prague. Do not overdo, he told them. Know your own constitution. "If one of you can do with less food than another, it is not my wish that he who needs to eat more should try to imitate the first," he said. Warning the brothers that he would not order up another midnight meal, Francis told them that it was his "desire and command that each and every one, while respecting our poverty, give his body what it needs."

One friar at Rivo Torto evidently took advantage of Francis's compassion and paid the price. Not only did the unidentified man pray little, do no work, and never go begging, "for he was ashamed," according to the *Legend of Perugia,* but he committed the cardinal sin of eating too much. "Go your way, Brother Fly," Francis said to the gluttonous friar, "for you wish to eat the fruit of the labor of your brothers, while you remain idle in the vineyard of God." Brother Fly evidently left without further ado, with Francis's damning words ringing in his ears. "You resemble Brother Drone who gathers nothing, does no work, but eats the fruit of the activity of the working bees."

Whatever standard Francis held for his friars, he was very hard on him self. He fought human appetite, according to Thomas of Celano, by rarely eating cooked foods, and when he did, "he either mixed them with ashes or destroyed their flavor with cold water." He fought the "temptation of the flesh," as exhibited in the thornless rose garden at the Porziuncola, by throwing his naked body either into brambles or "into a ditch full of ice, when it was winter"; there he remained "until every vestige of anything carnal had departed." He fought the comfort of a good night's sleep by either sleeping on the bare ground or sleeping sitting up, using a piece of wood or a stone as a pillow. And he fought vanity by ordering his brothers to rebuke him. "And when that brother, though unwilling, would say he was a boor, a hired servant, a worthless being, Francis, smiling and applauding very much, would reply: 'May the Lord bless you, for you have spoken more truly; it is becoming that the son of Peter of Bernadone should hear such things.' "

Francis's strategy at what was essentially a boot camp for friars was to instruct his brothers by his example, and by every account he succeeded. Like Francis, the early brothers threw themselves into thornbushes, went without shoes and food, worked as laborers for no pay, and cared for lepers. They deepened their spiritual life by fighting sleep to add prayer time, roping themselves erect, or wearing wooden girdles; they spoke only when necessary, walked with downcast eyes so they could cling to "heaven with their minds," and lived, communally, in quiet thanksgiving. "These were the teachings of their beloved father, by which he formed his new sons, not by words alone and tongue, but above all in deeds and in truth," writes Celano.

They also finished restoring another little church, San Pietro della Spina. Located vaguely by St. Bonaventure "a little farther from the city," it has since been identified more accurately by Francis's contemporary biographers as a chapel a mile or so from San Damiano. But we never find it.

The expensive, English-speaking guide we hire in Assisi takes us to quite a different San Pietro and insists it is this rather massive San Pietro that Francis restored. But perhaps it is just as well. San Pietro della Spina has evidently returned to the same derelict condition it was in when Francis and his friars started to repair it. Owned by a farming family, the little chapel is evidently used now as a storage barn for hay and farm equipment.

· · ·

I leave the Sacred Hovel at Rivo Torto somewhat puzzled by the sculpted prone figure of a sleeping Francis in one of the cells when my mind's eye has him sleeping sitting up, to look at the sanctuary's stained glass windows. All are of scenes from Francis's life—Francis touching a leper, Francis listening to the San Damiano cross, Francis receiving the stigmata, et cetera, but I do not see, though I may be mistaken, an event that took place at Rivo Torto and was reproduced by Giotto in the basilica in Assisi.

As recounted by St. Bonaventure, a "chariot of fire, of marvelous splen dor" entered the hovel in the middle of the night and moved "hither and thither" three times, leaving the brothers "amazed" and "affrighted." Some even saw Francis, who was away at the time, riding in the chariot toward heaven, mirroring the ascension made by the prophet Elijah, who had guided the Jews. When Francis returned to Rivo Torto the next day, he in terpreted the friars' vision as a friendly prediction from on high that the first few friars would grow "into a multitude." Francis's words both soothed and reassured the friars that "they would be most assuredly safe and blessed in following his life and teaching."

It isn't until we leave the church that I realize why I hadn't seen that part of the legend in the stained glass windows: The episode is portrayed in a colorful mosaic on the façade—Elijah ascending toward the heavens in his chariot of fire. A second mosaic tells another famous Rivo Torto story: the passage nearby of the emperor Otto IV in 1209 to be crowned in Rome by Pope Innocent III.

The story is quintessential Francis. As Thomas of Celano tells it, the fri ars were living right "next to the very parade route" and must have wanted mightily to see Otto's procession with all its "clamor and pomp," but Fran cis wouldn't let them. Nothing represented more the evil and material ways of the world that Francis and his friars had rejected than the emperor and his gaudy procession. Instead, Francis instructed his brothers to remain in side the Sacred Hovel and immerse themselves in their far better spiritual world of contemplation and prayer.

But Francis always had a knack for the dramatic. He excused one of his friars from his prayers and dispatched him to penetrate the procession, get as close to the emperor as possible, and continuously call out that "his glory would last but a short time." The unfortunate friar presumably returned to Rivo Torto with at least a bloodied nose, but Francis had made his point. "The apostolic authority was strong in him," Celano writes, "and he therefore refused entirely to offer flattery to kings and princes."

The brothers' idyll at Rivo Torto came to an abrupt end one day when a peasant burst through the door with his donkey and claimed the building for himself. Francis was evidently annoyed that the intruder had disturbed his companions' silent prayer and quickly decided that rather than share the already inadequate space, it was time for the brothers to move on. "I know that God has not called me to entertain a donkey," he said to them, as quoted in the *Legend of the Three Companions*. It was then that Francis and his first followers moved to the Porziuncola, where succeeding generations of friars remain to this day.

But Francis and his early companions were already well on their way in spreading the word about their particular vision of heaven on earth. From the beginning, when they numbered only four, they had set out to preach Francis's message of peace, goodwill, and penance. Taking his cue from the Gospels, Francis sent them on their journeys, like Jesus' disciples, two by two. And he went, too.

Francis would walk thousands of miles around Italy, through the hill towns and valleys of Umbria and Tuscany and over the Apennine Mountains to the Marches of Ancona. He would retreat to the solitude of mountaintop hermitages and to islands in Umbrian lakes and the Venice lagoon. He would try to take his message abroad, to France, to Spain, to Morocco, to Syria, and in 1219 he would finally succeed in taking it to Egypt. He walked barefoot in the heat and the cold, in the rain and in the snow, and when his health failed, he rode on a donkey.

He started from Rivo Torto in 1208 and walked for the next eighteen years. And we went with him, to some of the most beautiful places in Italy.

9

*The First Tour
to the Marches*

M y spirit falters as we head east across Umbria
toward the province of the Marches to follow
Francis and Brother Giles, his traveling companion, on
their first preaching tour. Looming on the horizon is a
high stretch of the Apennines, which we, like Francis
and Giles, will have to cross to achieve our mutual
destination. Unlike the gentle, mounded mountains of
Umbria, this range of the Apennines rakes the sky and is
the forbidding gateway to the province in central Italy
that runs thirty miles east from the mountains to the
Adriatic Sea. As the valley road we're driving on passes
through narrowing farmland and ever-encroaching,
steeper mountainsides, I brace for ultimate hairpin turns
and white-knuckle driving. I'm wrong.

We barely rise above sea level. The engineering
miracle of Italian tunnels—twenty-three in all on this
trip—makes our transition through the mountains from
Umbria to the Marches as level as sitting on a living
room couch. In between tunnels, the scenery is simply
staggering. Gigantic pinnacles of rock. Sheer cliffs and
chasms. Firs and pines rising seemingly on top of one
another. And there, on a far ridge, a still-visible ancient
rock "ditch" or *fossato* that Francis and Giles themselves
might have crossed the mountains on.

Little is known about Francis's first preaching foray

to the Marches, in the spring of 1208. But it was a journey, however arduous, that he would make at least six other times. The people in the Marches eventually embraced Francis and his teachings warmly—by 1282, according to the *Little Flowers of St. Francis,* there would be eighty-five Franciscan friaries established in the Marches, double the number in Tuscany or Umbria. This first trip, however, was not a success.

While Francis was evidently ecstatic walking through the forests of poplar, oak, and beech, and loudly "singing out in French, praising and blessing the Lord," the farmers and villagers he came across did not share his jubilation. A medieval biographer, the Anonymous of Perugia, re-counts that the people declared the wild-looking, barefooted Francis and Giles as "mad," "fools," or "drunkards." "Young women, seeing them at a distance, would run away," the biographer writes.

Not only did the people distrust these self-proclaimed messengers of God but they rejected their message. There was little interest in religion of any kind at the time, among either pagans or the tepid, uninterested Chris-tians. "Love and fear of God were non-existent almost everywhere and the way of penance was not only completely unknown, but it was also consid-ered folly," says the *Legend of the Three Companions.* "Lust for the flesh, greed for the world, and pride of life was so widespread, that the whole world seemed to be engulfed in these three malignancies."

Undeterred, Francis and Giles developed a routine. Francis would urge whomever they came across to fear and love God and do penance for their sins, while Giles would nod and say: "Believe him." But nobody did.

His other friars would fare no better on their first tentative forays, two by two through Umbria and toward the pilgrim path of St. James of Com-postela in Spain. Before the friars set out, recounts the *Legend of the Three Companions,* Francis predicted that though they would find some "faithful people, meek and kind," they would also find "many others, faithless, proud and blasphemous who will resist and reject you and what you say." He was right.

People were suspicious of the friars when they followed Francis's in-structions to greet them by saying: "God give you peace." Then there was the strange way the friars looked, with their bare feet and their threadbare habits. Were they charlatans and thieves? Were they savages? And why wouldn't they accept money as alms, like regular beggars?

The friars were chased, sometimes beaten, splattered with mud, even stripped naked. But they evidently clung to Francis's admonition to "to bear these things with patience and humility." The friars never fought back or deviated from Francis's message. "God give you peace," they said, over and over, then exhorted the curious and often hostile crowds to repent and shun evil before it was too late. "Who are you?" the suspicious people asked them time and again. The friars always gave Francis's answer: "We are penitents from Assisi."

Francis and Giles, the "penitents from Assisi" in the Marches, are thought to have gone to Fabriano, an established center in their time and now a sprawling industrialized city at the end of the twenty-third tunnel. Medieval Fabriano was known, and still is, as the papermaking capital of Italy. Not only did the city's master papermakers invent the watermark but they produced the singular high-quality paper that is still used for bank-notes all over the world. Contemporary artists, too, seek out Fabriano paper, as did the incomparable Leonardo da Vinci in the fifteenth century and the city's famous native son, Gentile da Fabriano, in the fourteenth.

We find modern Fabriano to be a rather cheerless city, but then again, when we arrive there it is midday, when everything in Italy seems to shut down, and it is also raining. We achieve Fabriano's cavernous and curiously empty medieval piazza and park the car to review the notes from our Italian-language book *I viaggi di S. Francesco d'Assisi nelle Marche*—The Journeys of S. Francesco of Assisi in the Marches—which English-speaking Italians along the way have generously translated for us.

Francis and Giles probably performed their routine in the piazza we're parked in, but there is no record of it. Who knew then that the ragged lit-tle madman from Assisi would soon become one of the most recognized figures in Italy? What is recorded in the book is the trip Francis made to Fabriano just two years later, in 1210, when he was better known. He stayed in a sanctuary called the Eremo di S. Maria di Valdisasso, a former

Benedictine convent for nuns just four and a half miles from Fabriano, near the village of Valleremita, and we set off to find it.

In one of the minor miracles that begin to govern our pursuit of Francis, we chance upon a young woman standing under an arcade in the lonely piazza who knows exactly how to get to Valleremita and the convent of Valdisasso. We happen to be parked in exactly the right spot, she says. Take a right at the next stoplight and drive for 5.5 kilometers. We do, following the edge of a narrow, densely forested gorge to the little, lopsided village of Valleremita tucked into the end of the valley. Turn right up the hill in the center of town. We do, though our anxiety begins to mount as the road turns to red dirt and we don't seem to be getting anywhere.

Francis was evidently just as anxious about finding the convent. Our Italian book tells the story of him asking a farmer he chanced upon to accompany him to Valdisasso. The farmer, who was in the middle of plowing his field, was reluctant, but Francis somehow talked him into it. When the farmer returned from delivering Francis to the convent, he found that his field had been completely plowed, and further, his oxen were entirely rested.

That field is still known locally as the "field of San Francesco," and we undoubtedly pass it before, miraculously, we too arrive at the charming Franciscan sanctuary of Valdisasso. It was here, in the beautifully restored medieval stone convent, that Francis stayed for the first, but certainly not last, time with four of his friars. The Franciscans would base themselves at Valdisasso off and on for the next six hundred years, lending it the nickname Porziuncola of the Marches.

The gate is locked, but there is room to walk around it to a manicured lawn terrace. An arched cloister with traces of frescoes on its walls and ceiling flanks one side of the lawn, the actual sanctuary, a second. There is a well-tended vegetable garden and flowers everywhere, in the window boxes of the sanctuary and in hanging baskets under the arches. Valdisasso is obviously inhabited, but by whom? We pull a cord to ring the sanctuary bell, but no one comes.

We don't feel we're trespassing. There are several picnic tables in a glade just off the lawn, trails cut through the woods, and a very full garbage bin, which signal its public recreational use. That, plus a sign in Italian saying to please eat at the tables, not to litter, and to observe *silenzio,* makes us feel welcome as we look out over the gorge at miles and miles of forested mountains.

We let ourselves into the sanctuary's tiny, restored twelfth-century church, which is billed in one Italian translation on the Internet as having the "beautifulest ceiling." The arched ceiling is indeed a marvel, but then so is the altarpiece, a copy of the coronation of the Virgin (the original was moved to Milan) attended by the various medieval saints who stayed at Valdisasso, including San Bernardino from Siena, San Giovanni of Capistrano, San Giacomo from Marca, and of course, San Francesco. All this unexpected beauty at the end of a dirt road in the seeming heart of nowhere.

Francis and Giles returned to the Porziuncola after their first visit to the Marches, trekking fifteen miles a day. In keeping with Jesus' command to his disciples—and Francis's to his—they took nothing with them on their journey and bartered their labor on farms and in villages along the way for food and lodging. From the beginning, Francis insisted that his friars work every day, preferably with their hands, or "with a trade they have learned," provided that it was in keeping with goodness and honesty. "Idleness," he wrote to his friars, quoting from the sixth-century Rule of St. Benedict, "is the enemy of the soul."

The early Franciscans' work requirement would stand them in good stead. As strange as they looked, their free toil shoulder to shoulder with everyone else in the vineyards and hay fields and their gratitude in return for a crust of bread and a night's sleep in a farm shed began to win them credibility. So did their work with the poor and the lepers. They lived what they preached—and with joy. "Let them be careful not to appear outwardly as sad and gloomy hypocrites but show themselves joyful, cheerful and consistently gracious in the Lord," Francis directed his friars in an early, written rule. Modern Franciscans still take that rule to heart. Every friar we meet on our many journeys through Italy is positively merry.

Soon after Francis returned to the Porziuncola, he set off again, this time with six of his friars. This second, and far more successful, preaching tour

Francis's body lay hidden for six hundred years deep under the Basilica of St. Francis in Assisi. We listen to Mozart here among the Giottos.

Spoleto's beautiful cathedral, where we don't find Francis's famous handwritten letter to Brother Leo.

The convent of San Damiano, whose little church Francis rebuilt after the cross there spoke to him. Clare would be cloistered here for forty-one years.

Francis stripped naked and renounced his father right here in front of the Bishop's Palace in Assisi's Piazza del Vescovado.

*Gubbio is famous for the
story about Francis taming
the wolf—but more important,
a family here saved his life.*

*The Abbazia di Vallingegno is
now an inn on the road to
Gubbio, but in Francis's time it
was the Benedictine monastery
of San Verecondo. The
inhospitable monks here put him
to work as a scullery boy.*

The skyscraping chapel at Pòggio Bustone, where Francis,
standing on a rock, wrestled with his conscience.

Francis turned from playboy to penitent and emerged a humble
pilgrim from the chapel's Grotto of Revelations.

Francis preached to the birds here at Pian d'Arca, the simple and hard-to-find roadside shrine near Cantalupo.

A fissure in the rocks at Sant'Urbano, one of many such crevasses in which Francis prayed and felt closest to the Lord.

Francis fasted here on the
Isola Maggiore in Lake
Trasimeno for the forty days
and nights of Lent.

My husband didn't.

*The lovely Tuscan sanctuary of Celle di Cortona,
where Francis founded one of his first hermitages.
He would write his Last Testament here near the
end of his life.*

The Virgin Mary, crowned
with a halo of electric
lightbulbs, atop the vast
church of Santa Maria degli
Angeli near Assisi, which
harbors Francis's tiny chapel,
the Porziuncola.

A naked Francis
fought devil-sent lust
by building a family
out of snow at
Sarteano, another
early and primitive
sanctuary. I gird
myself to access the
caves on my hands
and knees.

was to the Rieti Valley, a beautiful inland region of central Italy, halfway between Assisi and Rome, laced with forests and lakes and hills. Perhaps it was the valley's natural wonders and agreeable climate that tempered the suspicions of its residents and made them more accepting of the early Franciscans.

Unlike the people in the Marches, those in the Rieti Valley evidently listened to the penitents' sermons and converted in high numbers. The people in the hill town of Poggio Bustone, where we are headed, were particularly enthusiastic about Francis and his message. Maybe that is why he added a new and still locally celebrated greeting—*"buon giorno, buona gente"*—a lively, rhythmic phrase in Italian that translates quite dully into English as "good day, good people." So revolutionary was the greeting at the time, the people presumably never having been called "good," that the Italian phrase is engraved on a wall in Poggio Bustone and is commemorated every year on the fourth of October, when the town crier races from house to house at dawn, calling out, *"Buon giorno, buona gente."*

Given the friars' more harsh experiences elsewhere, it is not surprising that Francis would spend a great deal of time over the years—some say even more time than he spent in and around Assisi—in the hospitable Rieti Valley. He would establish at least five hermitages there, four of which exist to this day, in what has become known as the Sacred Valley of Rieti.

Yet for all the success of his first preaching tour to the Rieti Valley, this was not a happy time for Francis. He was reportedly beset with confusion and feelings of unworthiness when he first arrived at Poggio Bustone in 1208 and went on to a Benedictine friary by the same name high above the town. What should he be instructing his little band of brothers? What was their mission? What was his mission? Most important, how could he preach the embrace of poverty and selflessness when he himself had lived such a sinful, hedonistic life? What business did he have urging people to love and nurse the lepers when he had spent years running away from them? Would God forgive him? Could he forgive himself?

We, by contrast, are worried only about oxygen deprivation as we pass the town and start navigating the hairpin turns and switchbacks on the steep mountain road toward the old friary. Up and up we go, following the familiar gold cross sanctuary road signs through high olive groves and forests of ilex, pine, and oaks, until finally, around a last curve, we achieve the medieval stone church and friary of Poggio Bustone—only to discover the small parking lot is full. The white-paper ribbons festooning the cars signal a wedding is under way.

Being seasoned Francis hands by now, we do not find it surprising in the least to encounter a wedding going on at the top of the world. Everyone in Italy, it seems, wants to be married, baptized, or eulogized in a church associated with St. Francis. And Poggio Bustone *is* Francis.

I know from his biographers that Francis, not content with being at the already dizzying heights of the friary, climbed another thousand feet, to what is known as the Grotto of Revelations or the Upper Shrine, to beg for God's forgiveness. We set out on foot along the road next to the church, following signs to the Sacro Speco.

Our paperback guide to the hermitages in the Rieti Valley describes the route to the Upper Shrine as a "steep pathway." That is no exaggeration. For close to thirty minutes we labor straight up the cobbled mountain path, pausing only to pant and admire the wild, dwarf red cyclamen blooming in the woods.

Along the way we pass several stone shrines with open iron grilles, each giving us false hope that we have achieved the Upper Shrine. But no. Enclosed in the seventeenth-century shrines we pass are sacred rocks, one described by a wooden sign as bearing the imprint of Francis's knees; another encasing the footprint of an angel; a third, the twisted image of the devil. Still we climb, the church below receding to the size of a dollhouse toy, until we reach a large rock hanging precipitously over the valley. It is crowned with a rude wooden cross, a plastic water bottle bearing a single red poppy, and a wooden sign that translates: "The cross: from here St. Francis blessed the Rieti Valley."

For all that the sentiment must be reassuring to the residents of the valley, it does not seem quite accurate. The legend says that Francis wrestled with his conscience on this wild outcropping of rock and prayed for days for forgiveness. "He persevered there for a long time with fear and trembling before the Lord of the whole earth," Celano writes, "and he thought in the bitterness of his soul of the years he had spent wretchedly, frequently repeating this word: 'O God, be merciful to me the sinner.' "

I climb up on the rock to see if I can re-create the feeling of desperation Francis must have been experiencing, but what strikes me, besides vertigo, is the beauty of the valley stretching out below me. And the silence. There isn't a sound except for the occasional bird's call and the whisper of the wind in the trees—until the wedding ends.

I nearly meet God myself on the rock when the church bells suddenly start to peal below, followed by the blare of car horns and some celebratory gunshots. The adrenaline rush gets me off the rock and back on the path, so steep at this point that it becomes steps cut into the side of the mountain. And suddenly—unbelievably—we arrive at a very old church, clinging to the edge of a chalk cliff. There we are, alone with Francis, at what must be the doorway to heaven. But we are definitely not the first.

There are hundreds of little handmade twig crosses stuck in the netting holding the cliff in place, as well as a bell over the church entry with a celebratory rope for pilgrims to pull. Inside the sky-scraping chapel, through a tiny, unlocked wooden door, is an ancient fresco of St. Bernardino and more twig crosses propped up on the little altar, along with fresh roses, candles, and crucifixes. And there, in the rear of the fifteenth-century church, festooned with vases of fresh poppies and daisies and hyacinth along with more candles and handmade crosses, is the Grotto of Revelations itself, the cave where Francis repaired briefly to sleep before resuming his entreaties to God for forgiveness.

God must have responded positively, which is a blessing to all who for centuries have held Francis in such high esteem. Francis might very well have never come down from that mountaintop if he had not found absolution from his agony. But he did. "Little by little, a certain unspeakable joy and very great sweetness began to flood his innermost heart," writes Celano. "He began also to stand aloof from himself and as his feelings were checked and the darkness that had gathered in his heart because of his fear of sin dispelled, there was poured into him a certainty that all his sins had been forgiven, and a confidence of his restoration to grace was given him."

The Francis who finally returned to his worried friars waiting in the hermitage below "seemed changed into another man," notes Celano. And he was. Somewhere between the rock and the grotto, Francis had accepted his conversion from playboy to penitent to emerge the humble pilgrim of enduring legend.

It is little wonder, then, that so many people before us have made the uphill trek to the sacred Grotto of Revelations, though we haven't seen a soul. The handmade twig crosses and assorted fresh flowers are testament to the pilgrims' faith in the power of forgiveness and renewal personified by the "penitent" from Assisi. So is the church's guest book, the first such registry we have seen. Most of the messages are in Italian, some in German and French, and a few in English. "We traveled a long way from Dallas, Texas, and Rockall, Texas," reads one entry from the anxious autumn of 2002. "We pray for peace, love and understanding."

Returning downhill, we find more of Francis's legend at Poggio Bustone inside the now empty single-nave church. On one wall is a painting of Francis kneeling on the rock at the top of the mountain in front of a forgiving angel while his original six friars wait anxiously for him in the hermitage below. Another painting depicts the legendary exchange an older Francis had with the people of Poggio Bustone.

Francis is stooped and emaciated, and he is holding his hand over his heart in an attitude of confession. The image fits perfectly a sermon the ailing Francis delivered on a much later visit to Poggio Bustone when he publicly confessed to eating forbidden lard during a period of fasting. His "sin" was easily explained by the decision of a worried friar to cook his vegetables with a little lard to try to coax Francis to eat, but Francis chose to use the episode to broadcast his hypocrisy and to present himself as unworthy of any exaltation. "In this way, he often ascribed to pleasure what had been granted to him because of his infirmity," writes Celano. Such self-deprecation was one of Francis's most endearing and enduring characteristics. He was a human being like everyone else, he was telling the people, and just as prone to stumble on the road to salvation.

We make a quick tour of the cloister of the old friary behind the church with its intact thirteenth-century columns and the one remaining wall from the original church. Various scenes from Francis's life are painted on the semicircular fanlights that run along the entire cloister corridor, including the de rigueur scene of him receiving the stigmata. But it is Francis's original hermitage or Lower Shrine we're after, and we find the cave a short distance along a passageway.

No matter how many hermitages we have seen where Francis regularly withdrew from the world to meditate and pray, they never fail to amaze me in their starkness and complete discomfort. The hermitage at Poggio Bustone is no exception. Predating Francis and given to him and his friars by the resident Benedictine monks, the now restored hermitage is nothing but barren rock—rough rocks, big rocks, the rock of the hill behind it. No wonder Francis is said to have slept only two or three hours a night. The only luxury consists of two little windows that have since been fitted with stained glass: One shows Francis miraculously healing a child in the town of Poggio Bustone, whom legend tells us "had lived enormously swollen so that he could not even see his legs"; the other, a leper who was cured four hundred years after Francis died by washing himself in the water from a basin named after the saint farther up the mountain.

Francis returned to Assisi from the Rieti Valley, as do we, past the extraordinarily beautiful Lake Piediluco. We linger there, in far greater comfort than did Francis, at the Hotel del Lago, from which the view of the lake, tucked into the mountains and rimmed with cypresses, evergreens, and elms in early fall foliage, is hypnotic. As we watch the luminous morning mist lift off the silver lake, it is easy to understand why Francis believed everything, including the view, was a gift from God. "He rejoiced in all the works of the hands of the Lord, and saw behind things pleasant to behold their life-giving reason and cause," Celano writes. "In beautiful things, he saw Beauty itself; all things to him were good."

Francis also returned from the Rieti Valley with a great prize: Angelo Tancredi, the first knight to join his group of companions. "You have worn the belt, the sword, and the spurs of the world, long enough," Francis evidently said to Tancredi of Rieti. "Come with me and I will arm you as Christ's knight." It proved to be a most fortuitous union. "Brother"

Angelo would stay with Francis for the rest of his life, join Brothers Leo and Rufino in writing the *Legend of the Three Companions* after Francis's death, and be buried near him in the crypt of the basilica in Assisi.

Proof of Francis's extraordinary charisma came shortly after his return from the Rieti Valley when four more men from Assisi left their homes, gave all their possessions to the poor, and joined the "companions" at the Porziuncola. Many believe it was the joy and camaraderie exhibited by the early companions that fostered the growth of the all-male movement. Celano describes the "spiritual love" among the "members of this pious society" in detail: "Chaste embraces, gentle feelings, a holy kiss, pleasing conversation, modest laughter, joyous looks, a single eye, a submissive spirit, a peaceable tongue, a mild answer, oneness of purpose, ready obedience, unwearied hand, all these were found in them."

Francis demanded three vows from his charges—obedience, poverty, chastity—vows that are exhibited to this day in the three knots each Franciscan friar ties in the cord of his habit. They built their own thatched huts of mud and wood, raised as much as they could of their own food, and begged for the rest. Going door to door in Assisi for food handouts was particularly humiliating for the new friars, who had often been the ones to offer food to the poor. Quite naturally, they were frequently met with scorn and incredulity from their neighbors. If these crazy men hadn't given away all their property to the poor, the derision went, they wouldn't be at the door with their begging bowls.

But the nucleus of brothers, now eleven or twelve in number, remained steadfast, and seemingly content, in their voluntary poverty. Because they owned and wanted nothing, they had nothing to lose. "They were therefore, everywhere secure, kept in no suspense by fear; distracted by no care, they awaited the next day without solicitude," writes Celano.

But with the growth of Francis's following came danger. For all the good works of the friars, they were still for the most part evangelical laymen, wandering the countryside without license and preaching the word of God. They were bound, at some point, to become visible to the Church hierarchy in Rome and thus risk being branded as heretics. The Church was already at war with various breakaway sects, like the Cathars, which lived by their own rules. The Pope had tried to negotiate with the extrem-

ist Cathars, who had taken it upon themselves to administer the sacra-
ments and to preach against sex and food of any kind, but to no avail. In
1208, the same year Francis went to Poggio Bustone, a particularly vehe-
ment Cathar responded to the Pope's overtures by murdering the Papal
legate dispatched to talk to them.

Francis's regimen for himself and his friars was also considered extreme
by Assisi's clergy. Bishop Guido had urged him to ease his dedication to
ultimate poverty, but Francis refused. The rule Francis followed, after all,
was from Jesus himself in the Gospels. He had no intention of adopting
one of the rules of the already established orders: the Benedictines, for example, owned vast amounts of property and were cloistered for the most
part, and the Augustinians concentrated on apostolic activity in the
churches and universities.

Francis was determined that he and his followers remain pilgrims for the
Lord, carrying their message of peace and repentance to ordinary people in
the smallest villages and most remote forests. But he also wanted recogni-
tion from the Church. So one morning, in the spring of 1209, the cheeky
Francis gathered his friars together and announced they were going on a
trip: they were leaving immediately for Rome to see the Lord Pope.

10

*The Pope
Has a Dream*

*ROME, where the Pope first thinks Francis a swineherd
but then remembers a nightmare*

Francis and his disheveled brothers arrived
unannounced at the splendid Lateran Palace on the
Piazza San Giovanni in Laterano, a district in Rome.
The ancient and imposing palace, with its front hall that
boasted eleven apses, was the official residence of the
Pope and had been for nine hundred years by the time
Francis arrived. The gift of the first Christian emperor,
Constantine, to Pope Melchiades in 311, the palace sat
next to Christendom's first cathedral, the equally
splendid St. John, which Constantine had constructed
over a razed horse-guard barracks.

Francis was not intimidated in the least by the
opulent palace, which the poet Dante would later
describe as being beyond human achievement. Francis
had come to Rome not to challenge the Church, after all,
but to offer himself to the Pope as a humble messenger
for its teachings. The challenge was how to get to the
Pope.

How he accomplished that is depicted in one of
his most endearing legends. As recounted by Omer
Englebert in his biography, *St. Francis of Assisi,* Francis
and his ragged companions were walking through the
corridors of the Lateran Palace one day when they
chanced upon the Pope, then Innocent III. Seizing the
opportunity, Francis pressed the Pope to sanction their

preaching but was instantly rebuffed by the Pontiff, who mistook the wild-haired, smelly bunch for swineherds.

"Go find your pigs," Innocent reportedly said to Francis. "You can preach all the sermons you want to them." Ever obedient, Francis went out to the nearest pigsty, preached to the occupants, and presented himself again to the Pope. In this version of the legend, Innocent was so embarrassed he had treated Francis so badly that he told him he would grant him an audience—after he had cleaned himself up.

The more logical rendition of how Francis met the Pope is the age-old dynamic of who-you-know. Assisi's Bishop Guido happened to be in Rome at the same time and was quite naturally startled to see Francis there. When Francis told him he wanted the Pope to sanction a rule he had written for his followers, a delighted Bishop Guido introduced him to Cardinal John of St. Paul, the bishop of Santa Sabina in Rome, who was the Pope's confessor and one of his most respected right-hand men. The cardinal, in turn, questioned Francis closely about his intentions and like some before—and many afterward—urged Francis either to adopt an already approved rule or to soften the Rule he had brought to present to the Pope. "Fearful that the holy man might fail in such a lofty proposal, he pointed out smoother paths," Celano writes. But Francis refused.

He was wedded to the Rule that Jesus had written for his disciples, which Francis had adopted for his first few followers the year before in Assisi: "If you wish to be perfect, go, sell what you have, and give it to the poor, and you shall have treasure in heaven"; "Take nothing for your journey"; and "If any man will come after me, let him deny himself."

Francis surely based the written Rule he had brought to Rome on those biblical directives of extreme poverty and humility, though the original text has never been found. Franciscan scholars more or less agree that the Rule must also have included allegiance to the Pope and the Church of Rome as well as specific directives for his friars, among them the minimal dress of one tunic, hood, and cord; the practice of chastity, obedience, charity, harmony, prayer, preaching, and work for which they were forbidden to accept money. "Their greatest joy shall be to mingle with victims of leprosy, beggars and other wretches," Englebert suggests was in the Rule.

· · ·

The cardinal was evidently charmed by Francis, regardless of his reservations about the Rule, and soon arranged for the Assisian to be invited back to the Lateran Palace for a proper audience with the Pope. What a scene it must have been—Francis and his friars, barefoot and in rags, prostrating themselves in front of the Pope and his council of cardinals, satined and jeweled and gilded from toe to miter. The contrast would prove irresistible to generations of artists, including Giotto, who memorialized it on the frescoed walls of the basilica in Assisi.

This time it was Innocent himself who questioned Francis, and he, too, was evidently moved by Francis's devotion and candor. It was the harshness of the Rule that concerned the Pope. He and many of his opulently dressed cardinals questioned whether it was humanly possible to live the literal interpretation of the Gospel. And how could a religious order sustain itself without property or income? Add to that the humiliating thought of a priest actually begging for alms and a groundswell of disapproval began among the mitered mighty.

"My dear young sons, your life seems to us exceptionally hard and severe," the Pope said to Francis. He took note of their "great zeal," according to the *Legend of the Three Companions,* but cautioned: "We must take into consideration those who will come after you lest this way of life seem too burdensome."

But then the Pope remembered a disquieting dream he had had a few nights before Francis arrived. The Cathedral of St. John was teetering on its edge and would have collapsed were it not for a small and shabby man supporting its weight on his shoulder. "When he awoke, stunned and shaken, as a discerning and wise man, he pondered what this vision meant to tell him," recounts the *Legend of the Three Companions.* The answer to the dream, which Giotto also painted in the basilica in Assisi, was suddenly before the Pontiff, in all his smallness, shabbiness, and zeal.

So Francis, against all odds, achieved his ultimate goal: a blessing from the Pope and permission to preach penance. It never occurred to him that the Pope's reservations about the Rule's severity were prophetic and eventually and inevitably would cause a rupture in his order. Nor did it occur to him that becoming a legitimate arm of the Church bore within it the seeds of the destruction of his passionate dream.

Instead, on bended knee, an ecstatic Francis pledged obedience and reverence to the Pope, and his friars, in turn, pledged the same to Francis. The new Order of Friars Minor, as Francis named them, spent the next few days in Rome, having their heads tonsured as befitted clerics and praying at the various churches, including St. Peter's, where four years before Francis had first donned the clothes of a beggar, and Rome's first cathedral, St. John in Lateran.

We are standing in the piazza in front of St. John, looking up at the colossal marble sculptures of Jesus, his apostles, and assorted saints rimming the top of the eighteenth-century façade. Constantine had dedicated his fourth-century version of this cathedral to Jesus the Savior, and the oversize statues would have projected a clear Christian challenge to the pagan gods of Rome.

We enter the oldest Christian church in the world, now one of the four major basilicas in Rome, where we are reminded of the cathedral's historical significance. *"Mater et caput omnium ecclesiarum urbis et orbis,"* the inscription reads on a pillar: "Mother and head of all the churches of the city and the world." In keeping with its status, the cathedral boasts incomparable relics, including the heads of St. Peter and St. Paul, and a portion of the wooden altar from which St. Peter supposedly celebrated mass.

The cathedral has changed dramatically since Francis and his friars prayed here in 1209. One Pope after another felt compelled to leave his architectural mark on the structure, enclosing the ancient stone columns in massive pilasters and destroying some Giotto frescoes in the process. The cathedral complex, which included the old Lateran Palace, was also periodically sacked, almost entirely destroyed by a ninth-century earthquake, and badly damaged by fires fifty years apart in the fourteenth century.

The fate of this first Papal complex was sealed in the early 1300s, when the unrest in Rome forced the French-born Pope, Clement V, to relocate to France. The headquarters of the Catholic Church was set up in Avignon, and for the next sixty-eight years nine Popes held sway from there. When the Popes returned to Rome in 1378, the Lateran Palace and the Cathedral of St. John were in ruins. The decision was then made to relocate the residence of the Popes and the seat of the Holy See to the current—and more easily defended—Vatican complex across town, elevating St. Peter's Basil-ica, then a pilgrimage church, to the focal point of the Catholic presence in Rome.

Some vestiges remain of the original St. John in which Francis and his friars prayed. High in the apse are the fourth-century mosaics that miracu-lously escaped being destroyed during a nineteenth-century enlargement of the apse and were reinstalled in the new, bigger one just as they were in the original. I always feel a certain frisson when I see with my eyes what Fran-cis saw with his, and looking up at the mosaic figure of Jesus surrounded by the mosaics of nine angels brings on the familiar tingle.

I have the same feeling in the beautiful medieval cloister, once part of a Benedictine monastery, adjoining the cathedral. Francis surely found refuge from the brawling city in this serene space and admired, as I do, its graceful spiral columns of inlaid marble and its thirteenth-century mosaics. St. John in Lateran is in fact nicknamed after the Benedictines, who dedi-cated their monastery to St. John the Baptist and St. John the Evangelist and officiated at the cathedral's services. The official and cumbersome name of the church is Patriarchal Archbasilica of the Most Holy Savior in the Lateran.

There are no traces of Francis or his meeting with the Pope across the pi-azza in the Lateran Palace. The original palace was destroyed in the four-teenth-century fires and rebuilt far more simply in the 1600s. The current, hulking, three-story palace now houses a branch of the Vatican Museum on the ground floor and the offices of the cardinal vicar of Rome upstairs.

But there are other treasures dotted around the Piazza San Giovanni that predate Francis and were certainly there when he was. One of them is the ancient baptistry, which Constantine also built, next to the cathedral. How could Francis not have been in the baptistry and seen the seventh- and fifth-century mosaics in the oratories or the sunken, green basalt baptismal basin in which Constantine himself may have been baptized?

I see Francis as well in the Sancta Sanctorum, the medieval Popes' pri-vate chapel and the lone survivor of the fourteenth-century fires that rav-aged the Lateran Palace. Inexplicably moved in the sixteenth century to what is now a noisy traffic island just off the piazza, the chapel is reached by twenty-eight marble steps known as the Scala Santa. Legend has it that these are the "holy" marble steps Jesus mounted to Pontius Pilate's house in Jerusalem and that were brought back from the Holy Land by Emperor Constantine's Christian mother, St. Helena. Modern pilgrims mount these steps on their knees, and I imagine Francis did, too.

It is not clear where Francis and his friars stayed on this triumphal trip to Rome. On subsequent visits Francis often stayed at a hospice attached to a Benedictine church and monastery in Trastevere, the Soho of Rome. His cell is still there in the red church that was given to the Franciscans after Francis's death and renamed San Francesco a Ripa, so that is where we go after leaving St. John in Lateran.

Our visit to San Francesco a Ripa on the small Piazza San Francesco d'Assisi turns out to be somewhat fraught. Mercifully, we are in good humor after a delicious outdoor lunch with friends at Sabatini, a nearby restaurant, because the custodian we encounter at San Francesco a Ripa definitely is not. He is frantically setting up extra chairs for some sort of cer, emony and has little interest in unlocking the door to the left of the altar that will lead us to Francis's cell.

Grumbling, he finally relents and leads us up a flight of stairs to another locked door guarding the smoke-blackened cell, or *stanza di San Francesco.* Inside, he hovers impatiently while we admire a copy of a fourteenth, century portrait of Francis and an ornately carved and painted altar and silk altar cloth, which tradition says was sewed by Clare. There used to be a gold crucifix on the altar, but it has been moved to Assisi. The stone Francis used for a pillow, however, remains. *"Sasso dove pasava ii capo il serafico padre San Francesco,"* reads a sign in the cell. "The rock where rested the head of the seraphic father San Francesco."

The altar is said to contain a thousand relics from various saints, but not the heart of St. Charles of Sezze, which was pierced by a ray of light dur, ing prayer. The heart, which had been housed upstairs, was stolen years ago. More recently, the offering left in Francis's cell was also stolen, which explains all the locked doors between the church and the cell and the oblig, atory presence of the agitated custodian in a white lab coat. "Hurry! Hurry!" he keeps saying. "You finish." We succumb to his anxiety and leave both cell and church after taking in Bernini's orgasmic seventeenth-century sculpture of Blessed Ludovica Albertoni, a Franciscan tertiary, in one of the church's chapels.

The location of Francis's other resting place in Rome—the palazzo of Lady Jacopa de Settesoli—is in ruins. But she played such an important role in Francis's legend that she must be noted here, with or without her palazzo. Francis is thought to have met the "pious" twenty-two-year-old widow during the huge gathering in Rome in 1215 for Innocent III's Fourth Lateran Council. The Pope was evidently arranging lodging for the hundreds of faithful attending the council at St. John Lateran, and Lady Jacopa drew Francis as a houseguest. Their friendship would last the rest of his life.

Francis often stayed with "Brother" Jacopa, whom he made an honorary friar, on his many trips to Rome and even took a break from his austere diet of food mixed with water or ashes to indulge in her signature *mostacciuoli,* a concoction of almonds and sugar ground with a mortar. In return, on one of his visits he gave her a lamb, which became her "inseparable companion." According to St. Bonaventure, the lamb accompanied her to church and was so pious itself that if the poor woman slept late, the lamb "nudged her with its horns and woke her with its bleating, urging her with its nods and gestures to hurry to the church."

Life must have seemed as sweet to Francis as Brother Jacopa's sugared almonds when he and his friars left Rome to return to Assisi with the blessing of the Pope. They had become official men of God, with no boundaries set for the range of their preaching. Every soul in the world was theirs for the saving. They took their time, traveling north on the ancient Via Flaminia, which essentially parallels Italy's major modern highway, the A1, through the hill towns of Orte and Narni.

In his jubilation, Francis preached to everyone and everything in sight. He believed all natural things to be creations of God, and along the way, he exhorted the flowers and the cornfields and the vineyards to praise and serve the Lord. He issued the same call to stones and forests and fountains of water and "the green things of the gardens," as well as to earth, fire, wind, and air. And, in probably the best-known sermon of his life, he stopped on the way home to preach to the birds.

11 *Desperately Seeking Francis and the Birds*

PIAN D'ARCA, *the elusive roadside shrine where Francis preaches to the birds* · ORTE *and* NARNI, *where he dallies* · THE MARMORE FALLS, *where we hope he went* · ASSISI, *where his preaching wins Clare*

The little stone shrine at Pian d'Arca stands on the road near Cantalupo north of Bevagna, across from a gas station. We miss it three times. Everyone we ask for directions—the roadside vendor just outside Bevagna slicing lunchtime pork from a whole roasted pig on a spit, the woman walking her dog along the road in Cantalupo—sends us back the way we have just come. Our problem is that we presume, after having seen the grandiose monuments surrounding Francis in Assisi, that this shrine, too, will be a megastructure. It isn't.

⁂ The place where Francis first and famously preached to the birds turns out to be a lonely, simple, tree-shaded shrine by the road on the edge of a field. There is no parking lot, no sign, no nothing. It is not until we let ourselves into the low wrought-iron fence enclosure around the arched shrine and see its haloed painting of Francis with a bird on his shoulder, another on his hand, and still another flying toward him that we know we're in the designated place for one of his best-known and most beloved legends.

⁂ Francis was on the road near Bevagna, possibly this one, when he saw a gathering of "a great multitude of birds," including doves, crows, and magpies. He ran toward these common-a-day birds, symbolic of his own humility, and was surprised that they did not take flight, even when he walked among them. "Filled with great joy," he then asked the birds to listen to the word of God.

According to Celano, Francis exhorted his "brother birds" to praise and love the Lord. "He gave you feathers to wear, wings to fly, whatever you need," Francis told the attentive flock. "God made you noble among His creatures and gave you a home in the purity of the air." The birds responded by stretching their necks and spreading their wings and welcoming his touches on their heads until he blessed them and gave them permission to fly away.

This charming story is one of the most re-created by artists, including Giotto in the basilica in Assisi and the fifteenth-century Florentine Benozzo Gozzoli in the San Francesco church-museum in nearby Montefalco. The sermon to the birds also spawned a new audience for Francis, who left the field chastising himself for having neglected animals. From then on, writes Celano, "he carefully exhorted all birds, all animals, all reptiles and also insensible creatures, to praise and love the Creator."

The lovely legend appears to have drawn many others to this unassuming shrine on the side of the road. There are offerings of flowers in tin cans and an assortment of religious candles at the base of the shrine, partially obscuring the defining inscription, which begins: *"Questo luogo Santo Franceso insegnò le laudi di dio creatore."* There are also acorns scattered on the ground, one of which I still carry in my coat pocket to recapture the image of Francis preaching to the birds.

We had come to the little shrine from Orte and Narni, the two hill towns named by his medieval biographers where Francis stopped on his way home to Assisi from Rome. Celano writes that he spent fifteen days in a "place near the city of Orte," while another biographer, Julian of Speyer, writes that Francis spent forty days there. Regardless, the consensus is that Francis used the time not only to preach in Orte with his newfound license but to give his now legitimized friars a refresher course in humility and abstinence.

Francis reportedly sent his friars, one by one, into Orte, dramatically perched on a volcanic tuff cliff, to beg door to door for food. The lesson in humility was followed by a positive lesson in collective deprivation—

Francis instructed his friars to share among themselves the small amount they had received "with gratitude and joyful hearts." On the odd occasion that they had a crust or two of bread left over, writes Celano, they hid it in a "deserted and abandoned tomb, so they could eat it at another time."

We choose not to hide our lunch but to eat our prosciutto-and-watercress sandwiches in a cobbled minipark at the top of the small stone city. A young boy is whizzing around on his training-wheels bicycle, which suggests one of the miracles Francis performed in Orte. An unfortunate medieval boy was so crippled that his head was bent to his knees until Francis made the sign of the cross over him and the boy uncoiled. Francis also rid a man of a tumor "the size of a large loaf of bread" by blessing him. As I sit on a bench, lulled by the autumn sun and the bucolic view over Orte's surrounding fields, it all seems possible.

Francis ambled on toward home through Narni, the most southern medieval hill town in Umbria, fifteen miles beyond Orte. The Rough Guide describes Narni as an "intimate and unspoilt hill-town" with a "stage-set medievalism." We achieve center stage of that medieval set by following the Via Garibaldi, the original route of the ancient Via Flaminia on which Francis must have entered Narni; through the Piazza Garibaldi, from whose medieval cistern under the central fountain Francis might have drunk; past the cathedral, whose eleventh- and twelfth-century façade Francis definitely saw; then through a Roman arch into the Piazza dei Priori, Narni's small and quiet civic center, rimmed entirely by old palazzos. I could have spent weeks in the piazza's outdoor café, situated across from the intricately carved exterior stone pulpit from which St. Bernardino of Siena, a fifteenth-century Franciscan friar, railed against the biblical evil of usury.

Chatting with the other people at the café, including a retired doctor from Foligno who warns us not to trust anyone from Perugia, I visualize Francis entering the medieval piazza to preach. The people would naturally gather around the strange little man, who starts off by wishing them peace, then moves quickly into saving their souls. He is a troubadour and entertains the crowd by singing to them in French, often accompanying himself by strumming a stick to imitate a lute; he's an actor, whirling this way and that and gesturing wildly with his arms while he promises re-demption; he's a man of God, but unlike the stuffy priests who preach in Latin, he speaks to the people in their own language. And he seems gen-uine. Unlike the corrupt priests who condemn sin but father children and who grow fat while others starve, Francis obviously practices the poverty he preaches—just look how emaciated he is in his rags—and he is clearly in love—with Jesus.

No wonder people imbued him with otherworldly powers. Celano re-counts at least two miracles Francis performed in Narni—the curing of a paralytic who could "only move his tongue and blink his eyes" and the restoration of sight to a blind woman. Other miracles would cure people from Narni after his death: a crippled orphan restored to health after pray-ing at Francis's tomb; a sick boy cured after his mother pledged he would follow the spirit of Francis; a man crippled for six years made whole after he dreamed of Francis and felt his hands on his leg and foot.

The truth, however, is that Francis did not like performing miracles. He despised the resulting exaltation of him when, in fact, he believed such miraculous power came from the Lord; he was only the conduit. A perfect example occurred during a later preaching tour through the diocese of Narni, when Francis and three of his friars were invited to stay with a man of "very good reputation" whose unfortunate wife was possessed by a demon. Francis's host quite naturally asked the guest to exorcise his wife's demons—but humble Francis turned him down. "The blessed Francis pre-ferred in his simplicity to be held in contempt rather than be lifted up by worldly honor for some display of holiness, so he refused," Celano explains.

Francis's abhorrence of "vainglory" is a constant theme in all the early stories about him, and this refusal to perform an act that would win him praise is no exception. But in this case he finally bowed to pressure from the husband's friends. He placed his friars in the corners of the wife's room so the devil could not hide in them, then, after praying, commanded the devil to depart the woman, who was "twisting miserably and screaming horri-bly." It worked, in fact, too well. The devil abandoned the woman "with such swiftness and with such a furious roar" that Francis thought the devil had duped him. Overpowering the powerful demon could not have been so easy, and Francis quickly left, ashamed.

So convinced was Francis he had failed that on a subsequent visit he re-fused to speak to the grateful woman, who ran after him down the street, kissing his footprints, to thank him. Only after his friars and her friends in-tervened and convinced him that he had indeed delivered the woman from the devil did Francis relent and speak to her.

Francis is still very much a presence in Narni, so much so that we are lucky to have prebooked a room over the Internet in the Hotel dei Priori just off the piazza. A convention of Franciscan historians is about to de-scend on the town, after having attended the beatification ceremonies for Mother Teresa in Rome, and they take over every available hotel room, in-cluding those of the charming dei Priori.

That they are coming to Narni is not surprising. One of the most im-portant hermitages Francis founded, Sant'Urbano, is nearby. Tradition holds that Francis first stayed at the already existing Benedictine monastery in 1209 on his way back to Assisi from his triumphant visit with Pope In-nocent III and soon established a Franciscan hermitage there. He and his original friars would stay at Sant'Urbano often on their way to and from Rome, and subsequent generations of Franciscan friars would maintain a presence there for the next three hundred years.

I am obviously eager to see the medieval monastery, but this time I want to make sure I know what I will be seeing. My Italian is simply not good enough to communicate confidently with some of the enthusiastic friars we have met at other hermitages, so this time I have e-mailed ahead to the tourist office in Narni to inquire whether there is an English-speaking friar at Sant'Urbano and, if not, to engage a translator.

The young woman in Narni's tiny, one-person tourist office, I quickly discover, has outdone herself. Yes, indeed, there is an English-speaking friar at the hermitage, she tells me, and he is expecting us. And to make our visit there even more fruitful, she has translated into English an entire book for me on Francis at Sant'Urbano. I am dumbfounded by her generosity and enormous investment of time in the translation—but then I read it. Though her English is certainly better than my Italian, sentences like "if us put out from the wall of town-walls of small courtyard the open, here per-haps, down under, the mountain road for which Francis reached to you," and "Come you instead six here" do not shed much light on Francis at Sant'Urbano. But we are reassured by the promise of the English-speaking friar. Wrong again.

We achieve the hermitage in a mountain forest high above the morning mist and are greeted in the stone courtyard by an expectant Father Paolo. "Ah, Inglese, Inglese," the cheerful Italian friar says in welcome and rushes off to return with Brother John Lee, an English-speaking Korean friar from Seoul. Only he barely speaks English. I think he tells us that he is one of 170 Franciscan friars at the Seoul convent and is a guest of the three Italian friars in residence at Sant'Urbano, but who knows? The charming young man hands me an Italian-language guide to the sanctuary, which I can't read and he can't either. Faced with my questions, he darts away and returns with his own Korean-language guide to the sanctuary, which he tries gamely to translate into English. And so, haltingly but with good cheer, we begin our escorted tour of Sant'Urbano.

It is a magical and historic sanctuary, which has served as a spiritual refuge for countless saints dating back to 1000. We wend our way through the pots of miniature pomegranates in the courtyard and past an ancient well with its rusty water bucket into the tiny chapel of San Silvestro. It is easy to conjure up Francis praying and attending mass with his original friars in this simple stone chapel, which couldn't hold more than twenty people. Saints, including John the Evangelist, Silvester, Girolamo, Catherine of Alexandria (who is immortalized at St. Catherine's monastery in the Sinai Desert), and of course, Francis and Clare, march through the restored fourteenth-century frescoes.

We move on in time through the fourteenth-century Franciscan cloister to the timber-roofed refectory, where the resident friars ate their meager meals at the old plank tables. Upstairs are the convent cells established by St. Bernardino of Siena, and back across the courtyard is the sanctuary's "modern" sixteenth-century church, with its carved wooden choir or *coretto* used by the later friars.

But we have come to see Francis at Sant'Urbano, and with a big smile, Brother John leads us into the *Cisterna dell'Acqua,* the site of one of Francis's most famous miracles. A well, rimmed by four upright paving stones in the floor of the big, vaulted room, and the rusty old helmet on the wall tell the story of the *Miracolo del Vino,* or the Miracle of the Wine. On one visit to Sant'Urbano, a seriously ill and weak Francis yearned for some wine, but the friars told him there was none. So Francis asked instead for water, which they fetched by dipping the helmet into the well.

Francis, who must have enjoyed performing this miracle, made the sign of the cross over the water, and presto, it turned into wine—and snatched him back from the jaws of death. "At the taste of it, he recovered so easily that it became evidently clear that the desired 'drink' was given to him by a bountiful Giver not as much to please his sense of taste as to be efficacious for his health," St. Bonaventure writes. The healing power of the miraculous water evidently lived on; four hundred years later, water from the same well was dispensed among the people suffering from the pestilence of 1686 and saved many lives.

At the time of the original wine miracle, the gravely ill Francis was living in an "infirmary" cell his friars had built for him along a forest path above the sanctuary. We ask to see it, but Brother John, shaking his head, points to a barrier of orange netting blocking what used to be the path and is now a flight of wide stone steps leading up the hillside. "Closed," he says. I look so crestfallen that he relents, and scooting under the netting, the three of us climb up what is known as the Via Crucis or Avenue of the Procession, to emerge onto a plateau snuggled against the sheer rock face of the mountainside. It is a veritable Franciscan treasure chest.

There, straight ahead, is the Sacro Speco, a narrow cleft in the towering rocks where Francis repaired to pray. He is said to have felt closest to Christ in such rock clefts, believing they were created by the earthquake that rocked Jerusalem after Christ was crucified. Near it is the cell the friars built for the ailing Francis by piling the easily dislodged square rocks from the cliff behind it. Inside the cell, and preserved behind an iron grille, is the roughhewn wood bed where Francis was confined during his sickness.

Close to the infirmary cell is the Oratorio di San Francesco, a tiny stone chapel his friars built so that the bedridden Francis could join in their prayers. The gate to the chapel is locked, but clearly visible on the wall is a fresco of a prone Francis about to receive the miraculously healing glass of watertowine from one of his friars. And just outside the chapel is a cross topped column of stones, la Colonna dell'Angelo, where one night, in his suffering, Francis heard an angel sing.

To have missed this moving and utterly authentic panorama of Francis at Sant'Urbano would have been devastating—but there is a reason the plateau is blocked off. The mountain is moving and spewing its rocks and trees down on the plateau, which accounts for the various pieces of heavy machinery scattered about. Workmen on the cliff above the plateau are stabilizing the mountain's fragile face by cutting down the trees whose roots split the rock and are also adjusting the guy wires and heavy netting they hope will hold the cliff together.

Brother John has to leave us hurriedly for noon prayers, and one of the workmen takes a break to show us a towering chestnut tree, known as la Castagno di San Francesco. The tree is part of the Francis legend at Sant'Urbano and is believed to have grown from a staff Francis planted in the ground to celebrate his recovery. That the tree is said to be eight hundred years old tweaks the skeptical mind, but why not? It is enormous—and plentifully healthy. The ground around it is strewn with big, glossy chestnuts, which, under normal circumstances, pilgrims would have spirited away as living relics. Because we are the only visitors to the plateau, the workman fills our pockets with the miracle chestnuts to take home.

We go back down the stone steps of the Avenue of the Procession, imagining the medieval friars mounting the steps, as they were wont to do, carrying flaming torches and singing praises to the Virgin Mary and Francis. A local story holds that on one night in 1704, angels were seen climbing the steps to pay tribute to Francis and his spiritual legacy.

The medieval biographies do not make clear where Francis journeyed next on his way home to Assisi, but one of his modern biographers suggests Francis and his friars paused at the spectacular falls of Marmore in the River Nera Valley. Only five miles or so from Terni, the five-hundred-foot-high falls were created by the Romans in 271 B.C. as part of an elaborate engineering project to drain the perpetual flooding of the Rieti Valley. Twenty-three centuries and many alterations later, the falls power hydroelectric stations in the industrialized Terni basin—and are turned on and off by a switch.

Francis and his friars would not have thought of the falls as a power source, nor even, perhaps, as a gift from God since they were created by man. But he would have reveled in the beauty of the shimmering cascades of water crashing down the travertine sides of the mountain and been grateful for the shelter provided by the many natural caves in the area. We are grateful, too, not for the shelter of caves but for arriving at the falls on a Saturday afternoon in October when they are turned on.

We set out on an ancient footpath up the right side of the cascade, which has long since been designated a nature trail or *sentiero natura*. If Francis walked anywhere, it was along this path, through the more than two hundred species of plants and forests of maple, beech, and holm oaks. Immersed in such natural beauty, I can well understand why Francis instructed his friars not to cut down an entire tree but to leave enough so that the tree "might have hope of sprouting again." As we pass through groves of wild cyclamen and lavender, I can also understand why he insisted that any friar planting a vegetable garden leave space for "sweet-smelling and flowering plants."

Wild boar, wolves, and wildcats are said to live again in this protected forest at Marmore Falls, and I keep my eyes peeled as we walk along. But I feel so close to Francis at this point that I know exactly what to do if faced with a wolf. I'll just tell it to come, sit down next to me, and be a good wolf. And it will.

Considering Francis's affinity to all living things, it is little wonder that the birds flocked to hear him speak along the road near Bevagna. From here it is only eight miles or so to Assisi, an easy walk for Francis and his friars as they completed their journey from Rome. What they did not anticipate, however, but certainly must have welcomed, was the very different atmosphere that would greet them.

The Pope's stamp of approval on his Rule and the permission to preach transformed Francis and his friars from objects of ridicule to sought-after speakers. The local clergy gave Francis the church of San Giorgio, where he'd had his rudimentary schooling, but San Giorgio wasn't big enough. So many people clamored to hear him from the Sunday pulpit that the venue had to be changed to San Rufino, Assisi's new cathedral. Every Saturday night Francis walked the thirty minutes or so from, at first, Rivo Torto and later the Porziuncola to spend the night in a hut in the canons' garden so as to be ready to preach the next day.

Remarkably, there is no record of what he actually said. It fell to his more modern biographers, like the highly respected Paul Sabatier, a nineteenth-century French Protestant pastor turned biographer, to imagine the charismatic power of Francis's words. "He spoke as compelled by the imperious need of kindling others with the flame that burned within himself," Sabatier writes. "When they heard him recall the horrors of war, the crimes of the populace, the laxity of the great, the rapacity that dishonored the Church, the age-long widowhood of Poverty, each person felt taken to task in his or her own conscience."

Francis also continued to instruct his friars in humility and obedience. The *Little Flowers of St. Francis* describes the trial of Brother Masseo, a handsome, silver-tongued man who always managed to secure the most tasty alms. Lest Masseo become cocky, Francis decided to add contemplation to his education and, for a period of time, ordered Masseo to be Rivo Torto's cook, porter, and almsgiver, which required him to eat his meals outside and alone. Only when the other friars pleaded with Francis to release him, saying Masseo's disproportionate workload was distracting them from their prayers, did Francis relent and welcome Masseo back into the fold.

Francis orchestrated another rather cruel trial in obedience, this one for Clare's cousin Rufino. Rufino, who is described in the *Little Flowers of St. Francis* as being "so absorbed in God . . . that he became almost mute," was timid and had neither the "courage nor ability to preach the word of God." Nonetheless, Francis, who was presumably trying to instill confidence in Rufino, ordered him one day to go to Assisi and preach "whatever God would inspire him to say" in the cathedral.

Rufino's ordeal was set in motion when he pleaded with Francis to rescind the order. Because Rufino had not obeyed him "at once," Francis not only reissued his order but added the requirement that Rufino preach to the people in his underwear. The reaction was predictable. Poor Rufino, who evidently stuttered as well, was being subjected to ribald laughter in the cathedral until a contrite Francis suddenly burst in, clad only in *his* underwear. Francis then proceeded to give such a moving sermon on the "nakedness and humiliations" Christ had suffered on the cross that the congregation stopped laughing and was moved to tears.

Rufino evidently recovered from his harsh lesson in obedience. He would remain loyal to Francis for the rest of his life and play a central role in the drama already stirring among the parishioners at San Rufino.

Nobody knows whether the young Clare Offreduccio was in the congregation on the day her half-naked cousin mounted to the pulpit. But Clare, whose family lived right next to the cathedral, had been hanging on Francis's every word in the two years or so since he returned from Rome in 1209 and started preaching in San Rufino.

She was sixteen at the time and Francis, twenty-eight. And an unknowing Assisi was soon to be rocked by another family scandal.

THE PORZIUNCOLA, *where Francis receives the runaway Clare* · SAN PAOLO DELLE ABBADESSE, *where she is threatened by her uncle* · SAN DAMIANO, *where she pines for Francis, who calls women "honeyed poison"*

Assisi awoke on March 18, 1212, to an ordinary Palm Sunday. The families attended a Palm Sunday service conducted by Bishop Guido at the Cathedral of San Rufino, and each received a palm frond at the end of the service to take home. The only odd thing about this particular Palm Sunday was that Clare Offreduccio did not approach the altar with the other parishioners to receive her palm frond but sat frozen in a pew. Bishop Guido, who is thought to have known what was soon to take place, left the altar to hand-deliver Clare's palm.

Later that night, in what was an amazingly daring move, Clare and her coconspirator cousin, Pacifica, wrestled away the stones and wooden planks from the family palazzo's "door of the dead," jumped to the ground, and stole away into the dark. They headed toward the woods and the Porziuncola three miles away, where Francis and his friars were waiting for them.

The young women's arrival must have been a moving one. Thomas of Celano, who authored Clare's official biography as well, writes that the "brothers, who were holding a prayer vigil before God's little altar, welcomed the virgin Clare with candles." Other biographers add that the woods resounded with the singing of the brothers, some of whom lit their way with flaming torches. The scene was undeniably romantic. And it grew more so.

Francis received Clare himself and led her to the altar of the tiny chapel in the woods, where she became the first woman to take the Franciscan vows of poverty, chastity, and obedience. Then, while she knelt before him, bathed in candlelight, he slowly and methodically cut off all her long blond hair. Remnants of these tresses are identified as relics in Clare's basilica in Assisi, and while this claim may strain credulity, there is no doubt that Clare was "tonsured." Completing the induction ceremony, Clare then "abandoned her colorful baubles," in Celano's words, and exchanged her fine clothes for the rough, woolen habit worn by the friars and thus, renouncing the world, was "united to Christ."

In retrospect, Clare's dramatic flight from Assisi seems understandable. She had admired Francis ever since he defied his earth father in front of the Bishop's Palace and turned to a heavenly one. She was only thirteen at the time and is said to have marveled at his piety and bravery. Her parents were already talking about her marriage prospects, which filled her with dread. Clare had somehow managed to stave them off, but it is thought that her time had run out at seventeen, and she was indeed betrothed. How she must have wished that she could renounce her father, Favorone, just as Francis did his, and thereby cancel the wedding arrangement. But Clare did not make a scene—then.

Instead she clung resolutely to religion. It is not clear how much of her recorded history is revisionist, but even as a child, Clare is said to have been well on her way to becoming a saint. As penance, she wore a rough hair shirt under her elegant clothes, was so modest that she never left the house except to go to church, prayed for hours on end, and saved the best morsels of food on her plate to feed the poor. She is also said to have secretly supplied meat as sustenance for the friars restoring the Porziuncola.

Her spirituality was undoubtedly encouraged by her pious mother, Ortolana, who had reportedly made three pilgrimages. Omer Englebert, in his biography *St. Francis of Assisi,* writes that after Clare's mother told her daughter the story of the hermit Paul counting off his three hundred daily prayers in the desert with pebbles, Clare started saying and counting three hundred Our Fathers a day. Even her name was deemed a spiritual prophecy. Or-tolana had named her Clare, or Chiara, meaning "light," after she had a vi-sion during her pregnancy that her child would bring light to many souls.

What Ortolana had presumably not counted on was that her teenage daughter, listening to Francis preach in San Rufino, was falling in love. Just what sort of love is a subject of debate. Was Clare drawn to Francis by his fervor for the Lord, a fervor that mirrored her own? Was she swayed by the example of her cousin Brother Rufino, who had been one of the first nobles from Assisi to join Francis? Was her impending marriage so horri-ble to her that she would do anything to get out of it? Or did the seventeen-year-old girl simply fall in love with Francis?

In any event, Clare was so desperate by 1211 that her cousin Rufino brokered secret meetings between Francis and Clare, presumably in the woods. Clare was chaperoned by a sympathetic family servant, and Fran-cis, as added moral insurance, brought along another of his friars, the im-peccable Philip the Tall. The immediate subject in these dangerous meetings must have been her distress about her upcoming marriage. And sooner or later, Francis and Clare reached a decision. She would not marry the man to whom she was betrothed. She would elope with Christ.

The old Benedictine monastery church of San Paolo delle Abbadesse stands at the entrance to a large cemetery in Bastiola, a suburb of Assisi also known as Bastia Umbra. The church is so plain and unassuming that we walk right by it and spend what turns out to be fascinating time in the cemetery searching for it. Dozens of highly styled family mausoleums line the pristine gravel paths, some designed to look like mini-cathedrals, others like ancient chapels, and still others, ultramodern smoked glass and chrome structures like Giorgio Armani showrooms. One mausoleum is even fronted by a greenhouse, filled with flowering cyclamen and gerani-ums. And all bear framed, weather-sealed photographs of their occupants.

Exhausting our search, we head back toward the parking lot and sud-denly realize that the biggish, brick and stone, rather institutional-looking building we had passed on the way in is the very church we are looking for. There is no identifying plaque on the outside walls, but inside we find an inscription bearing the words "Santa Chiara," or St. Clare. A wall plaque identifying the building as the medieval church of a Benedictine monastery for women (or "virgins" as the plaque notes) cements its significance as the very monastery that briefly harbored the runaway Clare—and was the stage for the violent showdown with her family.

For Clare to remain with the friars at the Porziuncola was out of the question, so when Pacifica left to return to Assisi, Clare was quickly escorted to San Paolo delle Abbadesse. The Benedictine nuns here were expecting Clare, but they hadn't bargained on the ruckus that followed her family's discovery of her defection.

Clare's uncle, Monaldo, came after her—with a vengeance. Though it would be nice to think that her family simply missed her company, the bottom line, as it often was with the relatives and prospective heirs of Francis's converts, was money. There is some thought that Clare's father had died, so she already had her considerable inheritance. If her relatives didn't get her back, they would lose her family property to the poor. So Uncle Monaldo came after Clare with some of her male relatives and for several days, according to Celano, harassed her "with violence, venomous counsel and bland promises in order to convince her to withdraw from such a lowly state." The terrified nuns fled to their quarters, which were protected from intruders by Papal edict, but the shouting and cursing continued.

Clare finally faced down her uncle at the old stone slab altar that, on the day we are here, is covered with fresh sprays of baby's breath and Clare's favorite flower, roses. Who knows whether there were flowers on the altar eight hundred years ago, but Celano reports that there was an altar cloth, to which Clare clung with both hands before exposing her shorn head to her uncle. He finally realized that she had made an irrevocable leap of faith, and after trying, and failing, to convince her to accept money for the properties she owned rather than lose them to strangers, Uncle Monaldo and his relatives withdrew. But it was not over.

A week later Clare's fifteen-year-old sister, Catherine, decided to follow Clare's path. She had been visiting Clare every day and decided one day not to return home. When the nuns at San Paolo learned Catherine's intentions, they expressed such terror of a repetition of the consequences that Francis quickly spirited Clare and Catherine away to the stouter hearts of another convent of Benedictine nuns at Sant'Angelo Panzo, on the other side of Mount Subasio. It soon became all too clear that the nuns' fear had been justified.

This time Uncle Monaldo was livid. Two nieces, two inheritances—in a week. Without further ado, he set upon the convent with a dozen armed servants. The wily Monaldo evidently sweet-talked his way into the convent, but once inside, he commanded Catherine in no uncertain terms to return home. She refused. And the legend turns ugly.

One of the mounted servants grabbed Catherine by the arm, wrestled her outside, and started to drag her through the woods toward Assisi. Catherine cried out to Clare to help her, which Clare did in her own way—she fell to her knees in prayer. That was of little apparent use to Catherine, who was being dragged along the ground, leaving bloody smears on the rough stone and snatches of her hair on the thornbushes. But a curious thing was happening. Catherine's body was becoming heavier and heavier. Uncle Monaldo ordered the horsemen to pick her up and carry her, but they couldn't. "It seems as if she has been eating lead all night," one of the horsemen called out.

At that, Uncle Monaldo lost all restraint and lifted his arm to strike his niece, only to find that his arm was frozen in place. Monaldo's roar of pain scared off his horsemen, who fled toward Assisi, followed shortly by Monaldo himself. Poor Catherine, her clothes torn, her body bloodied, was left on the ground. She was barely conscious when Clare found her, but at Clare's touch, Catherine's wounds miraculously healed and she returned with her sister, unscathed, to the convent.

It was obvious to Francis, after all this violence, that Clare and her sister needed a safe place of their own. And it was then that the prophecy he had made while rebuilding San Damiano, that someday it would be a sanctuary "for the holy virgins of Christ," came true. He installed Clare and Catherine, who would adopt the name Agnes, at San Damiano, and the Second Franciscan Order, known as the Poor Ladies, was born.

Francis and Clare would have a very complicated relationship. On the one hand, he was devoted to her. He referred to her as his "little flower" or his "little plant." "As the first tender sprout, she gave forth a fragrance like a lustrous untouched flower that blossoms in springtime," writes St. Bonaventure.

On the other hand, Francis was so terrified of any compromising situa/ tion in his relationship with Clare that he rarely saw her. Public perception of his order was of paramount concern to Francis, and the last thing he wanted was even a whisper of impropriety. The Roman Church was fraught with sexual scandal at the time, as it is today, and Francis was de/ termined that he, as well as the men and women who joined his orders, re/ main above suspicion.

It was not easy. Because it would have been unseemly for the Poor Ladies to wander the countryside begging for alms, Francis had to assign friars to San Damiano to look after the sisters and collect their food. But there was danger in that as well, because the friars were, after all—human. So Fran/ cis issued strict guidelines. "I do not want anyone to offer himself of his own accord to visit them, but I command that unwilling and most reluc/ tant brothers be appointed to take care of them, provided they be spiritual men, proved by a worthy and long religious life," Celano quotes the anx/ ious Francis.

His concern about the friars' contact with women extended to any visits to any sisters at other monasteries. (Italians call the dwelling places of nuns "monasteries" as opposed to the American custom of calling them "con/ vents.") One instance recorded by Celano involves a friar who wanted to take a gift in Francis's name to two sisters he knew at an unidentified monastery. The friar evidently protested when Francis refused his request to go, prompting Francis to "rebuke him very severely by saying things that should not now be repeated." Francis then dispatched the gift with another friar, "who had refused to go."

All this could be chalked up to the vows of obedience and chastity sworn by all of Francis's followers and the spiritual value Francis placed on the denial of human wants, but his harsh punishment of friars who came in voluntary contact with women speaks more to the sexuality Francis both felt and steadfastly fought. When one unfortunate friar paid a sympathy call on a monastery without permission from Francis, Francis imposed his own delusting ice/water remedy on the poor man by making him "walk several miles naked in the cold and deep snow."

That Francis is so human while struggling so hard not to be is one of his greatest appeals. His efforts to distance himself and his friars from any temptation vis-à-vis women, however, border on paranoia. He referred to women as "honeyed poison" and warned his friars of the consequences of looking a woman in the face. "All of us must keep close watch over ourselves and keep all parts of our body pure, since the Lord says 'Anyone who looks lustfully at a woman has already committed adultery with her in his heart,' " he wrote in an early Rule for his friars.

Francis, who was so chaste he boasted that the only female faces he knew were those of Clare and "Brother" Jacopa, discouraged his friars from even talking to women—"He declared that all conversation with women was unnecessary except for confession or, as often happens, offering very brief words of counsel." When Francis himself was forced to talk to a woman, he did so, according to Celano, "in a loud voice so that all could hear." But talking to women at all had its perils. "Avoiding contagion when conversing with them, except for the most well-tested, was as easy as walking on live coals without burning his soles," Celano quotes Francis in *The Remembrance of the Desire of a Soul*.

Even Celano seems taken aback by Francis's negative attitude toward women and their "inappropriate chattering." "Indeed the female even troubled him so much that you would believe this was neither caution nor good example, but fear or terror," Celano writes. He may have been right. But it wasn't that Francis feared women per se; it was that he loved them too much. He would spend anguished hours begging forgiveness for the "sins of his youth," which most certainly involved the pleasures of the flesh. And in more than one sermon, he would portray himself as unworthy of flattery because he might yet father "sons and daughters."

Francis revered women, perhaps to a fault. He had been very close to his mother, Lady Pica; he "married" Lady Poverty; he worshiped the Virgin Mary and founded his community at St. Mary of the Angels; and it was his decision, after all, to welcome Clare into his fledgling order.

It was not just his personal weakness but the management of his Second Order for women, and the inherent temptation posed by the rapidly growing number of Poor Ladies, that threatened Francis. "God has taken away our wives and now the devil gives us Sisters," he once remarked. He never really resolved his inner conflict about women, but in one wonderful story, he did come to peace with his feelings toward Clare.

According to the *Little Flowers,* a tired and troubled Francis was resting with Brother Leo by a well on the night road from Siena when Francis suddenly said: "Brother Leo, what do you think I have seen here?" Leo replied: "The moon, father, which is reflected in the water." And Francis replied: "No Brother Leo, not our sister Moon, but by the grace of God, I have seen the true face of the Lady Clare, and it is so pure and shining that all my doubts have vanished."

Clare, by contrast, seems never to have had any doubts about Francis. She referred to him as "Blessed Francis" and to herself as the "little plant of the most blessed Father Francis." She readily embraced the vows of poverty, chastity, and obedience at San Damiano, which Celano calls "this harsh cloister." Her only regret seems to have been the absence of Francis.

Francis had written a very short rule for the Poor Ladies soon after Clare and her growing number of followers had settled into San Damiano. Known as "The Form of Life Given to Saint Clare and Her Sisters," the one-sentence missive simply states Francis's promise to the "daughters and servants of the most high King" that they will have the "same loving care and special solicitude" from him that he has for his friars. But that solicitude, while undoubtedly genuine, did not translate into action. For all that Francis "cared" about the sisters, he prayed with his friars, fasted with his friars, instructed his friars, and left Clare and the Poor Ladies pretty much on their own.

There are very few accounts in the early biographies of any face-to-face meetings between Francis and Clare, but the ones there are were all instigated by Clare. One such famous meeting involved a lonely Clare yearning to have a meal with Francis. He kept refusing until his friars intervened on her behalf. Making the argument, as recorded in the *Little Flowers of St. Francis,* that Francis owed her at least the favor of a meal, Clare having given up "the riches and pomp of the world as a result of your preaching," the friars finally persuaded Francis to honor her request. He even made the grand gesture of inviting her to the Porziuncola for the occasion, because she would "enjoy seeing once more for a while the Place of St. Mary where she was shorn and made a spouse of the Lord Jesus Christ."

When the day arrived, Francis sent some friars to escort Clare and a sister companion to the much-anticipated meal. But it was never eaten. No sooner had they all sat down on the ground to share whatever crusts of bread there were than Francis began to speak about God "in such a sweet and holy and profound and divine and marvelous way" that the dinner guests were overcome by rapture. The food was forgotten as their spiritual fever reached such a pitch that it lit up the night sky over the Spoleto Val-ley.

People in the surrounding towns, including Bettona, on the far side of the valley, thought the Porziuncola and the forest that surrounded it were on fire, and they rushed to put it out. But seeing Francis and Clare and their entourage in religious ecstasy, they quickly realized that it had been "a heavenly and not material fire" and they withdrew, with "great consolation in their hearts." (We tested the Bettona part of the legend and found that Santa Maria degli Angeli was indeed clearly visible across the valley.) The dinner party ended when "later, after a long while," Francis and his guests regained their senses, and Clare and her escorts returned to San Damiano, sated from that untouched "blessed meal."

Another bittersweet legend about Francis and Clare explains her love for roses. Again, it is Clare who desperately wants to be with Francis, and again, it is Francis who rebuffs her. This time the two of them are walking back to Assisi from Spello, an impossibility, of course, because Clare was cloistered at San Damiano, but regardless, the two of them are walking along in the winter snow and cold, and they are both depressed. They have evidently stopped at several houses to beg for food and water, and though they were given it, they also heard lewd insinuations about their relation-ship. The ever-sensitive Francis then told Clare that they would have to walk apart on the last part of their journey.

A disconsolate Clare took his words to mean for the rest of their lives, and after trudging on alone through the snow, with Francis following at a respectful distance, she suddenly cried out: "Francis, when will we see each other again?" to which he replied: "When summer comes and the roses are in bloom." And suddenly, roses in full bloom sprouted from snow-covered bushes and trees. Clare carried a bouquet back to Francis but knew in her heart they would be parted. Which is why her favorite flower became the rose, which still blossoms every summer on the bushes in her tiny garden at San Damiano.

True to his sense of decorum, Francis withdrew even further from con-tact with Clare. Did she pine for him? Probably. But she never deviated from the path she had chosen. Year after year, decade after decade, she re-mained cloistered at San Damiano, making altar cloths, caring for the sick who were brought to the convent's infirmary, praying, and looking after her sisters. It was for them, perhaps, that she sent message after message to Francis, entreating him to come to San Damiano to preach and instruct her and her followers on how best to serve the Lord. He finally came in 1221—but left them with a puzzle.

Clare and the Poor Ladies were waiting eagerly in San Damiano's choir to hear Francis utter the words that had stirred so many. When he fi-nally entered the tiny church, they watched expectantly as he knelt, raised his eyes to heaven, and began silently to pray. But then, instead of loosing his golden tongue, he called for ashes to be brought to him, some of which he sprinkled on his head and the rest around him in a circle. The Poor Ladies held their breaths, waiting to hear his explanation, but instead he recited the Miserere, the penitential psalm asking God for mercy—and left.

Though Clare must have felt disappointed, she evidently understood the lesson of the pantomime. The universal interpretation of Francis's per-formance is that he, like everyone else, is a sinner and worth no more than ashes. The only path to the Lord is through prayer and not through the words of an intermediary, however stirring. Some biographers also suggest that the ailing Francis knew he was nearing the end of his life—he deliv-ered the odd "sermon" five years before his death—and wanted the Poor Ladies to wean themselves from any spiritual dependence on him. It seems to have worked, for after Francis left Clare and the Poor Ladies sitting in the choir at San Damiano, it is said that Clare doubled the already consid-erable time she spent in penance and prayer.

What a fascinating and poignant relationship Francis and Clare shared. It is easy to read all sorts of innuendo into it, especially in their early years, but such snickers do not lend themselves to Francis's hard-fought war against temptation and Clare's deeply committed spiritual life. Their rela-tionship does not appear to be the steamy and forbidden stuff of *The Thorn Birds*. Theirs was a shared passion for Christ.

The deep devotion that joined Francis and Clare had extraordinary ramifications. Together, they humbled the arrogance of the Church by embracing the path of holy poverty and caring for the sick and needy. In modern jargon, Francis and Clare talked the talk and walked the walk, and they inspired the foundation of hundreds of Franciscan missions throughout the world, many of which continue to this day.

The rapid spread of Francis's visionary influence is also due largely to Clare. At one point after she entered San Damiano, Francis had a crisis of purpose. Part of him wanted to be a hermit and spend his days and nights in solitary prayer. The other part wanted to preach and save as many souls as he could. To resolve his "agony of doubt," according to the *Little Flowers of St. Francis,* he sent Brother Masseo to two of his followers with a request—to ask God in their prayers the question of what he should do and come back to him with the Lord's message.

The second person on Francis's list was a particularly devout friar, Brother Silvester, who was living in solitude on Mount Subasio. The first was Clare. And each came back to Brother Masseo with the same message for Francis from the Lord: "He wants you to go about the world preaching because God did not call you for yourself alone, but also for the salvation of others," the *Little Flowers* reports.

Francis was immediately transformed at the news. "As soon as he heard this answer and thereby knew the will of Christ, he got to his feet, all aflame with divine power, and said to Brother Masseo with great fervor: 'So let's go—in the name of the Lord.' " And off Francis went—again—to ever more beautiful places in Umbria and Tuscany.

*Eating Well and
Tuscany's First Hermitages*

LAKE TRASIMENO, *where Francis spends forty days with a rabbit* · CELLE
DI CORTONA, *the hermitage where he gives away his new cloak* · CETONA,
now an inn and restaurant · SARTEANO, *where Francis foils the devil by
sculpting a snow family*

The first glimpse of blue water is tantalizing. We have been up and down so many mountains and hiked the steep cobbled streets of so many hill towns that seeing the vast, flat, blue expanse of Lake Trasimeno elicits a disproportionate thrill. Just six easy miles west of Perugia, the lake is the fourth largest in Italy and seems almost an inland sea, rimmed by villages both new and very, very old.

Francis arrived on the shore of Trasimeno, then known as the Lake of Perugia, in the early spring of 1211. He had not come for the sport or recreation that currently draws summer hordes to its shallow, balmy waters. Francis was here to spend the forty days and nights of Lent secretly fasting in prayer and solitude on one of the three small islands in the lake, the Isola Maggiore.

Making sure his Lenten vigil would be undisturbed was characteristic of Francis. He did not want to be interrupted in any way during the periods when he communicated most directly with the Lord. So he persuaded the man he was staying with on the mainland to row him out to the island "during the night before Ash Wednesday," according to the *Deeds of Blessed Francis and His Companions*, "so that no one would know about it." The man was to return for him on Holy Thursday.

We are looking not for someone to row us out to the Isola Maggiore but for the passenger ferry that leaves every hour or so from the resort town of Passignano. The town's public parking lot seems a long way from the ferry pier, which is some indication of the crowds in summer, but we are here in October and miraculously find a parking place in town, almost directly across from the pier. It's a good omen for what turns out to be a magical day.

The morning haze begins to burn off as we board the 11:50 A.M. ferry for the twenty-minute run to the island. There isn't a whisper of wind, and the glassy surface of the lake reflects the passing clouds overhead. Cormorants are busy diving for their midday meal, but there are only a few fishing boats around, nothing like the swarms of summer speedboats that make swimming offshore a risky contact sport.

Unlike Francis, who landed on the thickly forested shore of Isola Maggiore and found—nothing, we disembark at the island's tiny, one-street fishing village lined with tourist kiosks, restaurants, and a hotel. "Since there was no shelter where he could rest, he crawled into a dense thicket where thorn bushes had formed an enclosure," continues the *Deeds of Blessed Francis and His Companions.* He would stay here for the next forty days and forty nights, "neither eating or drinking," his only company a wild rabbit that never left his side.

We set out to look for the "dense thicket," following the Lungo Lago, a pleasant perimeter dirt path hugging the lake's shore. We come upon a statue of Francis in such short order that it is almost anticlimactic. The modern statue is of a young Francis raising his hand in a blessing, his youth confirmed by his prestigmata hands and feet. We feel quite let down until we continue along the path to discover a much older stone shrine with a small, ragged wooden statue of Francis set in an alcove and, under it, a grilled opening into a small cave. We have arrived.

A narrow path leads up the hill behind the shrine, and we follow it to a second old stone shrine, with a bigger grille enclosing a larger cave. The carved sign just under the peak is almost illegible, but the inscription definitely ends with the words "Francesco d'Assisi." This must be the two-cell hermitage his friars later established on the island, where perhaps Francis had sought shelter in 1211. Local legend holds that he weathered a fierce

storm on the island, and this cave is well above the water and far more protected than the one below.

There is a wonderful smell of earth and pine needles at the shrines and
the persistent cry and wingbeat of a nearby male pheasant. We linger in the
lovely spot, looking out over the lake, struck as ever by Francis's fortitude
in spending more than a month here, all alone save for the rabbit.

We have a ferry to catch, however, and we hurry up the path and over
the hill, pausing briefly in an olive grove to admire the lovely twelfth-
century church of San Michele Arcangelo. But we've lingered too long
and miss the 12:50 ferry by seconds. And that turns out to be a gift. We
have an hour and a half before the next ferry—and lunch is being served at
the end of the brick-paved main street under white umbrellas outside the
Da Sauro hotel.

I hesitate to interrupt the narrative of Francis's legend on the Isola Maggiore to wax on about lunch, but it turns out to be one of the best meals we
have on that trip to Italy. Our research schedule is such that we do not usually have the time to indulge in Italy's leisurely, multicourse cuisine. Our
norm is to eat lunch either on the road, at the frequent Auto-Stops, otherwise known as gas stations, or at coffee bars in whatever town we have followed Francis to.

We are hardly deprived. There's nothing lacking in a prosciutto, moz-
zarella, and arugula sandwich on freshly baked bread, washed down by a
glass of freshly squeezed blood orange juice and cappuccino. Dinner, too,
is often at the restaurant nearest to whatever hotel we are staying in, and
though the food is always good, it is not always memorable. But this simple
lunch is. My perfectly cooked crisp whitebait, *latterini fritti,* with a fresh
salad, and my husband's pasta and rich *vitello tonnato,* accompanied by a
glass or two of the house white wine, turn an already wonderful day to perfection. We ask the waiter to take a photograph of us, and I keep it on my
desk as a reminder.

My digression into lunch is not, however, that far off course. Food, or
the lack of it, is central to the legend of Francis's Lenten fast on the Isola
Maggiore. He is said to have arrived on the island with two small loaves of
bread—and nothing else. In what is considered a miracle by some, and an
example of the utmost piety by others, he had eaten only half of one loaf

when he was picked up by his secret boatman forty days later. And that tiny portion out of deference to Christ. "It is believed that Saint Francis ate part of one loaf so that with a little bread he would expel the poison of vainglory and thus the glory of a forty day fast be reserved for the blessed Christ," records the *Deeds of Blessed Francis and His Companions.*

However humble it was of Francis to eat just a little bread, so as not to emulate the forty-day fast of Jesus, it was not good at all for his health. Already sickly from bone tuberculosis and recurring bouts of malaria, Francis is thought to have developed chronic gastritis and a gastric ulcer from his ongoing anorexic regimen. Add to that his reluctance to drink water "even when he was burning with thirst," as Celano notes admiringly, and the scene is set for the slow degradation of all his internal organs. In the religious fever of the Middle Ages, such abstinence was believed to feed the soul, and there was no concept at the time of the harm it did to the body.

We leave Lake Trasimeno and head north into Tuscany, where Francis would establish three hermitages near Cortona, Cetona, and Sarteano. All hermitages, we soon discover, are not alike. A surprising number, like the Celle di Cortona, are still working convents, with resident friars and regular masses open to the public; several other Franciscan hermitages and convents, including the one at Cetona, house social programs like Mondo X, a Franciscan-led community for troubled youth; still others, like Sarteano, are little more than caves.

Regardless of what the hermitages are now, they were lifelines for Francis. Always frail, he needed time to recover both spiritually and physically from his far-ranging preaching tours. His friars, too, needed solitude and contemplation. The Franciscans spent so much time on the road that they required retreats along the way for camaraderie and spiritual renewal. New converts to the order, whose numbers were doubling every year, also yearned for places they could gather in their own locales. And so the number of hermitages grew and grew.

We are never sure what we're going to find on our hermitage quest; we simply circle on our maps the approximate locations of the hermitage names we have taken from the medieval texts. The treasure hunt through the Italian countryside, however, is always beautiful. Especially our drive to Cortona and its nearby hermitage through the rolling vineyards of Tuscany.

The Celle di Cortona is nestled into the end of a wooded gorge halfway up the side of Mount Egidio. There is no sign directing us to the *celle*, which makes the first sight of the extensive stone complex at the end of a windy mountain road all the more extraordinary. Nothing has prepared us for the beautiful and immaculate Franciscan convent, straddling a rushing mountain stream and a waterfall. There are terraced gardens, arched bridges over the stream, and wooden-railed paths lacing the grounds. The *celle* is the most "uptown" sanctuary we've found to date, though we don't see a soul. A sign at the entrance tells us there are friars in residence, and there is a bell to pull to summon them, but the solitude is such that we don't want to disturb it—or them. Besides, we miraculously find an English-language guide in a wall rack, so we are able to show ourselves around.

Local legend has it that Francis was directed to this rugged spot by someone he met in Cortona, just two miles away, and that he came to the *celle* for the first time in 1211 after his Lenten fast on the Isola Maggiore. There was already a cluster of small mills along the stream, but what evidently attracted Francis was a fan-shaped recess in the mountain's rock face. Like the rock cleft we had seen at Sant'Urbano near Narni, and similar split rocks at many of his retreats, the natural stone niche at the *celle* became a favorite place of solitude and prayer for Francis. The niche is incorporated now into the substantial building that houses the convent's current oratory, but portions of its rough face remain exposed.

Francis's physical presence at the *celle* is confined to two rooms: the sanctuary's low, timbered-ceiling oratorio, which served as a dormitory for the early friars; and Francis's tiny stone cell, enlivened with baskets of fresh lavender, a copy of his famous portrait by Cimabue, and a somewhat garish painting of the Madonna and Child. The cell, with its familiar stone slab bed, stone pillow, and wooden plank for a mattress, seems carefully recreated to evoke Francis, and it could be an exhibit in the Smithsonian. Even the coarse cloth or *impannate* covering the windows is authentic to the preglass times Francis lived in. The painting of the Madonna and Child on the cell wall is not; the thirteenth-century original was stolen some years ago, and this is a copy. The cell is fenced off now, effectively discouraging common thieves and devout pilgrims from taking fragments of plaster and wood as souvenir relics.

Francis's spiritual presence, however, is everywhere, along the paths and by the waterfall, making the legends about him at the *celle* seem perfectly plausible. One centers on a new cloak that his friars had gone to some trouble to find for him, only to have Francis give it away to a poor man who came to the *celle* grieving for his dead wife. Francis was smart enough to realize the man would probably sell the cloak and cautioned him not to "hand it over to anyone unless they pay well for it." But his friars, seeing the man leaving the *celle* with their hard-won cloak, were moved to act in a very uncharacteristic way. They tried to wrest the cloak away from the poor man so they could give it back to Francis, but the man "clutched it with both hands and defended it as his own." The legend says that the friars finally had to pay the man the price he demanded to get it back, which is also curious in that the friars were forbidden even to touch money.

But the friars were probably at their wits' end trying to keep Francis adequately clothed. He was forever giving away his mantle or parts of his tunic to anyone in need, and often to people, including his own "brothers," who simply asked for something he was wearing. The belief was that anything the holy Francis had touched would bring good fortune to its new bearer and ease his suffering, a belief so strong that often people did not even ask but simply plucked at his tunic to secure a lucky relic. Francis had to patch and repatch his tunic, but he remained so eager to "offer to others things he had denied his own body, even though they were extremely necessary for him" that he was finally ordered by the minister general of his order and the brother appointed as his guardian not to give away his clothing without their permission.

Knowing Francis's penchant for giving away his clothing, his friars must have been ecstatic on this first trip to Cortona at the generosity of their wealthy host. Known as Guido, the man promised to use his wealth to pay for all the Franciscans' future cloaks and tunics. Whether he did or not is unknown, because Guido shortly became a Franciscan convert himself and spent the rest of his life in a cave along the stream at the *celle.* That cave,

too, has been incorporated into one of the buildings and is now the convent's library.

The *celle* is also closely associated with Francis's most controversial friar,
Elias of Cortona. Elias, who would become head of the order in 1221,
after Francis resigned, lived off and on at the *celle* and added a third level
and five more cells, which still have ceilings made of reeds. But that isn't
what made him controversial. The debate remains whether Elias was
Francis's most loyal disciple or, as many think, his Judas.

The positive argument could readily be made that, without the far-
sighted Elias, there would not be a Franciscan Order today. Francis was a
dreamer, not a CEO. He would reluctantly make some changes to accommodate the order's burgeoning number of friars—in 1217, for example, he
would abandon his relaxed approach to his evangelical vision and accept
the geographical division of his flock into "provinces," each with a provincial minister—but Elias would go further, much further.

It was Elias, the organization man, who would translate Francis's romantic dream of the "Lord's wandering minstrels" into a sustainable
Catholic order by dividing the free-form body into seventy-two distinct
provinces; it was Elias, the public relations man, who would make Franciscanism global by multiplying the order's foreign missions; it was Elias,
according to the biographer Omer Englebert, who contrary to Francis's
embrace of solitude and hermetical worship, "promoted study, and urged
the friars to mix in politics"; and it was Elias, the pragmatist, who would
pressure Francis to relax his strictest rules to accommodate the exploding
number of would-be friars. Under Elias, for example, houses began to rise
for the Franciscan clerics and scholars who did not want to wander the
land barefoot.

All this may have been necessary to keep the order alive, but such depar-
tures from Francis's ideal of radical poverty and humility constituted a betrayal to the first, inner circle of friars and subsequent generations of
purists. And it got worse, much worse, after Francis died.

Elias, the showman, would build himself a house in the fanciest part of
Cortona and have a world-class chef; Elias, the brilliant architect and
builder, would design and construct the current and opulent basilica in
Assisi without regard to Francis's insistence on simplicity; Elias, the ven-

ture capitalist, would finance the construction of the basilica by soliciting financial contributions despite Francis's anathema toward money and build such a luxurious attached convent for the new breed of friars that the first friars grumbled: "All they need now is wives." Worst of all, several of the dissenting first friars were beaten and thrown in prison. One even died.

Elias's "sins" would not go unpunished. It was probably here at the *celle* that, well before Elias enacted all these changes, Francis had an apocryphal dream that Elias was damned and would die outside the order. Francis was so horrified by this revelation from God that he stopped speaking to Elias, even stopped looking at him. Elias, who was devoted to Francis in his way, finally forced Francis to tell him why he was being shunned, and on hearing about the prophecy, cried so piteously that Francis said he would pray to God for his forgiveness. And it worked—after a fashion. Though the dream would come true in that some three decades later Elias was excommunicated and defrocked for siding with the emperor against the Pope, a last-minute plea to the Pope from a sympathetic friar brought him absolution and returned him to the Franciscan Order in 1253, while he was lying critically ill at the *celle*.

But it is Francis, not Elias, whose spirit lingers on among the tumbled rocks and noisy streams at the *celle*. The guide we'd picked up quotes a 1705 chronicle that marvels at the "gentle fragrance which overcomes every odor of nature" in and around Francis's cell. Moving on in time, the guide recounts a miracle in 1882, when a construction worker, seeming crushed by a huge boulder, emerged "hale and hearty as before," and yet another miracle in 1959, when two men fell into the "stream in full flood" and survived with only minor injuries.

All this goodwill conspires to make us feel totally secure on the mountain road back down from the *celle* and the journey through the Chianti vineyards and ancient olive groves of southern Tuscany to the next hermitage Francis founded, at Cetona. And another surprise.

If ever there is a success story for the Franciscan involvement with Mondo X, it is the convent at Cetona. Near the "hermitage" cave of travertine rock Francis prayed in, the thirteenth-century Convento di San Francesco is now a sought-after restaurant and inn nestled on the side of a forested hillside. There are walking trails through the woods, a medieval church and chapel, cloisters and courtyards, terraces and gardens, and seven serene bedrooms, all with baths.

The Mondo X commune of young men and women at Cetona, one of thirty-five such communities founded by a Franciscan friar, Padre Eligio, worked together for twelve years to restore the beautiful convent and to transform the cells the early friars reserved for pilgrims into comfortable modern rooms, furnished with antiques, for paying guests. There is no television and no swimming pool, but there is a first-class restaurant run by the resident commune. So we settle down to a delicious six-course lunch, starting with *prosecco* in the garden and moving on through the multiple courses assembled from the fresh produce in the convent's gardens.

There are no Franciscan legends that we know of directly associated with Cetona, but that is not surprising. Geographical location was not a medieval criterion for the recounting of Francis and his legend, and many sites are referred to simply as "the place." But Cetona must have been important to the Franciscans then, because it certainly is now. A convocation of senior Franciscans in 2002 chose to meet at three places: the Porziuncola in Santa Maria degli Angeli; La Verna, where Francis received the stigmata; and the Convento di San Francesco in Cetona.

Thrilled by our discovery in Cetona, we press on with Francis to Sarteano, a photo-perfect Tuscan castle town just north of Cetona where Francis preached in the winter of 1212. He lived for a time within the walls of the tenth-century castle with some local monks and helped care for the sick in the hospital of Santa Maria outside the walls. But Francis, as ever, yearned for solitude and soon started climbing the hills above Sarteano to find perfect seclusion. He succeeded. And so, after many false starts, do we.

Unlike Cetona, the hermitage two miles above Sarteano is rich with documented legends about Francis. It was here that Francis so fixated on his injunction against the ownership of any property that when he overheard a friar saying he had just come from Francis's cell, Francis declared he would never use that cell again. It was from this hermitage that Francis, who claimed he could see Mount Subasio thirty-eight miles distant, dispatched Brother Masseo to San Damiano to ask Clare whether he would better serve God as a hermit or as a pilgrim. And it was at Sarteano that Francis had one of his epic fights with the devil.

On a cold, snowy winter night, the legend goes, the devil so tempted Francis with the desires of the flesh that Francis finally took off his habit and whipped his naked body with the cord so strenuously that he was covered in welts. But the devil's wicked lust continued. The bruised and naked Francis then confronted his desire by suddenly leaving his cell to build a family out of snow.

He sculpted a father and a mother, and two sons and two daughters, and a servant and a maid to take care of them all, then called out to his naked body: "Hurry, and clothe them all, for they are dying of cold. But if caring for them in so many ways troubles you, be solicitous for serving God alone." And with that, according to Celano, the devil withdrew "in confusion," and Francis went back to his cell, praising God.

All this makes it imperative for us to find where Francis built his snow family. We set out with the directions we've been given in a coffee bar and head up into the hills on the Via dei Cappuccini. We are heartened when we see a handpainted sign reading "Celle di San Francesco" and keep on going up an eversteeper dirt road until we come to a fork and another primitively handpainted sign to the celle. And then it becomes ridiculous. We take the fork and proceed straight up the evernarrowing, increasingly washedout road until the branches of the roadside bushes and trees cover the windshield and our wheels start spinning.

The prudent course is to back the car down that track until we can turn around and depart, but somewhere on that mountain is the hermitage of Sarteano. So my husband starts rolling the car backward, and I start hiking up the path, which is so steep that I need the walking stick I pick up on the side of the path to keep from sliding backward down the mountain. And then, suddenly, around a last gasping turn, I step onto a small plateau. In front of me is a massive, threestoryhigh boulder hollowed through at the base by a waisthigh natural arch and bearing another handpainted sign, reading "San Francesco." We have found the hermitage.

I crawl through the arch to find myself on the edge of the plateau and in the midst of a complex of caves on the back side of the rock, which I dis cover later are Ionic Age tombs. I stoop to enter one of the cells and dis- cover that I am hardly the first to do so. A hand-carved wooden sign inside reads, *"Una Notte Chiamo per Francesco,"* and there are unlit candles and slightly wilted flowers and passport photographs of families and children presumably seeking Francis's blessing. I shake my head in disbelief, think- ing I must be imagining these icons in such an impossibly remote spot, but my husband arrives on his hands and knees and sees the same thing.

We explore the other caves, which is not altogether easy. The mountain ledge is very narrow, and we have to navigate over the raised, intertwined roots of trees and then climb the crumbly rock to reach the caves. But the peril is well worth it. One of the caves we achieve is adorned with a rude cross chiseled into its stone wall.

Few people reading this book will probably make the difficult journey to this hermitage. And understandably so. There is no payoff of a me- dieval convent or a church with gorgeous art or splendid gardens or a wa- terfall. What there is, is the stark reality of a no-frills medieval hermitage and the literal experience of what Francis and his followers sought out and endured. "He often chose solitary places to focus his heart entirely on God," Celano writes. No other "solitary" place we would find on our journey with Francis would duplicate the rugged authenticity of Sarteano. It was among these caves, in the dead of winter, I remind myself, that he built his "family" out of snow.

Francis was well aware of the severity of life in the hermitages. He wor- ried about his friars who chose to live in the growing number of secluded cave complexes or primitive mountain huts, and in 1217, he wrote the Rule for Hermitages governing the friars' behavior and spiritual life. To ensure the close bonds of a "family," he limited their numbers to three or four per hermitage and decreed that "two of these should be mothers and they may have two sons or at least one." Having determined that the appointed "mothers" would look after their "sons" and "protect" them from out- siders, he also ordered that each would have his own cell, "in which he may pray and sleep."

Francis remained characteristically harsh on himself, however. During one cold winter, his friars grew so concerned for his health that they sewed an animal skin to the inside of his habit for warmth. Francis, being ever obedient, accepted the pelt next to his skin but insisted that another be added to the outside of his habit so everyone would know of his hypocrisy.

The way back down from the Sarteano hermitage is easier, of course, both for us and, presumably, for Francis. He would need the spiritual re-newal he had received here to continue his journey to save as many souls as was humanly possible. What was becoming increasingly apparent, how-ever, was that he was succeeding beyond expectation. The response to Francis and his traveling message of peace and redemption was bringing him so many new converts that he had to rethink the structure of his move-ment. The answer would come to him in the little Umbrian hill town of Alviano—and multiply his followers by the thousands.

14 *Shrieking Swallows in Alviano*

ALVIANO, *where Francis silences the swallows and considers a Third Franciscan Order* · SAN ROCCO, *the Third Order's Porziuncola near Montefalco* · *the tiny shrine of* SANT'ILLUMINATA *near* ALVIANO, *where Francis might have formulated the whole idea*

The drive to the picture-book castle town of Alviano is spectacular. The road hugs the banks of the Tiber River, then rises to run along a dramatic gully past a huge, artificial lake, the Lago di Carbara, and continues on to the Lago di Alviano and the Alviano Oasis. The "oasis," a huge marsh area created by the damming of the Tiber River, attracts some 150 species of migratory birds and is managed by the World Wildlife Fund. The WWF oversees the nature walks through the oasis and its "hides," from which bird-watchers can see migrating cranes and fish hawks and geese. There must be close to three thousand geese and ducks on the lake the October afternoon we are there.

Birds of a different sort are central to an important chapter of Francis and his legend at Alviano. It was here, inside the charming walled and turreted fortress town overlooking the lake, that Francis is thought to have created the Third Franciscan Order, this one composed of urban laypeople. And all because of a flock of swallows.

According to his medieval biographers, Francis came to Alviano around 1212 to preach but ran into a natural obstacle. There were so many nesting swallows making so much noise—"shrieking" is the word used by Celano—that the people gathered in Alviano's central piazza could not hear him. Francis solved the problem by simply addressing the birds. "My sister swallows, now it is time for me also to speak since you have already said enough," he advised the swallows, which according to Celano immediately fell silent.

According to the *Little Flowers of St. Francis,* the people were so astonished when Francis quieted the "shrieking" swallows that "they wanted to follow him and abandon the village." Francis dissuaded them—with a promise: "Don't be in a hurry and don't leave, for I will arrange what you should do for the salvation of your souls." It was from that moment, the *Little Flowers* claims, that Francis started formulating the idea of a Third Order, "for the salvation of all people everywhere."

It was a brilliant concept. People had been flocking to Francis wherever he preached. Married couples, widows, mothers, fathers embraced his teachings and wanted to live a Franciscan life. "Many of the people, both noble and ignoble, cleric and lay, impelled by divine inspiration, began to come to St. Francis, wanting to carry on the battle constantly under his discipline and under his leadership," writes Celano.

The challenge was that many of these new converts had family obligations and could not become itinerant preachers or enter convents or monasteries. They wanted to follow Francis in their everyday lives. The result is the subject of an ongoing debate among Franciscan historians. Some claim that Francis merely urged his secular followers to live godly lives in their own homes, while others, including several of his medieval biographers, insist Francis established what was known as the Brothers and Sisters of Penance, or the Franciscan Third Order, for both secular penitents and clerics. "Thus through Blessed Francis's perfect devotion to the Blessed Trinity, the Church of Christ was renewed by three new orders," says the *Legend of the Three Companions.* "His three distinct orders were each in due time approved and confirmed by the sovereign pontiff."

Whatever its original makeup, the Third Order would prove to be an enormous success. Francis had tapped into the religious resurgence sweeping the towns and cities of Italy, a resurgence due largely to his preaching tours. "It is an historical fact that around 1215 in the urban centers of Italy we see a sudden increase in the number of penitents, even among married persons," writes G. G. Messerman in his 1961 history of the penitential movement. The "unexpected increase" of urban penitents, he continues, is "attributed to St. Francis of Assisi."

Francis would write a "norm of life" for the Brothers and Sisters of Penance, believed to be his Letter to the Faithful, in which he exhorts his lay followers to follow a religious life of penance, charity, humility, and prayer. "Oh, how happy and blessed are these men and women when they do these things and persevere in doing them, since the spirit of the Lord will rest upon them," Francis writes. The consequences are dire, however, for those who don't. "No matter where or when or how a man dies in the guilt of sin without doing penance and satisfaction," Francis warns, "the devil snatches up his soul from his body with so much anguish and tribu-lation that no one can know it unless he has experienced it."

Approved orally by Pope Honorius III in 1221 and more formally in 1289 by Pope Nicholas IV, the first Franciscan Pope, the "rule" for the Brothers and Sisters of Penance contained a revolutionary provision: In the pursuit of peace, members of the Third Order were forbidden to carry arms and were instructed to avoid taking oaths. The result was a serious blow to feudalism and the ability of warring governments, communes, and landed families to order up armies. The prohibition so infuriated the belli-cose tendencies of some members of society at the time that yet another Pope, Gregory IX, had to issue a Papal bull in 1228 defending the right of the increasingly persecuted members of the Third Order not to carry arms or enter military service.

Nonetheless, the Third Franciscan Order attracted extraordinary people who wanted to follow Francis and his life of penance. Francis's close female friend "Brother" Jacopa in Rome joined the new order. So did members of some of Europe's royal families: the widowed princess St. Elizabeth of Hungary; the widowed queen St. Elizabeth of Portugal; King St. Louis IX of France; and King Ferdinand V and his queen, Isabella I, of Spain.

According to a Third Order website, Christopher Columbus also joined the Third Order, as did the artists Giotto, Raphael, and Michelan-gelo; the scientist Louis Pasteur; the musicians Franz Liszt and Charles Gounod; and the poet Dante, who is buried in the church of St. Francis in Ravenna, allegedly in a Franciscan habit. The Third Order would also produce many, many Popes and, beyond the "royal" saints, St. Margaret of

Cortona, a single mother turned penitent, and St. Rose of Viterbo, who converted an entire village by standing for three hours, unscathed, in a burning pyre.

Fraternities of the Brothers and Sisters of Penance sprang up all over Italy and soon spread through Europe. Some were laypeople, known today as the Secular Franciscan Order, or S.F.O.; others were clerics, who became known as the Franciscan Third Order Regular, or T.O.R. The men and women established their own convents and churches and eventually had their own Franciscan habits. By the mid-fifteenth century, they also had their own minister general and their own Porziuncola, at the Little Church of San Rocco near the Umbrian high hill town of Montefalco.

Because of its historical significance, we had gone to Montefalco to try to find San Rocco. Local legend holds that Francis established a convent here in 1215, the year the Third Order took hold, and miraculously caused a spring to appear to supply fresh water. But we also went to the sky-scraping Montefalco, known familiarly as the "balcony of Umbria," to see the vibrant fifteenth-century fresco cycle of Francis's life by the Florentine artist Benozzo Gozzoli in the old San Francesco church and to indulge in Montefalco's unique and universally celebrated red Sagrantino wine. It is tempting to think that Francis, who passed often through Montefalco, indulged as well in the wine from the town's ancient vineyards.

We found San Rocco with considerable difficulty in the adjacent and tiny village of Camiano. The ancient church stands now on private property in a small, gated community, and we never would have achieved it had it not been for a passing woman who unlocked the gate for us, insisting that, by law, San Rocco has to be accessible to anyone who wants to see it. What she neglected to tell us about was the dog that was presumably guarding the house next to the church and that immediately took a strong dislike to us.

Standing in front of the ancient, slightly peaked, almost windowless old stone church made our visit worth it, though. Solid and unadorned, San Rocco looks nothing like the tarted-up Porziuncola in Assisi. The old church breathes authenticity and seems a natural place for Francis's followers to have convened so long ago and to make pilgrimages to today.

The Third Franciscan Order continues to thrive worldwide, and its members reportedly number in the millions. We had met several members ourselves on our journey—the smiling, elderly sister who runs a hostel for pilgrims in Assisi, an attractive young woman at a convent in the Marches, an extremely helpful man in New York—and they all owe a spiritual debt to this little church of San Rocco, where six hundred years ago the Franciscan Third Order was formally organized, and to the miracle of the shrieking swallows in Alviano, where two hundred years earlier the idea was born.

That miracle is re-created and celebrated in Alviano in the Chapel of the Swallows off the beautiful Renaissance courtyard inside the reconstructed sixteenth-century castle. The fresco of Francis silencing the birds has a familiar quirk: One of the faces in the thirteenth-century crowd listening to him preach belongs to the seventeenth-century woman Donna Olimpia, who commissioned the fresco.

Because we are in Alviano, we feel compelled to visit the nearby hermitage of Sant'Illuminata. The Franciscans inherited the second-century convent and hermitage in the twelfth century, and Francis is said to have stayed there often in a grotto whose singular stone slab "bed" is surfaced with a *panno di velluto,* or cloth of velvet. That description is intriguing enough to draw us up the mountain. We stop to ask directions from an old woman walking along the mountain road, having learned that young people are less apt to know the whereabouts of Francis sites, and she directs us higher up toward Guardia. After several wrong turns, we see a tiny yellow sign with a cross on it, and turning down an unmarked gravel road through an olive grove, we chance upon the little cell in the side of the hill, bearing the small inscription "Crypta di San Francesco."

It would seem that, having visited so many Franciscan hermitages, we would be sated and even blasé about finding yet another. But these isolated caves, and the reverence they continue to inspire, never cease to amaze me. Here we are, on top of a mountain with nothing around for miles, in front of a roadside cave barely three feet wide and ten feet deep, and there are fresh flowers in the assorted tin cans outside the grated opening and candles burning inside on the altar.

A brochure we picked up in Alviano tells us that this little fissure in the rock was created in a "furious" earthquake and is a miniature La Verna, the much more dramatic mountain fissure where Francis would later receive the stigmata. But it is the "velvet" stone bed that has drawn us here, and we get the flashlight from the car to discover that the slab's surface does indeed have a velvety, porous texture.

Perhaps Francis rested and meditated here after preaching in Alviano, and perhaps it was in this very grotto that he formulated his vision of a lay order for his followers. It is a lovely, quiet spot with a splendid view of Lake Alviano from across the road. He must have been as reluctant to leave this tranquillity to return to the real world of preaching as he was from every hermitage, in which he often spent months at a time. "He sometimes feared that, under pretext of withdrawing into solitude to pray, his body was in reality seeking only to escape from the fatigues of preaching throughout the world, this world for which Christ did not hesitate to come from heaven on earth," records the *Legend of Perugia.*

But Francis did not give in to his fatigue. Instead, he expanded the geography of his evangelical zeal. As a younger man, he had dreamed of becoming a knight and forcefully routing the Muslim infidels from Jerusalem. In this year of 1212, he dreamed again of going to the Middle East, but this time to peacefully convert the infidels to Christianity.

He didn't make it.

*The Marches Again—
Green Fields, Blue Adriatic*

ANCONA, *where Francis sails, unsuccessfully, for Syria* · SIROLO, *where the returning Francis saves a man's life* · ÓSIMO, *where he preaches with an adopted lamb* · SAN SEVERINO *and* ASCOLI, *where he wins many new friars* · SAN LEO, *where he is given the mountain on which he will receive the stigmata*

We are sitting in a cafeteria in the busy Adriatic port of Ancona, watching the huge commercial ferries unload. One eighteen-wheel truck after another rumbles past the windows with ever-more-exotic route markings—Athens, Sofia, Skopje, Patras, Piraeus, Bucharest, Warsaw. Passengers and similar trucks join the loading line for other exotic ferry destinations: Zadar, Dubrovnik, Split, Izmir and Istanbul, Bodrum, Rhodes, and the Greek Islands. One ferry will go all the way to Alexandria at the mouth of the Nile.

🕮 The medieval port of Ancona was just as busy. European trade was brisk between North Africa and the eastern Mediterranean, and commercial sailing vessels regularly arrived from and departed to these same ports, carrying spices, cloth, salt, olive oil, gold, wine. The ships also transported merchants, Crusaders, pilgrims, and missionaries. One of the missionaries, in the summer of 1212, was Francis.

🕮 Francis was bound for Syria, determined, in the words of St. Bonaventure, "to preach the Christian faith and penance to the Saracens and other non-believers"— or die trying. Martyrdom for Christ was considered the pinnacle of perfect love by Christian extremists in the

Middle Ages, and Francis, whom St. Bonaventure describes as "burning with the desire for martyrdom," was no exception.

There was ample opportunity for Francis and other Christian evange/ lists. Muslim armies controlled most of what is now known as the Middle East but was then considered Greater Syria—modern Syria and Lebanon, western Iraq, northern Saudi Arabia, and most of Jordan, Israel, and Palestine. But the prize then, as it is today, was the holy city of Jerusalem.

Liberating Jerusalem was one of was Francis's lifelong dreams, a dream shared by many European Christians. Francis had been only six in 1187, when Jerusalem was wrested from the Christians by Muslim armies headed by the legendary Muslim Kurd general Saladin. Now he wanted to go in peace and succeed where so many others had failed.

Four unsuccessful Christian crusades had been launched from Europe by the time Francis arrived in Ancona. The third, and most ambitious, had been led between 1189 and 1192 by the crowned heads of Europe— the German emperor, Frederick Barbarossa (who fell off his horse en route and drowned); the French king, Philip II; and the English king, Richard the Lion/Heart. The royal armies did manage to recapture much of the coastline of Palestine, including the Crusader Kingdom of Acre, which would serve as a Christian stronghold for the next century.

But Jerusalem, though reopened by Saladin to Christian pilgrims, re/ mained securely in Muslim hands—and stayed so during the embarrassing Fourth Crusade, which never even reached the Holy Land. The Vene/ tians, who held the lucrative Papal contract to transport the Crusaders to the Holy Land, instead turned their sights—and their sails—on the frac/ tious Orthodox Christian city of Constantinople. Led ashore by the blind, octogenarian doge of Venice, the Venetians and their cargo of Cru/ saders forgot all about Jerusalem in the frenzy of sacking Constantinople.

That sorry crusade, which would leave Constantinople under the con/ trol of Rome for the next half century, ended in 1204, eight years before Francis decided to embark on his own crusade or, as some think, to join one already in progress.

Francis's arrival in Ancona in 1212 coincided with the so/called Chil/ dren's Crusade. The romantic and ultimately tragic version of this "cru/ sade" (unofficial because the Pope had not sanctioned it) involves the more or less simultaneous visions of Jesus by two twelve-year-old boys in France and Germany who were instructed to lead a crusade of innocents to liberate Jerusalem. Few of the forty thousand children who set out for the Mediterranean coast made it, however—and none reached the Holy Land. Crossing the Alps claimed the lives of most of the German children, and the French children who straggled into the port at Marseilles found the Mediterranean did not part for them as promised. The tragedy climaxed when the children who set out by boat ended up either shipwrecked or captured by pirates and sold into slavery.

An alternative version of the Children's Crusade—and the one that pertains to Francis—is less heartrending. According to linguists, the Latin word *pueri* means both "young boys" or "children" and "landless serfs." Accordingly, this theory purports that the Children's Crusade was in fact a ragtag army of the poor and disenfranchised who were caught up in the religious fervor of the time and believed that they, not armed knights or royalty, were chosen by God to liberate Jerusalem. Francis, the living symbol of holy poverty, may very well have been one of them.

And so he had made his way through the Marches to Ancona, as had many others, to try to get to the Holy Land. And he, like so many others, would fail. Francis managed to get himself on a boat, accompanied by an unnamed friar, but the vessel met strong unfavorable winds and, instead of sailing southeast via Rhodes for the three-week voyage to Acre, was blown ninety-five miles northeast across the Adriatic to fetch up on the Dalmatian coast. Some say Francis was shipwrecked and survived only by the protection of God, but whether or not there was an actual shipwreck, he was definitely stranded in the port of Zara, now called Zadar, in what is modern Croatia.

Today, the ferry trip from Zadar to Italy takes a few hours; for Francis the return trip turned out to be even more fraught than the outgoing one. According to St. Bonaventure, the stranded Francis had no money to pay for his passage, and the hard-hearted sailors of a ship going to Ancona refused his entreaties "to take him with them for the love of God." Francis had to resort to the age-old method of secretly stowing himself and his companion friar in the hold of the ship. They might very well have starved to death had not a well-wisher, "sent by God for this poor man," arrived at the ship just before it sailed and secretly handed the food Francis and his brother would need on the passage to a God-fearing sailor who was instructed to distribute it to them "in a friendly fashion in their time of need."

The time of need turned out to be universal aboard the ship as it ran into such a "great storm," according to Celano, that the sailors had to "spend many days laboring at the oars." The food supplies onboard dwindled until only the few alms miraculously provided for Francis remained—which prompted a second miracle. The small cache of food "multiplied so much that while they were delayed at sea for many days by the relentless storm, it fully supplied their needs until they reached the port of Ancona," writes St. Bonaventure. By then, the hard-hearted sailors had changed their attitude toward the stowaways, realizing that they had "escaped many threats of death through God's servant."

Francis, safely back on dry land, decided to save souls closer to home, in the Marches. He did not give up his determination to convert the Saracens: He would try, and fail again, in 1213 after falling gravely ill in Spain en route to Morocco. At this point in his legend, however, Francis left the port in Ancona and "began to walk the earth and to sow in it the seed of salvation," writes St. Bonaventure. His preaching tour started in Ancona and went on through the coastal towns and mountain villages of the Marches, "reaping fruitful harvests." After their initial mistrust of Francis, the simple, land-loving people of the Marches had become more receptive to him than the populations of any other part of Italy, and soon, Celano writes, "many good and suitable men . . . followed him devoutly in his life and proposal."

Following Francis on his preaching tour of the Marches turns out to be an unexpected delight for us. The entire eastern edge of the small province fronts on the sunlit Adriatic and on the west is bounded by the snow-capped Sibilene mountains. In between, the Marches' fertile land is a dazzling patchwork of farms and vineyards, and its old, inland hill towns are virtually tourist-free. We eat splendid Marche meals of fresh grilled fish; *coniglio in coccio*, rabbit cooked in white wine and milk; *olive Ascolane*, a Marche specialty of giant breaded and deep-fried olives stuffed with minced meat and cheese; and top it all off with a nightly bottle of Verdicchio, the local white wine.

Francis's first and very pleasant stop, as is ours, was in the tiny seaside resort village of Sirolo, seven miles from Ancona. Local legend holds that he stayed here in an inn built into the city walls, and we stay in that same inn, now a tony seven-room hotel called the Locanda Rocco. Francis is said to have performed a miracle from an upstairs room—he saved the life of a man who was about to fall from the inn's adjacent arch onto the cobbled stone street below. We stay in that room.

One of our windows looks straight out at the "miraculous" stone arch entry into the town, embedded with a Crusader cross. Another window overlooks the Adriatic, and still another frames the distant, floodlit, and mammoth pilgrimage Sanctuary of Loreto, which contains what the faithful believe is the original stone house of the Virgin Mary in Nazareth, flown here by angels in 1294. Francis reportedly predicted the airborne delivery of the Virgin's house to Loreto, then the site of a thriving Franciscan community, a prophecy that seems perfectly in keeping with the medieval ethos of the Marches.

The residents of the Marches, including the early native Franciscan friars, were noted for their poetic fancy and mystical natures. The *Little Flowers of St. Francis* was written by a friar from the Marches and includes many stories of Marche friars overcome by religious ecstasy. One, Brother John of Fermo, "would run as if drunk: sometimes through the garden, sometimes through the woods, sometimes through the church, as the flame and force of the spirit drove him." A later and popular Marche friar, St. Joseph of Cupertino, the patron saint for students taking exams, frequently levitated and flew through the air. His remains are preserved, under glass, at the church dedicated to him in Ósimo, a Marche hill town.

Sirolo is a perfect repository of that mysticism. An engraved stone plaque near a tiny old chapel just down the street from the Locanda Rocco tells the legend of the still-standing trees Francis planted here with his own hands, in 1212. Because of the bright color of their seedpods, the trees are known locally as the "cherries of St. Francis."

The "cherry" trees are just inside the walls of the Vetta Marina, now a private estate and the site where Francis was given a convent by a local noble either in 1212 or on a return trip in 1215. Massimo, the estate's caretaker and hunting friend of the owner of the Locanda Rocco, graciously shows us the ruins of the old convent, then takes us along a manicured gravel path to the edge of the estate's seaside cliff. According to local legend, Francis stood on this dizzying 330-foot-high cliff and preached to the fish that had gathered in large numbers in the milky blue sea below to listen to the holy man.

And the Marche legends only get more charming. It is the saga of Francis and a lamb that leads us along the cattailed road from Sirolo inland to the hill town of Ósimo. According to Celano, Francis and one of his friars, Brother Paul, were walking along this road when Francis saw what he considered a sacrilege—a lamb alone among a herd of goats. Francis identified lambs with Christ, but for all his love of animals, he evidently did not like goats. "Do you see that sheep walking so meekly among these many goats?" Francis asked Brother Paul. "I tell you, in the same way our Lord Jesus Christ, meek and humble, walked among the Pharisees and chief priests."

Francis wanted to buy the sheep to spare its humiliation among the goats, but he and Paul had no money, and the cheap tunics they were wearing were not sufficient for barter. Miraculously, a traveling merchant came on the scene and bought the sheep for them. So now, Francis and Paul had a sheep, which they took with them to Ósimo to visit the bishop.

Ósimo seems a rather cheerless, steep-streeted town when we arrive on a cold and gray morning, perhaps because we meet there with our first—and only—unpleasant encounter in all our Italian travels. We stop in a coffee bar for a warming cappuccino on our way up to the thirteenth-century Cathedral di San Leopardo, and a drunk in the bar apparently makes such rude remarks about us in Italian that an offended patron throws him out the door.

Francis's welcome was undoubtedly warmer than ours but not altogether satisfactory. He, Paul, and the lamb proceeded up the same steep street to the cathedral and right up the steps into the sanctuary, to be greeted by the startled bishop. Celano credits the bishop with being "touched in his heart" by the parable of the sheep—but he did not offer to take the animal from Francis. So Francis, after preaching to the good folk of Ósimo the next day, left the hill town with Paul and the lamb, with Francis beginning "to wonder what to do with the sheep."

His answer leads us from Ósimo some twenty-five miles across the Marches to the small and important medieval Franciscan town of San Severino, where Francis solved the sheep problem by presenting the animal as a gift to the Poor Clares cloistered there. Unlike the bishop in Ósimo, the Poor Clares in San Severino reportedly accepted the lamb "as a great gift from God." According to Celano, the "maidservants of Christ . . . devotedly cared for the sheep" and made a tunic for Francis out of its wool, a tunic he received back in Assisi "with great reverence and high spirits, hugging and kissing it."

The medieval center of San Severino, with its handsome elliptical, arcade-rimmed piazza, is rich with Franciscan lore. Francis was officially here at least twice and left a plethora of miracles in his wake—a boy cured of leprosy, a man restored to life after being crushed by a stone. Francis's preaching converted several sons of San Severino to his order, including Brother Masseo, one of his earliest and closest friars, and Brother Bentivoglia, whose thirteenth-century body was so graphically preserved and lit under glass in one of the town's many churches that it scared people. (His face is now covered more soothingly in wax, but his bony feet are natural.)

The enthusiastic Marche friars, in turn, converted other young men from San Severino, including an unnamed "very vain youth" who, the *Deeds of Blessed Francis and His Companions* notes, had previously been "noble, refined and lusty." And it was here, at the old Franciscan friary and church, that Francis made his most famous conversion of all.

Brother Fabio greets us at the church high on a hill overlooking the town. He is a Capuchin friar, a member of an autonomous branch of the Franciscan Order formed in the early sixteenth century in the Marches in protest of the more secular policies being practiced by the Franciscan heirs of Brother Elias. Brother Fabio is a young man and has a beard, as do all Capuchin friars, and he is wearing the brown habit and the order's signature peaked hood, which symbolizes the habits and hoods worn by Francis and the early friars; the small, round hood worn by other Franciscan orders is thought to symbolize the relaxation of Francis's primitive clarity. (The Italians' ever-present sense of humor seized on the Capuchins' light coffee-colored hood, or capuche, and used the name to identify the espresso coffee drink cappuccino, with its peaks of foam.)

But back to the famous conversion and the reason we are visiting Brother Fabio. It was in this small, twelfth-century stone church, he tells us, that the dramatic and unexpected conversion of the poet laureate of Emperor Frederick II's court, known as the King of Verses, took place. The imperial lyricist, William of Lisciano, whose sister was a Poor Clare, had come out of curiosity to hear Francis preach when suddenly he had a vision: Two shining sword blades in the shape of the cross of Jesus appeared on Francis's breast. "Stunned at once by what he saw, he began to resolve to do better," writes St. Bonaventure.

Brother Pacifico, as Francis named the poet laureate, became a major figure in the early Franciscan Order. In 1217 he was sent to France, where he established the first province there of the Friars Minor, and seven years later he was at La Verna when Francis received the stigmata. Pacifico is also credited with setting the sayings and songs of Francis to verse. And his vision and induction into the order happened right here, in 1212.

The church has changed, of course, since Francis's time. Brother Fabio tells us that the Poor Clares enlarged it in the fourteenth century to commemorate the canonization of St. Clare and added windows and a Gothic arch. The sisters left in the sixteenth century, and the Capuchin friars moved in—with disastrous results. The austere friars thought the frescoed walls of the church looked too opulent, so they stuccoed over them. In the eighteenth century, they added another window and a new floor. "They made so many changes, you can hardly recognize the original church," laments Brother Fabio.

Even so, standing in the old part of the church and looking up at the thirteenth-century crucifix over the altar, I easily feel the presence of Francis. And again outside in the convent's lush garden. And at the huge thirteenth-century Porta San Francesco at the top of the hill near the ruins of his church. And in the extraordinary art in the Pinacoteca Civica, San Severino's municipal art gallery, which boasts a fifteenth-century Pinturicchio altarpiece, *Madonna della Pace,* and two fourteenth-century altarpieces from the old monastery of the Poor Clares by Paolo Veneziano. There is also a whole room of vibrant fresco fragments from the old Chiesa di San

Francesco, among them Francis with Pope Honorius III and an anguished Francis holding up the church on his shoulder.

Francis was even more successful gathering new friars—thirty in all—in the stunning Marche city of Ascoli Piceno, some forty miles from San Severino. Ascoli sits on the Via Salaria, the ancient but still heavily traveled Roman road from the Adriatic coast in the Marches and over the Torritao Pass through the Apennines to Rome. The approach to this busy border city through the urban sprawl of sixteen-story apartment buildings is not auspicious, but its medieval heart turns out to be sensational.

Many of the piazzas and the sidewalks are paved in local travertine stone, as are the details on many of the houses. Everything gleams in the sun and also, unfortunately for us, in the rain. But nothing dampens our enthusiasm for this old but also affluently modern city, with its medieval buildings and many cafés and restaurants.

We follow Francis to the Piazza Arringo, in front of the sixth-century Cathedral of Sant'Emidio, where he is said to have delivered the impassioned sermon that won him so many new friars. The piazza is being repaved, and a lunchtime crowd has gathered to watch the skilled mason set each perfectly matched cobblestone in place, then tap it three times with the handle of his trowel to secure it in the sand below.

For centuries, the Piazza Arringo was the site for all of Ascoli's public assemblies. Politicians, firebrands, and roaming religious, including Francis, spoke to the assembled hordes from under an elm tree, but the tree appears to be gone. The lunch crowd gathered around the piazza, however, is reminiscent of the crowd that greeted Francis—except that it is far more orderly.

His reputation as Christ on earth had preceded him, according to Francis's biographers, and his arrival in Ascoli caused a near riot. One version, commissioned by Francis's friend Pope Gregory IX, appears in the thirteenth-century versified life of Francis by Henri d'Avranches.

> *He is entering the city of Ascoli when all*
> *The sick come to him; and a struggle there is*
> *To see if they can touch even the hem of his garments.*

For they regard his very garments as relics,
And so they tear them off him that he goes around
In tatters. And they offer him loaves which he blesses;
A crumb of which, seasoned with faith, mitigates pains,
Alleviates ailments and brings riddance to injuries.

Celano's version of Francis in Ascoli is only slightly less dramatic. "There he spoke the word of God with his usual fervor," Celano writes. "Nearly all the people were filled with such grace and devotion that they were trampling each other in their eagerness to hear and see him. Thirty men, cleric and lay, at that time received the habit of holy religion from him."

The strong impression Francis made on Ascoli continues in its art galleries and churches. A sweet thirteenth-century fresco in the church of San Gregorio Magno, believed to be one of the earliest depictions of Francis, shows him looking very young, preaching to the birds. Francis is also portrayed, among other saints, in the Pinacoteca Civica, by the fifteenth-century artist Carlo Crivelli, who had to flee Venice after an adultery scandal and fetched up in Ascoli. Tucked away in a poorly lit corner is a huge, very dark painting of Francis receiving the stigmata, attributed, unbelievably, to Tiziano Vecellio, otherwise known as Titian, the sixteenth-century Venetian genius. The museum also displays the gorgeous thirteenth-century gold-and-silver-thread Papal cape worn by Nicholas IV, the first Franciscan Pope and a son of Ascoli.

In between galleries and churches, the rainy weather gives us the perfect excuse to hang out at the splendid Art Nouveau Caffè Meletti on Ascoli's central piazza, the Piazza del Popolo. Tout Ascoli appears to assemble daily at the Meletti's white Carrara marble tables and velvet sofas for coffee, platters of prosciutto, and the café's signature *anisetta* aperitif, and we eagerly join them.

Looking out from the warmth of the Meletti at the panorama of medieval buildings framing the marble Piazza del Popolo easily fills a morning respite. One of these structures, occupying an entire end of the piazza, is the massive thirteenth-century church of San Francesco.

We have long since learned to hire English-speaking guides in important Franciscan locations like Assisi, Perugia, and San Severino. Our guides in Ascoli—Leila, who has her fourteen-month-old son, Leonardo, with her, and her more fluent friend, Emanuella—point out details in the intricately carved travertine portico around the main entrance into the church that we never would have known: The triangular peak of the portico represents Christ speaking to the world through the Franciscan figures at the ends of all the upper flutes; the twelve descending roses represent the apostles, and the one open rose, fourth from the top, represents the four evangelists, Matthew, Mark, Luke, and John; the seventy-two diamonds represent the pairs of the first thirty-six Christians spreading the word of Christ; the figures of St. Francis and St. Anthony hold books to identify them as preachers. And so on.

Leila points out the dents in the rounded travertine flutes flanking the door to the church. The dents have been formed by pilgrims who rap the flutes with their knuckles, she says, because the resulting sound is that of organ pipes. We follow suit. She's right. "It is music for Franciscans close to God," she says.

Mass is being said inside the cavernous church, so we tour it in whispers. Some of the stained glass windows tell old stories—Francis and his first meeting with Pope Innocent III, Francis preaching in Ascoli—but others are startlingly modern: One depicts Pope Paul VI addressing the United Nations in New York in 1965, and another, a professorial-looking, youngish man wearing wire-rimmed glasses and dressed in prison stripes.

He turns out to be Maximilian Kolbe, a Polish friar and sainted martyr who was sent to Auschwitz by the occupying Germans during World War II for harboring two thousand Jews at his convent. Kolbe was killed in the death camp after voluntarily taking the place of a young father condemned, with nine others, to death by starvation in retribution for the escape of three POWs. Kolbe is said to have buoyed the spirits of the starving men by leading them in prayer and song day after day until he was the last left alive. The Germans then injected him with carbolic acid.

Francis must surely have been a model of courage and conviction for Brother Kolbe, which is somehow comforting in light of the horrors he endured. Had Kolbe been in Ascoli some seven hundred years before, he might very well have been among the thirty men Francis converted to his order, all of whom, like Kolbe and Francis himself, would court martyr-dom.

After a last, nostalgic cappuccino at the Caffè Meletti, we leave Ascoli via the Roman bridge over the River Tronto. Francis performed a miracle here, saving a man who had fallen into the river, but our crossing is un-eventful. We are bound, via the elegant palace city of Urbino (through which Francis may or may not have passed), to the most important—and well documented—town Francis visited in the Marches: San Leo.

To see San Leo is to blink and think your eyes are deceiving you. It does not seem possible that a town could exist on top of a rock spur that rises over nineteen hundred feet—the equivalent of a twenty-three-story build-ing—straight, and I mean straight, up from the surrounding plain. That Dante modeled his version of Purgatory on the terrain of San Leo seems completely apt. And here we are, at its formidable base, with road signs di-recting us to San Leo's sky-scraping center as if it were just some ordinary destination. As we begin corkscrewing toward the summit on the road cut into the rock, I fight feelings of vertigo I never knew I had, and wish I had brought a parachute.

Francis was not intimidated but excited when he and Brother Leo reached the foot of San Leo in the spring of 1213. High above them, they were told by villagers, there was a celebration going on at the castle of Montefeltro to honor the knighting of one of the Montefeltro counts. The feasts and tourneys had drawn nobles from all over the region to San Leo, which Francis saw as a good recruiting opportunity. According to the *Lit-tle Flowers of St. Francis,* he said to Leo, "Let's go up to that festival for with God's help we will gather some good spiritual fruit."

So up Francis went, as do we. He arrived in San Leo's small main square, named after Dante, as do we. Our mirror dance continues when we check into the small Hotel Castello over a restaurant on the main square to discover that our windows overlook the elm tree and stone wall in a corner of the square where Francis addressed the assembled nobles. "And in fervor of spirit he climbed onto a low wall and began to preach," the *Little Flowers* continues. Speaking, as ever, in the vernacular, Francis so electrified the partying nobles with his sermon of penance and deliverance that they fell silent and listened to him "as though an angel of God were speaking."

Among the nobles in the piazza was Count Orlando, a "great and wealthy Count from Tuscany" who was already an admirer of Francis by reputation. The count was so moved after seeing and hearing Francis in person that he took him aside to discuss with him the "salvation of my soul." Ever the diplomat and mindful that he had crashed the nobles' party, Francis suggested that the count spend the day with his friends, "since they invited you to the festival," and meet with him that night, after the feast.

The building in which they met that night, the Palazzo Nardini, turns out to be directly across the piazza from our hotel. But there is a problem. It is locked, and only the parish priest, Don Sergio, has the key. Romina, the Castello's nice young owner, phones Don Sergio and makes a date for me to meet him at the legendary palazzo the next morning at 8:15. And thus begins an urgent search for an English-speaking interpreter.

Romina apologizes that she can't do it; breakfast is a busy time at the Castello for locals going to work. Perhaps Francesca, across the square at the tobacco shop, can translate for me. Francesca is enthusiastic about the idea and anxious to practice her English—she is taking English lessons—but the tobacco shop is also very busy in the early morning and her ailing father cannot cover for her. Perhaps her English teacher can help. She'll give him a ring. If that fails, the plan is for me to see the inside of the Palazzo Nardini with the padre, then adjourn with him to the tobacco shop so Francesca can translate any questions I might have.

I already know the story of the all-important meeting between Francis and Count Orlando from Francis's medieval biographers, but I do not want to miss a word or detail about where the meeting actually took place. This transaction would change not only Francis's life but religious history.

"Brother Francis," the *Little Flowers* quotes the count, "I have a mountain in Tuscany which is very solitary and wild and perfectly suited for someone who wants to do penance in a place far from people or who wants to live a solitary life." The mountain, which the count told Francis he would give him in return for the salvation of his soul, was—and is—

named La Verna; there, eleven years later, Francis would become the first person on record to receive the stigmata.

Francis, who was always looking for remote spots to lose himself in contemplation, praised God for this unexpected turn of events and thanked the count, saying that after the San Leo celebrations ended, he would send two of his friars to the count's home in Chiusi, just a mile or so from the promised mountain, to see if it was suitable for "prayer and penance."

According to the *Little Flowers,* the dispatched friars got lost but finally arrived at Orlando's castle to be greeted "as though they were angels of God." To make sure nothing untoward befell the friars on their exploration of La Verna, the count sent fifty armed men with them. The friars evidently found La Verna suitable and, locating the perfect plateau on the side of the mountain, set to building a little hut out of branches with the help of their escorts and their swords.

And so the Franciscan stewardship of La Verna began, attested to in a remarkable document from Count Orlando's brothers and sons after the count died. The document, dated July 9, 1274, makes legal, forever, the oral gift the count had made to Francis on May 8, 1213, in San Leo. The deed also promises the return to the friars of a tablecloth that Francis, Count Orlando, and his children ate meals off, a wooden wine cup and bread bowl used by Francis, as well as Count Orlando's leather belt, which Francis blessed and used to "girt" the count when he received his habit, presumably that of the Third Order. And all this began right across the piazza from our hotel.

While we await word about the interpreter, we tour tiny San Leo, taking in the ninth-century parish church of Santa Maria Assunta, with its Roman pillars and assorted Byzantine capitals recycled from a pagan temple to Jupiter. It is Sunday, and a steady stream of Italian families file through the church, lighting candles until there are none left. A group of visiting choristers suddenly breaks into song, and *Nobis Domini Gloria* fills the air.

Francis was most certainly in this wonderfully simple, rough stone church, lit only by three small windows, and was probably at the nearby twelfth-century cathedral, which is now covered with scaffolding and closed to visitors. He would not have been at San Leo's main attraction, however, the massive fifteenth-century fortress even farther up the rock spur, which was commissioned by the duke of Urbino and later used as a national jail.

The fortress's most famous prisoner was the eighteenth-century intellectual, alchemist, and Mason the count of Cagliostro, who was convicted of heresy in Rome and sentenced to life imprisonment in the fortress. He survived for four years in a solitary cell into which his food was lowered through a trapdoor in the ceiling so that his jailers would not have eye contact with him and succumb to his charisma. As further punishment for his embrace of science during the absolutist and hideous Inquisition, his only window, with a triple iron grid, looked out on the churches of San Leo. The Inquisition theme continues back in San Leo's museum. Every conceivable medieval torture device—spiked tables, spiked neck collars, spiked chairs, spiked castration belts, along with graphic illustrations of how they were used—is displayed.

I am more interested in the elm tree under which Francis preached in 1213. The tree collapsed of old age in 1637, a date ingrained in the minds of San Leo's many amateur historians; its remains were taken to the Franciscan convent of Sant'Igne farther down the rock, where it has gradually disappeared, bits picked away by pilgrims as relics. The current tree was planted in 1937—with great ceremony; it was carried up the rock in a carriage, accompanied by young people in medieval dress and Franciscan friars singing Gregorian chants; the scene is reenacted every year in May. So dear is the tree to San Leo that it appears on the town's coat of arms, making San Leo the only town in Italy, the historians assure me, to honor the memory of Francis officially.

I am at the ready for my tour of the Palazzo Nardini at 8:15 the next morning. A thick fog—which I realize later is a cloud—has enveloped San Leo, and I hear Don Sergio arriving in his car before I see him. Don Sergio is in such a hurry that he leaves his car engine running and his headlights on. We hurtle into the palazzo and up the stairs to the second floor into what is known as the Oratorio di San Francesco, but there is little here to commemorate Francis's meeting with Count Orlando. A modern painting of St. Francis with some angels at La Verna hangs on the wall. There's a marble altar, which could use a dusting, and what looks to be office furniture scattered about. And we're back out the door.

The English teacher, Ugo Gorrieri, has arrived at the tobacco shop next door, but Don Sergio has driven off into the fog, and there is nothing for my interpreter to translate. He is not surprised by my disappointment. When Countess Nardini lived in the family palazzo, Ugo explains, the room, which the family had previously used as a bedroom, was converted into a chapel. A piece of the original tree was displayed there, the chapel was furnished with medieval furniture, including a simple wooden altar, and catechism classes were held there. The chapel was a source of great pride to San Leo. It was opened every day, by one of Countess Nardini's servants, for anyone to visit. But the room was essentially abandoned after the countess died twenty years ago. She left the house and its chapel to the local parish, and . . . Ugo raises his eyebrows and shrugs.

The parish priest also controls entry to the convent of Sant'Igne, which Francis established on another trip to San Leo, when he was lost in the dark. *Igne* translates to "fire" and describes the miraculous light that suddenly appeared around the lost Francis, illuminating the road he was looking for. Francis promptly founded a hermitage there, which he named Sacred Fire. It grew into a sizable monastic complex over the centuries and is said to be very beautiful, but Don Sergio is nowhere to be found, and and the caretaker, Romina's cousin Angelo, says he can't open the convent without the priest's permission. We are reduced to groping our way to Sant'Igne through the dense fog on the way down the rock pinnacle, but we can barely see the road, let alone the convent.

I am relieved to emerge into sunlight halfway down the pinnacle. San Leo and all its wonders are completely invisible as I look up, and I wonder, briefly, if the magical place ever existed. It occurs to me as we drive toward Rimini on the coast, the same route Francis took in reverse to San Leo, that he, too, might have been enveloped in a similar cloud, and that it was the cloud, not the darkness, that the "Sacred Fire" had penetrated.

Our tour of the Marches with Francis ends, regrettably, in San Leo. (I've spared you the many lesser documented and beautiful places that local legends hold he also visited, including the breathtaking hermitage of Soffiano, at the end of a forested gorge.) Francis went on from the Marches to preach in other provinces, of course, saving more souls over the next few years and winning more friars. Many more. No fewer than five thousand Franciscan friars, an astonishing number, would gather at the Porziuncola in the spring of 1219 for a general chapter of the order.

However gratified Francis must have felt that so many had answered his call, he did not feel his missionary work was done. His friars were already fanning out around Christian Europe to try to set up foreign missions, and the first tentative forays were being launched to Morocco.

But Francis had a larger vision of converting the Saracens. He had twice failed to reach the land of the Muslims. This time, he made it.

*Finding Francis
Along the Nile*

EGYPT: DAMIETTA, *where Francis preaches in the Crusader camp and
foretells a disastrous battle* · FARISKUR, *where he meets and befriends the
sultan* · ACRE, *where he receives devastating news from Assisi*

The view is hypnotic. One balcony off our hotel room overlooks the Nile and its peaceful fleet of bright blue fishing boats. The other balcony looks north over the Mediterranean and the lighthouse that guides the fishing boats to safe harbor. We are in Ras el-Bahr, a gated Egyptian resort near Damietta in the eastern Nile delta. It was very near here, in 1219, that Francis arrived by sea at the decidedly nonpeaceful mouth of the Nile to join the encamped Christian troops during the Fifth Crusade.

Francis had come to Egypt as a man of peace. His goal was wildly ambitious: to end the blood spilled on the sand, marshes, and mountain passes of the Holy Land by converting none other than the sultan of Egypt, Malik al-Kamil, to Christianity. The sultan's troops were presently defending the fortress city of Damietta from the Crusaders, or "Franj" as the Arabs called all Europeans. If Francis failed in his missionary mission, he might very well succeed, at least, in becoming a martyr.

We might have become involuntary martyrs ourselves on the chaotic road to Damietta from Cairo—one report notes that more foreigners die in traffic accidents in Egypt than in any other country—had we not once again been blessed with good fortune. A friend in New York has put us in touch with a former Egyptian ambassador to the United States, Dr. Abdel Raouf el-Reedy, who lives in Cairo. The ambassador, it turns out, was born in Damietta and graciously arranges a visit to his family still living there to coincide with our research on Francis in Egypt. We make the three-and-a-half-hour trip to Damietta in a rented minivan with the ambassador, his sister, and a driver, Mahmoud, giving silent thanks all the way that we had not rented our own car and attempted to follow the road signs, almost every one of which is in Arabic, through the slalom course of cars, trucks, and buses to the nontouristy, industrial port city.

Our good fortune continues when we arrive at Ras el-Bahr, a tiny spit of land jutting out from Damietta into the Mediterranean, to discover that the hotel the ambassador has booked us all into, the Beau Rivage, is at the epicenter of Francis in Egypt. The ambassador is unaware of the fine points surrounding the Fifth Crusade and had chosen the hotel simply because it is owned by English-speaking Egyptian friends.

These friends, Anwar Hamdoun, a Ph.D. who taught Arab Islamic culture and civilization at San Diego State for five years, and his wife, Susu, who holds a Ph.D. in education from Temple University and has applied it by designing graduate-degree programs in Saudi Arabia, are also unaware of the fine points of the Fifth Crusade. The Crusades are not a popular subject in Egypt, and neither one of these charming academicians turned hoteliers realizes that the location of their hotel is nothing short of miraculous for our research.

The Crusaders, some sixty thousand strong, were camped on the west bank of the Nile, near the convergence of the river and the sea. That happens to be our exact location on modern Ras el-Bahr. It is entirely possible that our balcony view of the resort's palm-shaded esplanade along the river and behind the hotel, Ras el-Bahr's neat grid of summer homes, would have been of the thousands of tents and pavilions that sprawled through the dusty Crusader camp.

The medieval camp teemed with people, unlike the very few we see in the off-season Ras el-Bahr, some of them additional security the hotel has laid on because we are American. Even in the summer, few foreigners these days visit this resort for middle-class Cairenes, a reality that stands in sharp contrast to the multilingual, multinational thousands encamped here eight centuries ago.

Many of the English, French, Spanish, Germans, and Italians were military men—knights, archers, foot soldiers, Levantine mercenaries—but as many as twenty thousand more were civilian camp followers, including pilgrims, servants, merchants, cooks, some of the knights' families, and several shiploads of French prostitutes. Many among the military men were indeed carrying the banner of Christ, but a sizable number were atheists or profiteers looking to scavenge the riches of Egypt.

This motley crew for the Fifth Crusade, scheduled to begin in 1217, had been assembled by Pope Innocent III, the same Pope who had approved Francis's Rule. Still smarting from the failure of his Fourth Crusade thirteen years earlier, which had ended with the sacking of Constantinople, Innocent had advanced this crusade with the skills and verve of a top public relations man.

In written word and traveling sermons, the Pope demonized the seventh-century prophet Muhammad, the founder of the Islamic faith, as a "pseudo-prophet," the "son of perdition," and "the beast." He charged the Saracens, Muhammad's religious heirs who had wrested Jerusalem from the Christians in 1187, with defaming the Christian holy places and holding Christian captives, including women, in "dire imprisonment" and "most severe slavery." And he issued his trump cards: the promise of eternal salvation not only to anyone joining this particular army for Christ but also to those who paid for "suitable" men to go in their stead.

The Pope's definition of "suitable" turned out to apply to virtually anyone who agreed to join the Crusade. Because of the urgency to recruit as many people as quickly as possible, "Innocent no longer insisted on an examination of the personal fitness of the candidates," writes one Franciscan scholar. The Pope even went so far as to revoke the indulgences formerly granted to those who chose to go to Spain to fight the Moors or to Provence to fight the heretics, thereby increasing the recruitment pool—and the incentive—for participation in the Fifth Crusade.

Francis surely heard the Pope's call himself. It is widely believed that Francis attended the Fourth Lateran Council in 1215 in Rome, where Innocent III made it incumbent upon every Christian in Europe to rid the Holy Land of its demon Muslims. Though Francis may have been somewhat distracted in Rome—it was at the Fourth Lateran Council that he first befriended his hostess, "Brother" Jacopa, and it is thought he also met the Spanish preacher Domingo de Guzmán, later St. Dominic, who would found the Dominican Order of Preachers—he could not have missed hearing Innocent's call for a holy war. And the call continued from Pope Honorius III after Innocent died suddenly the next year in Perugia while trying to persuade the eternally warring factions there to direct their weapons at the Saracens and not at each other. Only Francis, it seems, sought a peaceful resolution.

Francis arrived on the shores of the Adriatic in June 1219, probably at the port of Ancona, with a substantial number of friars who were eager to go with him to convert the Saracens. The captain of the ship who consented to take them to Egypt drew the line at such a crowd, however. He would take twelve friars, no more. Francis could not bring himself to choose which friars would go and which would be left behind—so he turned to a small boy who happened to be there and asked him to pick the eleven friars who would accompany him to Egypt by pointing. The boy's selection process is re-created in the Marche town of Ósimo by a huge fresco in the church formerly dedicated to St. Francis and since rededicated to St. Joseph of Cupertino, with Ancona's domed duomo clearly visible in the background. So that's a vote for Ancona as the departure point, but then again, every region—and every port—in Italy competes for Francis.

The six-week voyage that followed was marked by storms, hunger and thirst, disease, and even death. Francis's shipmates included mercenaries and priests, criminals and impoverished men hoping to find salvation by answering the Pope's call. There is talk of mayhem and even murder onboard. But this time, on his third try, Francis achieved the land of the Saracens.

It is also not clear whether the ship landed first at Acre, the Christian stronghold on the coast of Palestine where huge medieval Crusader halls have recently been unearthed. There was already a Franciscan contingent in Acre, headed by the controversial Brother Elias, who held the imposing title Guardian of Syria. But Francis would not have lingered in seductive Acre, which Julien Green describes in *God's Fool* as "Granada as we know it today, in all the splendor of its Moorish beauty." Acre, now the northern Israeli town of Akko, sported fountains and hanging gardens, cypress-lined paths, and cool, tile-floored houses, all of which Elias relished but which would have offended the austere Francis. His goal was to meet the sultan at the heart of the Christian-Muslim conflict in Damietta, two hundred miles to the southwest.

By the time Francis arrived in the Christian camp in the late summer of 1219, the Crusaders and their hangers-on had been here for more than a year. Francis was evidently appalled at the dissolute nature of the camp, especially among the knights he had idealized all his life. There was so much savagery, drinking, and whoring going on that at first he put his idea of converting the sultan on hold and instead concentrated on saving the souls of the Christians who had gone astray. He was evidently quite successful, so successful with virtually everyone he talked to that the bishop of Acre complained he was losing his staff members to the Franciscan Order. But Francis's chief conversion goal remained the sultan, whose forces were defending the nearby fortress town of Damietta on the eastern bank of the Nile, with its Muslim population of eighty thousand.

The seemingly impregnable city, with its double and triple walls, high ramparts, and one hundred red ocher towers, was surrounded by natural defenses—the Nile on one side and on the other Lake Manzaleh, a marshy body of water that, in more peaceful times, was—and still is—a lively refuge for migrating herons, storks, pelicans, and flamingos. Damietta, a rich trading center, sat two miles upriver from the sea, and to protect it from attack from the Nile, the Egyptians had ingeniously blocked river access by installing a huge iron chain that stretched from the city's ramparts to a citadel on an island near the opposite bank of the river.

That citadel, we are told by historians, was clearly visible from Ras el-Bahr, which means, unbelievably, that the view from our hotel balcony encompasses the area where the great chain blocked the river. To further strengthen Damietta's defenses, the Egyptians had blocked the mouth of the river during an earlier crusade with huge stones plucked from the Pyramid of Zosa, the oldest step pyramid in the world. The then sultan had considered taking even bigger stones from the great pyramids at Giza but settled for the smaller Zosa at Sakkara, whose stones are still submerged in the Nile. That explains why the fishing boats we see going out every day have to leave and reenter the Nile through a very narrow channel.

Damietta's seeming impregnability had turned back one Crusader assault after another until the Christians came up with an ingenious plan of attack: They lashed two ships together and constructed a tower of sorts the same height as the well-manned citadel. In August 1218, a year before Francis's arrival, the Crusaders floated their tower upriver, successfully stormed the citadel with scaling ladders, and cut the chain. With that stroke, they had not only made Damietta more vulnerable but opened the Nile all the way to Cairo. But al-Kamil's army continued to defend Damietta successfully.

The suffering and devastation that greeted Francis in the Christian camp convinced him the only road to peace lay in his mission to convert the sultan. The Crusaders and the Muslim troops had engaged in innumerable but inconclusive skirmishes, with heavy losses on both sides. Floods had drowned many of the Crusaders' horses and ruined their store of food; dysentery and disease had ravaged Christian and Muslim alike, the high fevers leaving them with blackened skin, and an outbreak of scurvy had killed as many as ten thousand Christians. Still, the bloody attacks and counterattacks continued into the summer of 1219.

Francis did what he could, caring for the sick and injured, comforting the dying, and praying for their souls. His own health, already fragile, deteriorated further. The hot and squalid camp was thick with flies, which spread disease from one to the next, and Francis was not spared. He developed an eye infection, thought to be trachoma, which led to chronic watering of his eyes, painful sensitivity to light, and clouding of his vision. He became jaundiced and, for the rest of his life, is thought to have suffered from hepatitis.

He was also pained by the dangerous schism that had developed in the camp between the military commanders and the Pope's representative, Cardinal Pelagius. The arrogant and stubborn Spanish cardinal, who dressed himself—and his horse—in scarlet, was constantly challenging the

military strategy of King John of Jerusalem, who was recognized by everyone except Pelagius as the senior military officer in charge.

On August 29, 1219, their wrangling led to a disaster, which Francis
had seen coming. The troops in the camp, who wanted nothing more than
to go home, were on the verge of mutiny. Pelagius, thinking military action
would lift morale, ordered the reluctant King John to send the troops to attack al-Kamil's camp, some three miles away at Fariskur.

Francis spent the night before the siege in prayer and in the morning, as
recorded by Celano, faced a dilemma. "The Lord has showed me that if
the battle takes place . . . it will not go well with the Christians," he told
Brother Illuminato. "But if I tell them this I will be considered a fool: if I
am silent, I will not escape my conscience. What therefore seems best to
you?" Illuminato advised him to follow his conscience and "to fear God
rather than men," but predictably, when Francis relayed his prophecy to
the Christians and presumably to Pelagius himself, his warnings fell on
deaf ears. Instead, and just as predictably, the Christians ridiculed Francis
and branded him a coward.

But Francis was right, and the siege turned into a complete rout for the
Christians. Al-Kamil had cleverly concealed his horsemen in palm groves
around his camp and waited to unleash them until the Crusaders, having
met little resistance, entered Fariskur. Meanwhile Francis, who was anxiously waiting back at the Crusader camp, kept sending Illuminato out to
see what he could see of the battle, but there was nothing until his third
foray. "And behold, the whole Christian army was turned to flight and the
battle ended in shame, not triumph," writes Celano.

It also almost ended with the death of Francis. The majority of the Crusader forces had panicked and fled from the surprise onslaught of the Muslim forces, many to be run down and hacked to death. Only the Spanish
knights held their ground and tried to stem al-Kamil's counterattack, but
most were slaughtered. The Muslim troops came very close to overrunning
the Christian camp and killing all who were in it. Only the last-minute
stand by the seventy-year-old King John with his small contingent of
knights managed to turn back the Muslims and save the camp.

Francis's prophecy that the battle would not go "well" for the Christians
turned out to be a stunning understatement: Six thousand Crusaders were

either killed or captured in the carnage. Francis mourned "especially over the Spaniards when he saw that their greater impetuosity in the battle had left but a few remaining," writes Celano. The Muslims compounded their victory by beheading fifty knights from each of the military orders and displaying the heads on wooden stakes along the way to Fariskur, leading the British biographer Adrian House to wonder wryly whether Pelagius realized the date of his impetuous battle orders coincided with the beheading of John the Baptist centuries earlier.

The extraordinary loss of life moved Francis to act on his conviction that the only way to end this bloody clash between faiths was for him to go see the sultan. Francis was convinced that once he showed al-Kamil the light, the Muslim sultan would embrace the teachings of Jesus Christ, his soul would be saved, and the hostilities would cease. (Francis had held the same conviction the year before in his failed attempt to reach Morocco to convert the *miramamolin,* as the commander of the believers or sultan there was known.) This time, soon after the massacre and with Pelagius's grudging approval, Francis set out with Illuminato for the sultan's camp.

We are sitting in the office of the governor of Damietta, Dr. Abdel Azir, who is a friend of Ambassador el-Reedy. The governor is not familiar with the details of the Fifth Crusade and has never heard of Francis of Assisi. It is the Seventh Crusade or Franj War that he and everyone else in Damietta is familiar with, the Crusade that ended in an overwhelming Muslim victory in 1250. Once again the Crusaders had besieged Damietta, leading the then sultan to raze the fortress city at the end of the thirteenth century and move it four miles inland to a new, less vulnerable position, where we're presently sitting, sipping coffee.

The defeat of the Seventh Crusade is a source of great pride to the people in the province of Damietta. The Muslims not only took prisoner King Louis IX of France but slaughtered many of his army of ten thousand. The Muslim victory is commemorated in a museum in the nearby city of El-Mansura, where the house in which King Louis was imprisoned along with two of his brothers has been proudly restored and all the paintings show either Crusaders bleeding to death or King Louis in chains. Sitting in the governor's office, I notice an elaborately carved wood bas-relief depicting the king of France on his knees in front of scimitar-wielding Muslim warriors, which is a little nervous-making, but the governor is charming. And, it turns out, very helpful.

He has assembled a group of local experts in an adjoining conference room to tell us what they know about the Fifth Crusade. Seated around the table are two men from the Department of Egyptian Antiquities, a local author and Crusade historian named Mahmoud Al Zalaky, and a Coptic priest, Bishoy Abdel Masih. (The Egyptian Coptic Church, founded by St. Mark around A.D. 61, is a still-flourishing Christian Orthodox religion with its own Pope.) There are also local newspaper reporters and photographers to record the meeting as well as a television crew.

Bishoy Abdel Masih offers a disquieting fact. During the Fifth Crusade, he says, the Roman Catholic Crusaders killed twenty thousand Egyptian Orthodox Coptic Christians on the western bank of the Nile because they were scared they would join the Muslims. He has much more positive feelings toward the Franciscans, however, who were allowed by the sultan to establish a convent in Damietta in 1250, the same year as the bloody end to the Seventh Crusade. It is now a Christian school run by a French nun for twelve hundred girls and boys. Would we like to see it? We would, and we feel heartened during our visit to see a bust of Francis in the school's church.

And would we like to go to Fariskur? Mahmoud Al Zalaky, the local historian, says he thinks he has identified the site of al-Kamil's camp to which Francis went. And so, after more coffee, gift exchanges, and many press photographs, we set out in a convoy of cars with the ambassador, the historian, the bishop, and a detail of armed guards to stop briefly at the Christian school and, from there, to pick up the trail of Francis.

Francis's journey along the three miles to Fariskur was far more dangerous than ours. The Saracen and Christian camps were so close to each other, St. Bonaventure reports, that "there was no way of passing from one to the other without danger of death." The peril was heightened, he continues, by the sultan's "cruel edict" that whoever brought back "the head of a Christian would receive as a reward a gold piece." To buoy their spirits as they trod the perilous path, Francis and Brother Illuminato recited the twenty-third psalm, which in the medieval texts translates, "Even if I should walk in the midst of the shadow of death, I shall not fear evil because you are with me."

The August heat must have been insufferable and the intense light painful to Francis's eyes, but on they trudged, these two men dressed in brown rags. Until al-Kamil's sentries pounced on them "like wolves," and beat them and insulted them and tied them up with chains. Why they weren't killed is a mystery. "Sultan, Sultan," Francis and Illuminato kept saying, which may have saved their lives. Al-Kamil was continually sending peace feelers to the Crusader camp, and the sentries might have thought that the two were bringing him back an answer.

The Fariskur to which the sentries brought Francis and Illuminato in chains was very different from the sprawling town to which the local historian takes us. What Francis saw was a sea of earth-colored tents in al-Kamil's almost one-mile-square camp. What we see is a shrine thought to be the location of al-Kamil's tent in the peaceful center of the busy town, dominated by a huge mosque with a green and white tiled dome. We are greeted by a crowd of curious schoolchildren who keep repeating "good morning," presumably their one phrase in English. Francis and Illuminato were greeted by the sultan's soldiers, today represented by the graceful equestrian statues of Muslim warriors flanking the town's entrance.

It is hard to imagine the actual meeting between Francis and the sultan. What preconceived notions did Francis have of the Muslim ruler? Did he consider him a barbarian? A "beast"? An ignorant Arab? And what did the sultan make of the small, tattered man brought before him? Was he a beggar? A spy? A deserter? The unlikely-looking emissary of peace he was hoping for from the Christian camp?

Francis's medieval biographers reflect the sultan's understandable curiosity. "When that ruler inquired by whom, why and how they had been sent and how they got there, Christ's servant, Francis, answered with an intrepid heart that he had been sent not by man but by the Most High God in order to point out to him and his people the way of salvation and to announce the Gospel of truth," St. Bonaventure writes.

The sultan was evidently intrigued by Francis. Hardly a barbarian or an ignorant Arab, al-Kamil was a former medical student and intellectual who delighted in reciting poetry and debating the logic of Aristotle and the origin of the universe. Like most Muslims, he was tolerant of other monotheistic religions and counted Coptic Christians among his closest advisers. Francis, whose persuasive sermons had moved so many, was obviously articulate and intelligent, regardless of his lack of education.

An empathy quickly developed between the two. Despite the ferocity of his troops, al-Kamil was a man of peace who had been thrust into defending his country from the Christian invaders. He had good relations with the Christian communities long established in Egypt as well as with European traders, and he wanted nothing more than for the Crusaders to pack up and leave. Francis, too, was a man of peace, but he clung to his conviction that converting the sultan was the way to achieve it. His zealous proselytizing nearly cost him his life.

The sultan sent for a retinue of theologians to hear Francis's arguments for Christianity. Al-Kamil certainly did not intend to convert—that would have been political suicide—but he had an intellectual interest in his guest's thesis. The sultan also needed a cover to enter into any sort of dialogue with such an unabashed proselytizer as Francis, proselytizing being forbidden by Islam. During the several days it took for the theologians to gather, Francis and Illuminato remained in the camp as the sultan's guests.

The meeting with the theologians, re-created by virtually every artist recording Francis's life, including Giotto, took place under the sultan's open-air canopy. To test his sincerity, the sultan's advisers had prepared by laying a carpet leading to the sultan's throne with gold crosses woven into it. Were Francis to step on the crosses, their reasoning went, he would be exposed as a sham for dishonoring Christ; if, however, he refused to walk over the carpet to greet al-Kamil, he would be dishonoring the sultan. But Francis neatly circumvented the lose-lose situation.

Entering the canopy and oblivious to the trap, he walked straight across the carpet to greet the sultan. When derided by the assembled theologians, Francis replied that Christians carried Christ's cross in their hearts, and that the crosses in the carpet he had stepped on were those of the thieves who died that day in Jerusalem with Jesus. Round one for Francis.

Round two was trickier. After listening to Francis continue to expound on Christianity and repeat his desire to save the sultan's soul through conversion, the sultan's advisers pronounced him guilty of proselytizing and urged the sultan to have Francis and Illuminato beheaded. But al-Kamil refused, citing the friars' good intentions.

Mercifully, round three never took place. According to different legends, either Francis or the sultan devised an ordeal by fire to test each other's faith. It is doubtful that this challenge ever existed, but it, too, is recorded by St. Bonaventure and many artists. According to St. Bonaventure, it was Francis who suggested to the sultan that he, Francis, and the sultan's priests walk into an "enormous fire"; if he came out unharmed, Francis said, and the Muslims did not, then the sultan would know the power of Jesus Christ and convert to Christianity.

The sultan demurred on his priests' behalf, having seen one of them "slipping away from his view when he heard Francis's words." So Francis made another offer. He would enter the fire alone, and if he came out unharmed, the sultan and his retinue would convert. But again the sultan turned him down. He told Francis that if, in fact, he emerged unscathed, the sultan still would not convert because he "feared a revolt among his people." A more generous explanation for the sultan's rejection of Francis's offer was that he had no desire to risk seeing his new friend burned alive.

And he did consider Francis his friend. The sultan called him Brother Francis and admired him for his bravery and the depth of his religious conviction. Francis, in turn, admired the sultan for his reason and humanity. More important, Francis's hard stand on Christianity being the only way to salvation softened. "When, during his stay among the Muslims, he experienced how God had graciously accepted them in the otherness of their religion and culture and blessed them with good gifts, he knew that he too had to accept the Muslims in their otherness and approach them with respect for God's sake," writes Dr. J. Hoeberichts in *Francis and Islam*.

When it came time for Francis to return to the Christian camp, the sultan tried to give him "many precious gifts," which St. Bonaventure claims Francis "spurned as if they were dirt." It is doubtful that Francis was so rude, and even questionable whether he did, indeed, turn down all gifts. Among the relics in his basilica in Assisi is a silver-and-ivory horn that he is said to have brought back from this visit. Al-Kamil also presented Francis with a far more precious gift: a pass guaranteeing him safe conduct to all the holy places. It is not known whether Francis ever availed himself of the pass to visit Jerusalem and Bethlehem, but it is known that when Francis and Illuminato left, the sultan had an honor guard escort them to the path leading to the Crusader camp. He also asked Francis to include him in his prayers.

If Francis was a changed man, Cardinal Pelagius was not. The sultan felt increasingly unable to continue his defense of Damietta: He was distracted by an attempted coup d'état in Cairo, famine spreading across Egypt, and a new threat from the advancing Mongol armies of Genghis Khan. An epidemic was also raging through Damietta, and he worried about the residents' defensive strength were the Crusaders to attack. In October 1219, while Francis lay ill in the camp, the sultan sent two captive knights to Pelagius with an extraordinary offer: He promised to give the Crusaders Jerusalem, Bethlehem, Galilee, and Nazareth if they would abandon their quest for Damietta and just leave Egypt.

King John of Jerusalem, who had barely saved the camp from being overrun because of Pelagius, advised the cardinal to accept the offer, as did many other European nobles. But Pelagius refused to negotiate with the infidels. (He was supported by the avaricious Venetians, who wanted to secure Damietta as a trading center.) In short order, Pelagius turned down the sultan's offer.

There is no indication that Francis was involved in the sultan's peace overtures, but he surely would have supported the bloodless return of Jerusalem. The carnage and pillaging he had already witnessed in the name of Christ must have shaken him to his core. And, just as the sultan feared, it got worse.

Shortly after Pelagius turned down the peace offer, he sent a scouting party toward Damietta; they reported that the outer wall was unmanned. On November 5, 1219, three months after Francis arrived at the siege of Damietta, the Crusaders swept into the city and took it with barely any opposition. Pelagius may have been vindicated, but Damietta proved to be a scene from hell. The streets were deserted, most of the inhabitants having either fled or died. Bodies were rotting in makeshift graves attended by vultures. The city's population had shrunk from eighty thousand when the Crusaders arrived to barely three thousand.

Was Francis witness to the subsequent looting of the rich city's booty, the rape of its women, the selling of the Crusader captives as slaves? Damietta's children at least were spared and shipped off to Christian-held Jaffa, where they were converted to Catholicism. But the anarchy among the Christian troops and fights over the division of Damietta's spoils went on for some three months before the city was brought under control.

Francis and his friars, more of whom had arrived from Acre, were given a house to use as a ministry. That the militant Christians were in need of a refresher course on the teachings of Jesus goes without saying, but perhaps the friars' most attentive audience were the "infidels" they set out, with considerable risk, to convert. "The Saracens gladly listened to the Friars Minor preach as long as they explained faith in Christ and the doctrine of the gospel," writes Jacques de Vitry, the bishop of Acre, in his thirteenth-century history of Crusades and the Holy Land. "But as soon as their preaching attacked Mohammed and openly condemned him as a liar and traitor, then these ungodly men heaped blows up them and chased them from their cities."

Secure in Damietta, the Crusaders turned it into a Christian town, installing a Roman Catholic as bishop, much to the disgust of the native Orthodox Coptic Christians, and converting the city's handsome mosque, the second oldest in Egypt, into the Cathedral of the Virgin. Francis surely prayed at the mosque turned cathedral, the remains of which, unbelievably, are still here. The building is being reconstructed now, as a mosque, which it became again only eighteen months after the Christians converted it to a cathedral. And again, all because of Pelagius.

Francis is thought to have departed Damietta for Acre in February 1220, leaving behind the increasingly belligerent Pelagius, who having captured Damietta, soon decided to march on Cairo and take all of Egypt for Christ. He failed in August 1221, and with him, the Fifth Crusade. The annual Nile flood would turn to mud the route the Crusaders were taking to Cairo. The sultan's forces added to the mire by demolishing the dikes holding back the surging river, leaving the Crusader forces completely stranded. Rather than lose his army to the surrounding forces of the sultan, Pelagius was forced to surrender Damietta and sign an eight-year truce. After three years of hardship and the loss of thousands of lives, the

Crusaders had come up completely empty—no Jerusalem, no Nazareth, no Bethlehem, no Cairo, not even Damietta. At least they were still alive: Instead of slaughtering them, the sultan let the Crusaders sail away—which was all, in fact, he had ever wanted.

The puzzle that remains is where Francis was between the late winter of 1220, when he is thought to have left the camp at Damietta with King John, and his next recorded sighting, in Acre, that summer. Nobody knows. The romantic explanation is that Francis used the sultan's gift of safe conduct to visit Jerusalem and the Church of the Holy Sepulcher, Christendom's holiest church, built on Golgotha by the emperor Constantine over the sites where Christ was crucified, buried, and rose again. But surely Francis's biographers would have recorded such a momentous event.

The more likely explanation is that Francis was lying sick in Acre, sick not only physically but at heart. He had failed on the two missions that led him to Egypt: He had not converted the sultan, and he had not been martyred. He had witnessed mass death, rape, pillaging, and epidemic disease. Moreover, his faith in the tactics and infallibility of the Church surely had been shaken. "He had also observed . . . that the Muslim al-Kamil had demonstrated a greater humanity and desire for peace than his Christian counterpart, Pelagius," writes Adrian House.

The news that a young friar brought Francis from Assisi in July 1220 was just as depressing. There were rumors at the Porziuncola that he was dead. The two vicars Francis had left in charge while he was in Egypt had summarily moved to bring the order more in line with other, traditional orders by changing the requirements for fasting and relaxing Francis's insistence on extreme poverty. They had even erased the Gospel dictum—"Take nothing with you for your journey"—from the Rule.

Clare and the Poor Ladies were also being pressured to abandon their rule of extreme poverty and, like the Benedictines, accept the ownership of property. Moreover, the friars who had been assigned to look after the Poor Clares and collect their alms were no longer allowed to see or even speak to them. The Third Order, too, was suffering and in danger of splintering. Was everything Francis lived for about to be lost?

His year in the Holy Land came to an abrupt end. Francis left Acre on the first Venetian galley to try to salvage his orders and return his friars to what Jacques de Vitry approvingly calls the Franciscan "life of the primitive church." But the wheels of modernization were turning too fast for Francis. His vision of his friars joyfully following his example of simplicity, humility, and poverty in the love of Christ was doomed.

17 Cruising the Venice Lagoon

The "DESERTED ISLAND" *where Francis strengthens his resolve ·* BOLOGNA, *where he vents his wrath ·* ASSISI, *where he resigns as head of the Franciscan Order*

The vaporetto cuts through the blue water of the Venice lagoon, heading toward the island of Burano. Gleaming behind us in Venice are at least three buildings Francis would have seen when he arrived here from Acre in 1220—the Palazzo Ducale in St. Mark's Square, the towering campanile that functioned then as a lighthouse, and the signature Basilica di San Marco. What does not show is the basilica's shady past. In 828 the ancient Venetians stole the body of St. Mark the Evangelist, founder of the Egyptian Coptic Church, from Alexandria and built Venice's most famous church to house it. Four hundred years later, the medieval Venetians stole the basilica's famous sculptures, the horses of San Marco, from Turkey during the Fourth Crusade. The life-size horses, among shiploads of other priceless treasures, arrived in Venice after the sacking of Constantinople in 1204.

Francis, too, figures into the lore surrounding the Basilica of San Marco. According to one medieval text, the *Kinship of St. Francis,* a Venetian abbot named Joachim foresaw his coming years before Francis was born and painted a portrait of him in San Marco wearing what would become his familiar "habit and cord." As further proof of his vision, the abbot pictured Francis in bare feet with the stigmata clearly visible, "maintaining he was a most holy man and should be honored by everyone."

Whether or not Francis felt honored by anyone when he arrived in Venice, he must have felt exhausted. He had been very sick on the voyage home, according to one of his modern biographers, suffering a recurrence of high malarial fevers as well as liver disease. His eye infection was also worsening, and he was plagued by sharp pains behind his eyes. Perhaps that is why he sought a place to regain his strength and the solitude to plan his reentry into the affairs of his fractious order. That place is identified vaguely by his medieval biographers as a "deserted island" in the lagoon of Venice.

Unbelievably, that island, which has been home to Franciscan friars since 1233, has long since been identified. It is known as the Isola del Deserto—and that is where we are headed.

There is magic in the way the afternoon light plays off the water in Venice. The ripples in the silver lagoon are alternately pink and gold as we move slowly in a fishing boat to the four-acre island through an allée of staked fishing traps. The Isola del Deserto is very near the colorful lace-making island of Burano, where per the instructions of the friars on the island, we have hired Alessio, Burano's garrulous former postman, to transport us in his boat. The twenty-five-horsepower motor driving Alessio's boat gives him time to regale us with stories about the Franciscan convent on the island.

Where once there were thirty to forty friars, now there are only seven, he tells us. The *frati* used to run a school on the island, but no more. As a child during and after World War II, Alessio would swim from Burano to the island, holding his clothes on his head, to get something to eat. "Everyone has forgotten how hungry the people were," he says.

The island looks as magical as the light on the water as we draw closer. Almost completely encircled by tall cypresses and a waterside walk, the island has only one sign of habitation visible from the water, the convent's tall bell tower. The little, sheltered dock we land at, however, reveals a quite substantial complex of buildings. We approach them along a tidy gravel path past a rude wooden cross and along a high brick garden wall to the sunbaked church, San Francesco del Deserto—to be greeted by Friar Antonino.

If the late actor Walter Matthau had been cloned, he would have reap-peared as the eighty-two-year-old Friar Antonino. The friar carries an En-glish script in his hand about the convent's history, which he delights in reading rapidly, theatrically, and virtually unintelligibly. We are with an Ital-ian friend, Angela Seriaccholi, who is also researching a book on Francis, and she implores him to speak in Italian, which she will translate for us, but no; Friar Antonino is on a roll and won't give up his performance art. So, uninformed but entertained, we dutifully follow him from the thirteenth-century cloister to the fifteenth-century cloister, from the fifteenth-century chapels of the Madonna and St. Bernardino to the thirteenth-century sacristy, with its original stone floor visible under glass, and on to the Oratory of St. Francis.

Francis reportedly chose this spot to pray in during his monthlong stay on the island. The oratory was outside then, and has since been enclosed, making the gaunt, life-size sculpture of Francis kneeling in prayer inside it visible through a grate in the inside oratory wall as well as from the outside. According to Friar Antonino, the site was enclosed and roofed in soon after Francis's death, at the order of St. Anthony. "Quick! Quick!" Friar Antonino ad-libs St. Anthony's instructions. "We must build a church and put in an altar, just in case Francis is canonized. Then this will be the *first* church dedicated to him."

However entertaining the friar's performance, I pause to admire a paint-ing of Francis with Venetian birds. According to St. Bonaventure, Francis and a "brother" were walking through the "marshes of Venice" when they came upon a "large flock of birds singing among the reeds." In what has become a familiar sequence of events, Francis, who wanted to recite the canonical hours with his friar, asked his "Sister birds" to stop singing so the two men could hear each other. The birds obliged until the "holy man of God" gave them permission to sing again and the birds "resumed singing in their usual way."

Near the painting are the remains of yet another tree that miraculously grew from a staff Francis planted in the ground here when he returned from Acre. The pine tree lasted for 481 years, until it collapsed in the eighteenth century. The stump of the *"giganta,"* as Friar Antonino describes it, is in the church. Outside—near the convent's extensive garden of cabbage, radicchio, eggplant, and fennel, and its orchard of apple, pear, apricot, cherry, fig, and persimmon trees—is the overgrown stone grotto where the tree had stood, shored up by guy wires in its last days.

The island is lovely and, it turns out, quite busy. The convent not only is open to the public, but according to a younger friar we meet, Friar Augustino, offers well-attended weekend spiritual retreats, counseling for engaged couples, a weeklong summer camp for young people, and a ten-day icon-painting course in June. In the spirit of Francis, especially after he returned from his meeting with the sultan, the convent also hosts meetings between representatives of different religions.

It is easy to see why Francis lingered on this serene island before tackling the problems that lay ahead. He began by writing a defiant letter of support to Clare, who was fighting the Church for her "right" to live in extreme poverty. "I, little Brother Francis, wish to follow the life and the poverty of our most high Lord Jesus Christ and his most Holy Mother, and to persevere in it until death," he wrote. "And I beg you and advise you to live always in this most holy life and in poverty. Beware of departing in any way from it because of the advice or teaching of anyone whatsoever."

Francis continued his hard line when he left the island to go on to Bologna. Our feelings are more mellow as we depart at sunset and head back to Burano through the inky shadows cast on the water by the island's sentinel cypresses. The night turns cold on the vaporetto, and we think of Francis girding himself to return to his divided flock.

Bologna is a nightmare for us—as it was for Francis. Our joint issue is lodging. For us, it is the international leather trade fair that has filled every hotel room for miles around. (We finally find a wildly expensive room in a suburban hotel, crammed with Pakistani leather dealers.) For Francis, it was not the lack of lodging but the abuse of it.

One version of the Bologna legend reports Francis arrived in the city to discover that the Franciscan convent established here years before by Brother Bernardo had been transformed into an elegant, comfortable residence, known as "the house of the brothers." The irate Francis promptly threw all the friars—including his dear friend Brother Leo, who was ill at the time—out of the house.

Granted, Francis was ill himself and undoubtedly irritable, but still, his actions seem severe. The convent had been a gift to Brother Bernardo from a local judge during the earliest days of the Franciscan movement after the judge had watched Bernardo withstand public abuse and derision while preaching in the main piazza. "They pulled his capuche, one backwards, one forward; some threw stones, and others, dirt," reports the *Little Flowers*. Bernardo's patience and cheerful endurance, made more poignant by the fact that he, who was now wearing rags, had studied law at the University of Bologna, moved the judge to offer him a house in which he could "serve God fittingly." That convent, the first established by the Franciscans, had been the source of great pride, but now, to Francis, it was a betrayal of holy poverty.

Another version of Francis's stern stay in Bologna is more complicated. He discovered that the Franciscan minister of Bologna, which was home to Italy's foremost university, had started his own library and center of study—without Francis's permission. This was anathema to Francis on two counts. Not only had the minister disobeyed the rule of obedience but he, too, had violated holy poverty. Francis was vehemently opposed to his friars' owning books, because books, which had to be hand-copied on parchment, were very expensive and tended to inflate the egos of their owners. "After you have a psalter," he had admonished a young friar, "you will desire and want to have a breviary [prayer book]; after you have a breviary, you will sit in a chair of authority like a great prelate and you will tell your brother: 'Bring me the breviary!' "

Francis also had an aversion to his friars' studying or teaching in universities, because he felt such intellectual pursuits diverted them from prayer and their spiritual relationship with God. Both these aversions converged in Bologna.

Francis was so incensed that he ordered the center and its library destroyed. The minister either ignored the order or rebuilt the center after Francis left, which leads to a truly horrifying story. According to the *Kinship of St. Francis,* Francis put a curse on the disobedient minister, who immediately fell ill. Even after two friars came to Francis and asked him to lift the curse, he refused. And the minister was doomed. As he lay on his bed "a fiery drop of sulfur came down from on high on his body, and it bored completely through him and the bed on which he was lying. And with a great stench, he expired."

It is difficult to lend any credence to the story of the cursed minister as we stand in Bologna's massive, palazzo-rimmed Piazza Maggiore, where Brother Bernardo endured such abuse in the name of a kinder, gentler Francis. Far nicer to imagine is the miracle Francis performed here, curing a half-blind boy by making the sign of the cross over him. Nicer still is to imagine the sermon Francis delivered in this piazza, the only sermon for which there is an eyewitness account.

Paul Sabatier, Francis's most respected nineteenth-century biographer, sets the date of the Bologna sermon as 1220, which would place it on Francis's stop here on his way home from Venice. Francis seems to have recovered some of his health: The eyewitness, an archdeacon in Bologna's cathedral, gives a traditional description of Francis as a "plain man . . . whose apparel was poor, his person in no respect imposing, his face not at all handsome." His words and his delivery on the theme of "Angels, people and demons," however, were anything but plain to "almost every person in the city," among them many "learned people who were there."

Francis did not threaten the assembled crowd with words of thunder and brimstone but spoke "with wisdom and eloquence." "His ways were those of conversation; the substance of his discourse rested mainly upon the abolition of enmities and the necessity of making peaceful alliances," the archdeacon reports. Francis's charisma was obviously still very much intact. Not only did he bring "peace and harmony" to the warring nobles in the crowd, says the archdeacon, but he so inspired the men and women of Bologna that they "flocked after him," trying to touch "the hem of his garment."

Francis is memorialized in Bologna by a massive, thirteenth-century, buttressed church, down the street from the Piazza Maggiore. Described in the Rough Guide as a "huge Gothic brick pile," it is nonetheless an important cultural and religious center. Friar Antonio Ranzini proudly shows us the church's three-thousand-book library (which Francis would surely have ordered destroyed) and a bust of Father Martini, a renowned Franciscan organist and composer, who instructed none other than Mozart. The library had recently been the setting for a concert by the Conservatorio Bologna—two hundred people came—and many more are expected to visit the annual mechanized Nativity scene that is being set up in the sac⁄risty.

Night is falling along with the drizzle as we tour the convent's gorgeous, hedged⁄in cloister and admire in one of the cavernous church's eleven chapels a stunning blue, white, and gold ceramic *arca* with scenes of Fran⁄cis receiving approval of his Rule from Pope Innocent III and preaching to the overflow crowd in the Piazza Maggiore. It is dark as we take our leave of Bologna to drive to our suburban hotel. Francis's stay here in 1220, how⁄ever dramatic, was short, and so is ours.

Francis had much on his mind as he pressed on to Orvieto to meet with the Pope. He knew, sadly, what he had to do to keep his movement from disintegrating. The answer had come to him en route in a dream of a little black hen who tried futilely to spread her wings wide enough to protect her many chicks. (We see several representations of this dream in paintings in southern Italy, the hen having been replaced by a giant clergyman shelter⁄ing many tiny friars in his black cloak.) His movement now had at least six thousand followers, and to survive it needed the formal, written protection of the Church. What had begun as a spontaneous movement of "compan⁄ions" was about to become an official order of the Church and subject to canonical law.

Pope Honorius III agreed in his meeting with Francis and, at Francis's request, named Ugolino, the bishop of Ostia, as the official protector of what had begun, simply, as the Penitents from Assisi. "The era of sweet evangelical anarchy was over and done with," writes Julien Green in *God's Fool*.

Francis did win some important concessions from Ugolino and the Pope. Honorius formally approved the secular Franciscan Third Order and informally lifted the "privilege" of property thrust on Clare. Clare won other concessions from Ugolino herself: A few friars were quietly per⁄mitted to return to collect alms for the Poor Clares, and the sisters resumed their charitable work in the neighborhoods outside their monasteries.

But there was no room for Francis and his zealous leadership in the newly official order. Whereas Francis had answered only to Christ, the new order would answer to the Pope. Francis knew he had to abdicate to make room for a new, more efficient leader, preferably a lawyer. The Pope knew it, too. So did Ugolino.

"From now on, I am dead as far as you are concerned," Francis announced to the stunned friars gathered in Assisi on September 29, 1220, for their annual meeting. "But I present to you my brother, Peter of Catania, whom we shall all obey, you and me." And with that, Francis stepped down as leader of the movement he had begun twelve years before with his first two converts.

He did retain some authority, however. The Pope and Ugolino had given him permission to write the order's official, new Rule. It was a task that came close to breaking his heart.

18 *Poor Francis*

P oor Francis. Ill and emaciated, he is sitting slumped at the feet of the minister general at the Pentecost chapter of the order in May 1221. A year has passed since the last chapter, and he is about to present the Rule he has written to the three thousand friars and provincial ministers gathered at the Porziuncola. It has not been a good year. His health is failing, and sadly, his friend Peter of Catania died six months after taking over as head of the order. The order's new minister general is Brother Elias, and without his permission, Francis cannot even read the Rule he has written to the assembled friars. One of his biographers describes him as having to tug at the bottom of Elias's habit to get his attention, and permission to speak.

The Rule that Francis presents reflects the many compromises from his original evangelical vision urged on him by the Pope and Ugolino. He has followed the Pope's instruction to require a probationary year for would‑be friars rather than accepting into his order anyone "desiring by divine inspiration to accept this life." He has reluctantly agreed to allow the Franciscan clergy to have books but "only the books necessary to fulfill their office"; similarly, lay friars who can read are allowed to "possess a psalter," or Book of Psalms.

The modern Adriatic port of Ancona, whence Francis first sailed for the Holy Land and was shipwrecked instead.

The gleaming travertine-paved Piazza del Popolo in Ascoli Piceno, with the imposing church of St. Francis in the background. Francis was mobbed when he preached in Ascoli.

*The incomprehensible pinnacle of San Leo,
where Francis crashed a noble's party and was
given the mountain of La Verna.*

The runaway Clare thwarted her furious uncle at the monastery church of San Paolo delle Abbadesse near Assisi. This is how it looks now.

A triumphant Muslim warrior in Fariskur, Egypt, where, during the Fifth Crusade, Francis offered to walk over hot coals to peacefully convert the Sultan. He failed.

Francis recuperated from his Egyptian ordeal on the Isola del Deserto in the Venice lagoon. Here he decided to resign as head of the Franciscan Order.

CAMPANELLO
DI
SAN FRANCESCO D'ASSISI

On a preaching tour of southern Italy, Francis summoned a crowd in Bari by ringing this bell, now enshrined here in the church of Santa Maria degli Angeli. We ring it, too.

Francis reenacted the first live nativity in a cave in this extensive, reconstructed sanctuary of Greccio. He also performed many miracles here.

Francis received the stigmata in the rocky wildness of La Verna and lived thereafter in excruciating pain.

His stone bed, strewn with pilgrims' offerings, at the hermitage of Monte Casale, near Sansepolcro, where the weakened Francis rested on the way home from La Verna.

The Pope ordered Francis to go to the important medieval city of Rieti for treatment of the eye disease he had contracted in Egypt. The Pope's doctors failed.

The tiny Chapel of the Magdalene at Fonte Colombo, a hermitage near Rieti, where another doctor vainly tried to cure Francis by searing his temples with a hot poker. INSET: *The Greek letter "Tau," Francis's symbol, was supposedly etched on the chapel's window frame by Francis himself.*

The Porta Ovile in Siena, through which Francis was carried, mortally ill, to the nearby sanctuary of Alberino on his final journey home.

The medieval church of San Stefano, in Assisi, whose bells rang spontaneously at the moment Francis died.

Further, the friars, when they are not fasting, are allowed to eat "whatever is placed before them," a departure from Francis's own abstemious habit of feigning eating while secreting the food in his lap. And the friars are to be allowed two tunics, one with a hood, unlike the original companions, whom Celano describes as being "content with one tunic, patched at times within and without."

Even so, many of the newer friars grumble that Francis's standards are out of touch with reality. Some friars embarking on preaching tours want to travel by horseback instead of on foot, and to take adequate provisions with them. Yet Francis has reinstated the Gospel instruction to his friars to "carry nothing with you on your journey, neither a knapsack, nor a purse, nor bread, nor money nor a staff," and not to "ride horses unless they are compelled by sickness or great necessity."

He has also continued to forbid the ownership of property—"The brothers should beware that . . . they do not make any place their own"—although that admonition has already been flouted. Houses are being acquired left and right by the order's ministers, and some friars, as Francis found in Bologna, are living much too comfortably. It has also become chic among some members of the Church hierarchy to have in their households resident friars, who presumably sleep in beds and share their meals. With all these temptations, fewer friars, except for his original companions and many in the Marches, are content to be pilgrims or live in the humble huts Francis had decreed should be made of mud and wood.

And so, the friars shelve Francis's Rule and instruct him to rewrite it. The presenting reasons are that the scripture-laced Rule is too long and too vague. But the underlying and long-festering sentiment is that it is too hard, much too hard. Poor, poor Francis. "In his whole life we scarcely find a sadder or more poignant moment," writes Julien Green in *God's Fool*. "Francis believed with all his heart that he had received this rule from God. Men judged otherwise."

19 *Following Francis to Italy's Boot*

APULIA: BARI, *where Francis turns money into a snake* · BRINDISI, *where he may have sailed to Egypt* · LECCE, *where he performs the miracle of the loaves* · GAETA, *where the stampede of admirers forces Francis to preach from a boat*

The light is different in Apulia, the province in the heel of southern Italy's boot. Compared with the crisp light in the high hill towns of Umbria and Tuscany, Apulia's light is soft and seems to bear within it its own shade. The diffusion comes from the salt in the air from the Adriatic Sea on Apulia's east coast and from the Tyrrhenian Sea on its west.

We go to both coasts, as supposedly did Francis on a preaching tour in the eighteen months between the rejection of his Earlier Rule in 1221 and the completion of its revision in 1223. It is hard to believe Francis had the strength to travel all the way down the Adriatic coast to Apulia, but several reputable Franciscan sources, most notably *St. Francis of Assisi—Omnibus of Sources,* record his whereabouts in 1221 and probably 1222 as southern Italy. Many of the dates associated with Francis are guesstimates and, like political polls, have an accuracy margin of several percentage points; but we haven't been to Apulia, so we put our trust in the *Omnibus* and head south, too.

We look for signs of Francis in the Crusader port city of Bari, where he was reportedly a guest in the huge, reconstructed twelfth-century seaside Castle Svevo. The centerpiece of Bari is the wondrous eleventh-century Papal Basilica of St. Nicholas, the patron saint of children and, of course, the model for Santa Claus, whose bones were spirited here from Turkey in 1087 and still lie in the basilica's crypt. But we find Francis in the aptly named church of Santa Maria degli Angeli, across the street from the castle.

A stone tablet in the entry to the church commemorates Francis's stay in the castle, and a padlocked, velveted niche off the nave holds the small bell, the Campanello di San Francesco d'Assisi, that Francis used to call the people to hear him preach. We ring the precious relic ourselves, with the permission of Don Filippo, the church's secular priest, giddy with the possibility that we're holding in our hands something Francis actually held in his.

We follow Francis farther south along the Adriatic coast road to the Crusader port of Brindisi, from which many think he set sail for Egypt. I fantasize that it is on this road, identified only vaguely by Celano as "near Bari," that Francis graphically illustrated the evil of money to a young friar. The legend involves a sack of coins lying abandoned on the road and the young friar who urged Francis to take the money and distribute it to the poor. But Francis suspected the sack of money to be a lure of the devil. Instead of touching the money, he "withdrew about a stone's throw and concentrated on holy prayer." He then ordered the young friar to pick up the bag, and suddenly, instead of coins, "a large snake slid out of the bag." The young friar had been taught a lesson he would never forget. "Brother," Francis said to him, "to God's servants money is nothing but a devil and a poisonous snake."

Padre Salvatore, a thoroughly modern forty-one-year-old Franciscan friar wearing jeans and a two-day stubble, greets us at the Franciscan church and convent. He takes us on the medieval pilgrim road, the Provinciale San Vito, to Brindisi's busy commercial port, passing the twelfth-century Tancredi Fountain, from which the Crusaders and possibly Francis drank on their way to embark for the Holy Land. The modern pilgrimage route is by air: UNESCO flies humanitarian aid to Iraq and Afghanistan from Brindisi.

So far on this journey to Apulia we have seen no indication that Francis preached here in 1221 or 1222. Most of the medieval history involving him along this coastal section of southern Italy concerns the Crusades and, in

Brindisi, includes the recently renovated fourteenth-century Crusader *os-pedale* or hospital of Santa Maria del Casale. Padre Salvatore takes us to see this stunning Crusader rest house, which the transient pilgrims and knights frescoed brilliantly with biblical scenes and depictions of Cru-saders with their horses, shields, and flags bearing the Crusader cross. Francis's connection to Santa Maria del Casale is that it was built over a lit-tle chapel in which he prayed and which contained one of his favorite paintings of Mary. A Franciscan convent was established after Francis's stay here, and the remains of its arched cloister still stand next to Santa Maria del Casale, shaded by palm trees.

We leave the jovial Padre Salvatore, who operates a local Franciscan radio station named Brother Sun, Sister Moon, and press farther south to the ornate, Baroque city of Lecce. Every inch of the many medieval palaz-zos and churches remaining in the old city seems intricately carved with saints, knights, flowers, animals, the sun and the moon. The dizzying dis-play of sculptured artistry, made possible by the honey-colored and easily worked local sandstone, makes our frustrating visit here worthwhile.

The frustration begins with our fruitless half-hour search for the Centro Storico, a sixteenth-century palazzo turned B and B we are booked in, somewhere in the maze of streets in the old city. Mauro Bianco, the young owner of the B and B, has anticipated the impossibility of visitors finding it on their own and offers his cell phone number with each reservation. We finally succumb and, humbled, follow Mauro on his motor scooter through one alleyway after another to fetch up at the beguiling B and B, where our funky bright red room is up fifty-two steps on the roof.

That frustration resolved, we move on to the next. According to local legend, Francis performed the miracle of the "multiplication of the bread" in Lecce, at the palazzo of the Perrone family. When he went to the palazzo asking for bread for his monks, as friars are called in Apulia, the servant said there wasn't any. Francis insisted that she look in the cupboard, and lo and behold, she found fresh, hot bread. The family is said to have com-memorated the miracle by carving an angel holding a piece of bread on the façade of their palazzo and adding an inscription describing the event in-side the palazzo's front door. But when we set out to find the building, which Mauro has located in a Lecce reference book of medieval palazzos, the address turns out to be an uncarved and quite modern building subdivided into apartments.

Our last hope of finding a trace of Francis is to locate the little cell where he is said to have rested during his visit here. We are successful in the thirteenth-century church of San Francesco, where just outside a chapel wonderfully frescoed with scenes from Francis's life we find a roped-off opening in the floor and, visible below, a stone cell only six feet long and three feet wide. Our thrill of discovery is dampened, however, by the date of 1219 the church custodian attaches to Francis's stay in the cell. That date, too, seems to involve the Crusades and supports those who believe Francis embarked for Egypt in 1219 from Bari or Brindisi and stopped in nearby Lecce en route.

We leave Apulia with some frustration and drive northwest to the Tyrrhenian seaport of Gaeta. For all of Apulia's pleasant, tourist-free wonders—the province's singular and ancient *trulli,* conical-roofed houses and farm sheds constructed, without mortar, with the area's thin, gray stone; the cactus-lined roads through back-to-back vineyards, which produce one-tenth of the wine drunk in Europe; and mile after mile of ancient olive groves—the dates remain wrong for Francis and his preaching tour of southern Italy. Our last hope is Gaeta, where St. Bonaventure reports that Francis, while preaching, had to take refuge in a small boat and finish his sermon from the sea after the overenthusiastic crowd on the beach "rushed upon him in order to touch him."

And bingo! It was sometime during the winter of 1222 and early spring of 1223, we are told by Professor Fernando Robbio, a former English teacher and local historian, that Francis delivered his seaborne sermon here. "We don't know why he came here, but the dates are certain," he says. Just where Francis stayed, nobody knows—his cell has never been found—but Professor Robbio thinks it is buried somewhere in the convent Francis founded next to the site where Gaeta's San Francesco church subsequently rose on a high cliff overlooking the sea.

We pace up and down the old convent's cloister corridor with Professor Robbio, who insists that Francis also walked up and down here in 1222. The convent is now a children's center, the Oratorio Don Bosco, which makes it difficult to conjure up a meditative Francis amid the teenage frenzy of an upcoming soccer game. But Dr. Robbio's enthusiasm is infectious—and understandably so.

Gaeta figures heavily in the medieval biographies of Francis. It was here that he vented his wrath on two brothers who let their beards grow long, cursing them for setting a bad example. His outburst over this seemingly innocuous transgression suggests that it occurred during the painful rebel-lion within his order. "By you, most holy Lord, and by the whole court of heaven, and by me, your little one," Celano quotes him as saying, "may they be cursed who break and destroy by their bad example what you ear-lier built up, and do not cease to build up, through holy brothers of this re-ligion!"

Francis also performed miracles in Gaeta, one the curing of a paralytic whose condition had been made worse by a doctor; the other a man named Bartolomeo, whose neck had been crushed by a wooden beam during the "construction of the church of blessed Francis." Bartolomeo was returned to life by a vision of Francis and eleven of his brothers bringing him a lamb. The next morning a healthy Bartolomeo went back to work on the church, startling his fellow workers, who "had left him half-dead."

The original thirteenth-century church in Gaeta that almost killed Bar-tolomeo was commissioned by Emperor Frederick II and was replaced in the nineteenth century by the current and gorgeous Gothic church built by another emperor, Ferdinand II, to commemorate Pope Pius IX's flight to Gaeta in 1848 during a revolution in Rome. Of all the churches dedicated to St. Francis, this splendid church in Gaeta, stuccoed in pale coral, be-comes my favorite, despite its imperfection.

A gale on February 9, 1999, blew a heavy exterior cross off its perch on the church and sent it crashing onto the roof, leaving a gaping hole. The church has been open to the elements ever since but closed to the public, disappointing many families all over Italy who had booked it months in advance for their children's weddings and baptisms. I can see its national appeal when Dr. Robbio, who is leading a local fund-raising effort to fix the roof, graciously unlocks the church and lets us into its wounded and poignant interior.

Life-size sculptures of the twelve apostles line the nave, covered with bits of the roof. The wooden pews are dotted with pieces of coral-colored stucco, and the marble floor is covered with bits of rock and fine grit. This haunted space, inhabited by pigeons and watched over by a carved wooden likeness of St. Francis in a wood-and-glass cabinet, is nonetheless spectacular. The light coming through the tall, narrow, green, yellow, and blue stained glass windows illuminates the church's massive coral-colored columns and their white tracery, bathing the space in a sort of orange glow. I feel like I'm sitting inside a Creamsicle and immediately contribute to the church's restoration fund.

It is not known from which beach Francis had to retreat by boat to escape the zealous natives of Gaeta. Our hotel is on the harbor, not the beach, and overlooks the USS *La Salle,* a command ship of the U.S. Navy's Sixth Fleet; we wake up every morning to "The Star-Spangled Banner" being played over loudspeakers. Gaeta's broad crescent beach, rimmed with hotels, is on the southern side of the rocky promontory and may well have been the site of Francis's sermon in 1222.

Another possibility is the nearby Grotta del Turco, or Turk's Grotto, at the base of Monte Orlando, where Saracen pirates terrorized Gaeta's shipping in the ninth century. The dramatic, wave-washed grotto is reached by steep stone steps through the sort of narrow rock cleft favored by Francis, and ends at the sea in the small Chapel of the Crucifix. The chapel is wedged between two towering rocks believed to have been rent when the entire mountain split in the earthquake at the moment Jesus died.

Francis, as we well know, shared that belief. And in the early spring of 1223, presumably after he left Gaeta, he headed north to the Rieti Valley, where he sought out a similar and equally dramatic rock fissure at the verdant hermitage of Fonte Colombo. It was at this historic hermitage, known as the Franciscan Mount Sinai, that Francis would spend the forty days of Lent looking for divine guidance in rewriting his rejected Rule.

20

The Beautiful Rieti Valley

FONTE COLOMBO, *the hermitage where Francis writes the Rule of 1223, only to have it mysteriously lost* · GRECCIO, *the hermitage where he stages the first living Nativity*

There is silence, absolute silence, as I enter the impossibly narrow rock cleft at the sanctuary of Fonte Colombo. Marked only by a rude wooden cross, the cleft is barely three feet wide and maybe nine feet long. There are no distractions, nowhere to go, nothing to look at save the dizzying view through a crack in the rock straight down the side of the high mountain. I can feel Francis in this extraordinary isolation, praying to the Lord to instruct him on the new Rule.

Right next to the fissure is the stark white cave where Francis prayed and slept during his forty-day vigil. Above the fissure, at the top of a steep path, is the tiny twelfth-century stone Chapel of the Magdalene, where Francis heard mass from Brother Leo. Barely big enough for ten people, the chapel still bears a tau cross, supposedly painted by Francis, in the recess of the window.

Francis had come to Fonte Colombo with his closest brothers, Leo, Rufino, and Angelo, as well as Brother Bonizzo, a canonical lawyer from Bologna. Leo presumably stayed in another cave, known as the Grotto of Brother Leo, along the steep mountain path. There is a third cave as well, identified as the Chapel of St. Michael, where perhaps the the friars prayed together while Francis stayed in solitude.

Meanwhile, the order's ministers were getting very impatient—the rewriting of the Rule was taking far too long. But Francis did not move to an earthly timetable. And so he prayed and fasted and talked to the Lord in this stark rock fissure. His close companions knew not to disturb him, and they waited and waited and waited. Finally he emerged.

Back up the path toward the little chapel is a three-hundred-year-old holm oak, very like the tree Francis sat under in 1223 while he dictated to Brother Leo the Rule the Lord had spoken to him. (The original tree was felled by a heavy snowstorm in 1622 and its wood used by a master carver to replicate the scene. The intricate carving is in the thirteenth-century church at the entrance to Fonte Colombo, and it tells the entire—and sorry—story.)

The new guard of Franciscan ministers suddenly decided the Rule was going to be unacceptable. It was obviously again going to be too long or Francis would have long since finished it. And it would undoubtedly be too hard, much too hard. In what can only be seen as a mutiny, several of the ministers decided to go to Fonte Colombo to confront Francis, using the head of the order, Brother Elias, as their reluctant spokesman.

Francis was startled to see Brother Elias, even more startled to see the ministers, whom he did not recognize. "Who are these brothers?" he asked Elias. Elias's reply, as recorded in the *Mirror of Perfection,* broke Francis's heart. "These are ministers who heard that you are making a new rule. They fear you are making it very harsh and they say, and say publicly, they refuse to be bound by it. Make it for yourself and not for them."

One can only imagine the pain Francis must have felt. Turning his face toward heaven, he cried out: "Lord! Didn't I tell you they wouldn't believe me?" And suddenly, the legend goes, the Lord's voice was heard throughout the forest: "Francis, nothing of yours is in the Rule; whatever is there is mine. And I want the Rule observed in this way: to the letter, to the letter, to the letter and without a gloss, without a gloss, without a gloss." The Lord's pronouncement had the desired effect, and the ministers fled, "confused and terrified."

The Rule of 1223, which Elias mysteriously lost after Francis delivered it to him, forcing Francis to rewrite it yet again, was heavily edited by Brother Bonizzo, Cardinal Ugolino, and even Pope Honorius III. The

Rule is short, only twelve chapters, as opposed to the twenty-four in Francis's rejected Rule of 1221. It is not laced with writings from the scriptures, as the earlier Rule was, and it is considerably toned down.

Gone is any mention of caring for lepers, though that was a central and nonnegotiable requirement for the early friars. Gone is the directive from Luke for traveling friars to "take nothing with you for your journey." The formerly barefoot friars can now wear shoes, if "forced by necessity." And the language, at least, about women has been softened. Whereas the chapter about women in the earlier Rule was titled "Evil Relations with Women Must Be Avoided," the parallel heading in the later Rule states simply: "The friars are forbidden to enter the monasteries of nuns."

The central spirit of the Rule remains constant, however. The friars are still bound to live in "obedience, without property and in chastity," though a chapter devoted to the condemnation of a friar for "fornication" has been dropped. The requirement continues for friars to work and "avoid idleness," never to accept money, and to beg for alms. "This is the pinnacle of the most exalted poverty, and it is this, my dearest brothers, that has made you heirs and kings of the kingdom of heaven, poor in temporal things but rich in virtue," the Rule reads.

The stern directive also remains that the friars "are to appropriate nothing for themselves, neither a house nor a place, nor anything else," though a way had already been found around that. Shortly after Francis threw the friars out of the convent in Bologna and condemned the learned, bookish minister to death, Cardinal Ugolino took ownership of the house and invited all the friars back as his guests. The practice would continue of property being "loaned" to the Franciscans, just as Lord Ripon did at San Damiano in the nineteenth century.

But the Rule, at last, was done. As I stand at the spot under the tree where Francis dictated the Rule to Leo and look down the mountain path at the rock cleft where Francis talked to the Lord, it seems almost unbelievable that that same Rule governs the Franciscan Order today.

Francis performed one last, great public act shortly after the Pope approved the Rule on November 25, 1223. It was getting on toward Christmas, and Francis decided to spend the holiday at one of his favorite hermitages, Greccio, also in the Rieti Valley. As a younger man, Francis had gone often to Greccio "to relax or tarry," according to the *Legend of Perugia*. He was so fond of the devout and poor people in the little cobbled village—and they of him—that Francis had told a village boy to throw a stick and wherever it landed, he would establish a hermitage. The stick flew a miraculous one and a quarter miles through the air and landed on the sheer rock wall of a nearby mountain. Lord John of Velita, who held sway over Greccio, promptly gave the mountain, with its series of interconnecting caves, to Francis. And it is to those caves, since converted into a substantial Franciscan sanctuary, we are headed.

From the road below, the complex seems as huge as it does gravitationally impossible: three- and four-story unfaced stone buildings rising straight from the edge of a sheer cliff and seemingly holding up the mountain behind. As we negotiate the last hairpin turns, I realize the road should have given us a clue that this is to be no ordinary hermitage—unlike any other sanctuary road we had been on, the road to Greccio is wide enough to accommodate tour buses easily.

One hundred thousand people a year visit Greccio. Our arrival coincides with that of a busload of Italians from Campobasso, and together, in reverential quiet, we tour the sanctuary. Though I should long since have gotten over it, seeing again the discomfort Francis and his early friars courted continues to amaze me. Francis's rough-rock cell is no larger than four feet square, and his friars evidently slept sitting up along the narrow corridor outside his cell, under crosses carved in the walls to mark their individual "beds."

Among the many legends that draw visitors to Greccio is a lesson in humility Francis taught his friars. Francis was so upset when he saw his friars sitting comfortably at a well-set table for Easter that he disguised himself as a poor pilgrim and entered the room, begging for alms. The obliging friars soon recognized the pilgrim as Francis, who chose to eat his alms on the floor by the fire. "Now, it seems to me, I am seated like a brother," he said to his companions. The story, as told in the *Assisi Compilation*, does not say what happened next, but it seems safe to assume that the chagrined brothers joined Francis on the floor for the rest of their meager holiday meal.

Greccio also has its share of animal stories, like the one about "Brother

Rabbit," whose life Francis saved on the way to the cooking pot, and the miracle of the local cattle whose lives Francis indirectly saved during a plague when a farmer "pilfered" his wash water and sprinkled it on the cattle. "From that moment, by the grace of God, the contagious pestilence ceased and never again returned to the region," writes Celano.

Another favorite story at Greccio involves Francis, secluded in prayer, sensing the presence of a friar who had walked ten miles from the city of Rieti to see him and Francis suddenly emerging to bless the dispirited, departing friar. Another is the bout an ailing Francis had with the devil, who was hidden in the feather pillow Lord John had given him for comfort during one of his illnesses.

Unable to sleep or pray because his head and knees were shaking so hard, Francis finally summoned a brother for help. "I believe there's a devil in this pillow I have for my head," he told him. The brother picked up the cursed pillow and was walking away with it when he became paralyzed. For an hour the friar stood frozen, unable to speak and powerless to drop the pillow. It was only when something miraculous moved Francis to call out to him that the friar's senses returned and he could drop the pillow.

Francis's rationale for the devil's attack, as recorded in the *Assisi Compilation,* is wonderfully complex. The cunning devil knew he could not hurt Francis's soul because of God's grace, but he could hurt Francis's body by denying its need for sleep and the strength to stand up for prayer. All this was devilishly designed, said Francis, "to stifle the devotion and joy of my heart so that I will complain about my sickness."

Francis was again not well on this trip to Greccio in 1223, presumably his first since he'd returned from the Middle East. His deteriorating condition is captured in a haunting portrait at the sanctuary in which he is wiping his weeping, diseased eyes with a white cloth. It is the only image, anywhere, of Francis and his eye affliction and was commissioned before his death by "Brother" Jacopa de Settesoli, the pious widow of Rome who is buried near him in Assisi. The original was lost, but this fourteenth-century copy shows Francis, sadly, as he actually was toward the end of his life.

His spirit, however, was high this Christmas season. He was planning a surprise and asked his friend Lord John to do something special at the hermitage that "will recall to memory the little Child who was born in Bethlehem and set before our bodily eyes in some way the inconveniences of his infant needs, how he lay in a manger, how, with an ox and an ass standing by, he lay upon the hay where he had been placed." And so the first, or at least the most recognized, living Nativity took place.

Celano's description of the ensuing pageant in a cave, which has since been incorporated into the Chapel of the Crèche, is as vivid as it is moving. The friars came from all their various hermitages. Men, women, and chil-dren came from the village, while farmers with candles and torches came up the mountain from their fields. "The woods rang with the voices of the crowd and the rocks made answer to their jubilation," Celano writes. "The brothers sang, paying their debt of praise to the Lord, and the whole night resounded with their rejoicing."

Francis must have been ecstatic to have re-created the birth of Jesus for so many people. Little did he know that he had started a tradition that would be celebrated all over the Christian world for centuries to come— and continues at Greccio to this day. That same Nativity scene is reenacted four times during the Christmas season and draws some thirty thousand people carrying candles and singing. It is also memorialized on the rough cave wall of the Chapel of the Crèche with two beautiful side-by-side fres-coes, one of Francis at the Nativity in Greccio, the other of Mary and Joseph with the baby in Greccio's twin city of Bethlehem. The still-vibrant thirteenth-century frescoes are the work of the Giotto School and rival those in the basilica at Assisi.

Francis had such reverence for Christmas and for the animals that at-tended the birth of Christ that he toyed with petitioning the emperor to de-clare an amnesty for animals on Christmas Day. Not only would the imperial edict spare animals from being captured or killed but it would guarantee them a Christmas feast. Francis wanted wheat and other grains scattered along Italy's roads by law on Christmas Day "so that our sister larks and other birds may have something to eat on such a solemn feast." Similarly, oxen and ass, the animals that flanked Jesus in his Nativity crib, were to be provided "a generous portion of the best fodder." Lest poor hu-mans be overlooked on Christmas Day, they, too, would benefit from the law and "be fed good food by the rich."

There is no record of Francis actually delivering his case to the emperor, but the concept of rewarding animals at Christmas is a lovely one and particularly valid in Italy, where the appetite for hunting is second only to a passion for *futbal*.

We linger at Greccio, as did Francis. Above the Nativity cave is a beautiful, tiny thirteenth-century chapel with blue and red stars painted on the vaulted ceiling; it is allegedly the first church dedicated to Francis after his canonization in 1228—despite the claims of the friars at the Isola del Deserto. And near the tiny chapel is the original thirteenth-century wood dormitory built by the friars shortly after Francis's death in 1226, with twigs still visible in the hardened mud walls as well as pages from medieval books plugging holes in the roof.

However disappointed Francis may have been by the institutionalization of his order and the sorry behavior of the new breed of friars, he must have left Greccio with gladness in his heart. He had done what he knew best: brought the joy of Christ to the hearts of the people. And he must also have felt relieved: The final Rule was written, and he had been freed from the management of his order. Francis could return to preaching the Gospels that he lived by and spending more time in the isolation of nature, where he felt closest to God. And so, in the late summer of 1224, Francis made his seminal journey to the sanctuary of La Verna in Tuscany. He would never be the same.

21

Touched by an
Angel at La Verna

The sacred mountain where Francis receives the stigmata

Anticipation mounts as we climb the winding mountain road to La Verna, the ultimate Franciscan sanctuary. We are in Tuscany, headed toward "that rock 'twixt Tiber and Arno," as Dante describes it in *Paradiso,* where Francis experienced the culmination of his mystical relationship with God: the stigmata.

Perhaps that is why everything about the approach to La Verna seems magnified, starting with the wider, more bus-friendly road than the approach to Greccio and the increasingly wild landscape we are passing through. The firs and beeches are bigger, the huge rocks more cracked and craggy. Through the trees we can see so many ledges, pinnacles, chasms, and caves that the whole mountain seems a parable of the legendary earthquake in Jerusalem. No wonder Francis came to La Verna so often during the eleven years following Count Orlando's gift of the mountain to him at San Leo.

There were just a few wood and reed huts built by his friars when Francis started coming to La Verna, and a little chapel dedicated to the Virgin Mary, which Count Orlando began to build for him in 1213. The chapel, Santa Maria degli Angeli, matches in name and exact proportion the similar small chapel at the Porziuncola and, in style, the church of San Damiano.

Fittingly, Count Orlando is buried in the chapel in this spiritual home away from home he created for Francis.

It was on an earlier visit to La Verna that Francis once again displayed the humanness that had won so many hearts. When a friar cooking a meal accidentally set the hut on fire, other friars quickly arrived to help him put out the blaze, but Francis withdrew into the woods. Not only did he have such respect for Brother Fire that he did not want to participate in quenching it but he also had a warm fox pelt to sleep under, which he spirited away with him. A chagrined Francis returned when the fire was out and confessed to his friars: "From now on, I don't want this hide over me since, because of my avarice, I did not want Brother Fire to consume it."

For all the rugged beauty of La Verna, Francis was visited there often by "demons." The devil's sometimes vicious attacks, presumably during the rancor in his order, led Francis to say wistfully: "If the brothers knew how many trials the demons cause me, there would not be one of them who would not have great piety and compassion for me." Still, he felt closer to God here, especially among La Verna's rocks, which he identified with the Lord. "Whenever he had to walk over rocks, he would walk with fear and reverence out of love for Him who is called 'The Rock,' " records the *Assisi Compilation.*

The journey from Assisi to La Verna in the summer of 1224 had not been easy for Francis or his closest companions, Leo, Masseo, and Angelo. All of them were beset by the troubles in the order and the dilution of the spiritual vision they had embraced from the beginning. Brother Leo was so troubled he even began to doubt his faith, an agony that he discussed with Francis on the long, hot journey and that resulted in the letter Francis later wrote to him in the mountain sanctuary.

That letter, one of only two in Francis's handwriting and preserved in Spoleto (see Chapter 3), is worth repeating here, in the context of the friars' rebellion and Leo's despair. "I place all the words we spoke on the road in this phrase, briefly, and [as] advice," Francis wrote, in part, to Leo. "In whatever way it seems best to you to please the Lord God and to follow His footprints and His poverty, do this with the blessing of God and my obedience. And if you believe it necessary for the wellbeing of your soul, or to find comfort, and you wish to come to me, Leo, come!"

The journey to La Verna was not only spiritually grueling for Leo but also physically exhausting for Francis. When they finally reached the base of the mountain, Celano writes, the friars persuaded a local peasant to lend Francis his donkey "to ride on, because he was not a little weak." The peasant grudgingly started leading the donkey carrying Francis up the mountain, but the way was so hot and so steep that somewhere en route the peasant "collapsed, exhausted by a burning thirst." The ensuing miracle, which Giotto frescoed in the basilica in Assisi, finds Francis praying and stretching "his hands towards heaven," then directing the peasant to a nearby rock, which suddenly produces "a flow of water."

The journey up the mountain paused again at the foot of an oak tree where Francis and his companions took a rest. It was here, the *Little Flowers* reports, that "a great number of different kinds of birds flew to blessed Francis with joy and song and sportive flapping of their wings." So welcoming were the birds that some "settled on his head, some on his shoulders, some on his knees and some on his hands." That scene, too, is replicated in a multitude of paintings and garden statuary, including a birdbath that adorned my grandmother's garden. It is memorialized at La Verna by the tiny seventeenth-century Cappella degli Uccelli, or Chapel of the Birds, along the steep old mountain road from the little town of La Breccia.

But Francis was not through with his journey up the mountain. When he reached the level top of the sheer cliff where the friars had built their huts, he insisted on going on alone—across a chasm bridged by a log—to a solitary cave in the face of the cliff. It was in this isolated place, "separated from the others," that Francis would spend the forty-day fast in honor of St. Michael, which fixes the dates in 1224 as between Thursday, August 16, and Saturday, September 29.

He laid out detailed instructions for his friars, two of whom, Rufino and Silvester, were already at La Verna. "None of his companions should come to him, nor should they allow anyone else to come except Brother Leo," reports the *Little Flowers.* He gave Brother Leo his own detailed instructions. Leo was to bring him bread and water in the morning and return for late night prayers—but with a proviso. He was to "approach him saying nothing but 'Lord, open my lips.' " If Francis replied, " 'And my

mouth shall declare your praise,' " then Leo was to cross the log to continue reciting the Night Office with him. If Francis did not reply, Brother
Leo was to leave.

But Brother Leo cheated. He kept a close eye on Francis, whether or not
Francis had given him the password to join him, and secretly saw amazing
things. We must bear in mind that the *Little Flowers* was written by a friar
from the Marches, where spiritual ecstasy was common, but it says that
Leo witnessed Francis on one occasion "elevated in the air to such a height
that he could touch his feet" and on another, "elevated to such a height that
he could hardly see him."

This routine went on for a month, during which Francis befriended a
falcon nesting near his cell. According to St. Bonaventure, the falcon became so attuned to Francis's late night prayer schedule that "it anticipated
him with its noise and song." Francis was grateful to the attentive falcon,
because "such great concern for him shook out of him all sluggish lazi-
ness." In contrast, when Francis was "more than usually burdened with
illness," he was also grateful to the sympathetic falcon for choosing to remain silent.

The miracle of the stigmata took place in stages, according to the *Little
Flowers.* The first occurred during one of Leo's late night forays to Francis's
cell. Francis did not respond when Leo called out "Lord, open my lips,"
but Leo pressed on anyway and, finding Francis's cell empty, snuck
through the woods to find him. At first, what Leo witnessed was common
enough. He found Francis praying on his knees, arms outstretched, his face
raised toward heaven. "Who are you, my most dear God, and who am I, a
worm and your little servant?" Francis kept repeating. But then, by the
light of the moon, Leo witnessed a "most beautiful flame of fire descending from the height of the heavens to the top of the head of Saint Francis"
and heard the flame speaking to Francis.

Leo, "afraid and retreating," tried to flee but was exposed when Francis
heard the "sound of his feet stepping on twigs." Francis then told the curious Leo that the flame was God and that God had asked him for three
things. Francis was puzzled, he told Leo. He had nothing to give God save
"a tunic, a cord and trousers," which he summarily offered. God's response to Francis, which he made three times, was to "put your hand in

your pocket and offer me whatever you find there." Each time Francis found a gold coin in his pocket and realized "that the threefold offering was figuratively golden obedience, the most exalted poverty and the most beautiful chastity," and thus a reaffirmation of the "holy goodness God has given me."

But God had told him something else as well. In a few days, Francis told Leo, God was going to perform "an astonishing miracle" on this mountain, "which the whole world will admire." Though it seems unlikely Francis would have said anything so boastful, he then ordered Leo to return to his cell "with God's blessing."

A few nights later, on September 14, a bright light, brighter than the sun, suddenly lit the sky, waking all the friars as well as the shepherds looking after their flocks in the valley below and many of the people in the towns. The light moved steadily toward Francis and was soon discernible, Celano reports, as a "man standing above him, like a seraph with six wings, his hands extended and his feet joined together and fixed to a cross." Francis rose to his feet, filled with feelings of fear, sorrow, joy, and confusion as to what this vision meant; he soon received the mysterious answer. Like those of the crucified man hovering above him, "the marks of the nails began to appear in his hands and feet . . . [and] his right side was as though it had been pierced by a lance." By the time the bright light receded, Francis had become the first earthly being to receive the five wounds of Christ.

Celano describes the marks on Francis's feet and hands as "round on the inner side, but on the outer side they were elongated; and some small pieces of flesh took on the appearance of the ends of the nails, bent and driven back and rising above the rest of the flesh." St. Bonaventure goes beyond Celano's description of the nails being flesh and describes them as being real nails. "The heads of the nails in his hands and his feet were round and black; their points were oblong and bent as if driven back with a hammer and they emerged from the flesh and stuck out beyond it."

Modern biographers, not surprisingly, are skeptical about the stigmata. Adrian House, a contemporary British writer, explores many rational explanations for the stigmata in his book *Francis of Assisi: A Revolutionary Life*. According to House's research, the explanations for Francis's wounds run the gamut from tubercular leprosy to lymph node tuberculosis, which is also known as scrofula or the king's evil. Other, more psychological explanations include "overexcited neural activity" or just plain hysteria.

Francis inadvertently added to the mystery by hiding his wounds from all but a few of his closest friars. "He did not seek to use this to make himself appealing to anyone in a desire for vainglory," Celano writes. "Rather, in every way possible he tried to hide these marks, so that human favor would not rob him of the grace given him." From that moment on, Francis either wore bandages on his hands or tucked them inside his sleeves. Leo helped by wrapping bandages around his feet and trying to keep a dressing on the wound in his side, "from which," St. Bonaventure writes, "his sacred blood often flowed, moistening his tunic and underwear."

Rational explanations aside, there is no doubt among Francis's medieval biographers that he was "the crucified servant of the crucified Lord." The biographers, all of whom were Franciscan friars, had a motive, of course: to establish the founder of their order as the chosen one of Christ and thus unequaled by any other religious figure at the time. And it worked.

The stigmata virtually assured Francis, considered a saint by many while he was alive, of sainthood after his death in 1226. Before the formal canonization proceedings even took place, Cardinal Ugolino, who became Pope Gregory IX in 1227, had commissioned Brother Thomas of Celano to write the *First Life of St. Francis* and authorized the construction of Francis's basilica in Assisi.

Father Roy meets us in the dining hall at La Verna, where, for sixteen dollars, we've been served an adequate no-menu meal of chicken, pasta, wine, ice cream, and coffee. (This is the only Franciscan hermitage to serve food, necessitated by the daunting volume of pilgrims and visitors to La Verna—one million a year.) A friend in nearby Arezzo has arranged for the English-speaking Father Roy to show us around La Verna, which turns into a treat for us. The thirty-three-year-old friar from Croatia regales us with stories about the sanctuary, one being the miraculous saga of a would-be suicide who deposited his hat and pipe on the edge of the cliff near the site of the stigmata and jumped—but to no avail. He somehow landed safely on the rocks below, climbed back up, retrieved his hat and still-smoldering pipe, and went home.

Father Roy, who has just completed a thesis on the Franciscan balance between preaching and contemplation, is so jovial that it is difficult, for me anyway, to try to experience, secondhand, the momentous event that took place here eight centuries ago. Instead, I momentarily abandon Francis to succumb to Father Roy's exuberance as he tours us through the convents, chapels, and churches that have sprung up at La Verna over the centuries.

Andrea Della Robbia's extensive and stunning fifteenth-century ceramic artwork scattered through the sanctuary's buildings makes a visit here worthwhile with or without Francis. The early Franciscans commissioned Della Robbia to commemorate this most sacred place because, says Father Roy, his enameled terra-cotta artwork was "not fit for a grand church but was cheap and in keeping with the Franciscan spirit of poverty."

The penurious Franciscans did not realize what a treasure they had given the world. While the frescoes that once adorned the walls at La Verna have either vanished or had to be restored again and again because of the mountain's dampness, Della Robbia's signature blue and white ceramic altarpieces, with their colorful borders of enameled apples, lemons, and oranges (including the largest altarpiece—nineteen feet, four inches by thirteen feet, ten inches—he ever created), look as fresh as if they were created yesterday. And they are gorgeous, though Father Roy mischievously points out that there is a mistake in the Latin inscription under every one of the ceramics.

We connect with Francis again in La Verna's dramatic and almost surreal natural surroundings. Down a steep flight of exterior steps is a chasm leading into a tree-topped jumble of huge, moss-streaked boulders, balanced precariously one on top of another. One edge of an upper rock protrudes over the chasm in a seeming mockery of gravity, and I gingerly follow Father Roy ever deeper into what is known as the Sasso Spicco (projecting rock), past a wooden cross and taus scratched into the rock walls by pilgrims, to the impossibly wild spot where Francis often withdrew to pray. "This is a wounded mountain," says Father Roy. "Francis felt he was entering into the wounds of Christ."

Looking straight up is even more surreal. The mountain seems to be split cleanly in two and is spanned, high overhead, by a small bridge. That man-made bridge has replaced, appropriately, the log that Francis crossed to achieve the solitude he was seeking during the fast of St. Michael when he received the stigmata. The solitary ledge he achieved, visited only by Brother Leo, is also overhead and has since been enclosed and transformed into the Chapel of the Cross. It bears within a haunting wooden figure of the wounded Francis sitting on a log beside his companion falcon, staring heavenward in pain.

We feel as though we are living inside the medieval legend at La Verna. Around the other side of the ledge overhead is a plaque on the edge of a sheer precipice. It marks the spot where, sometime during those forty days, Francis had such a violent encounter with the devil that he had to flatten himself against the cliff face and implore God to save him from being thrown to the rocks below. God responded, according to the *Little Flowers,* when "suddenly by a miracle, the rock to which he was clinging yielded to the form of his body and received him into itself." As proof, the absorbent rock is said to bear the imprint of "the shape of his face and hands"— though we had to stretch our imaginations to recognize the shapes.

We follow Father Roy back up the steps to the first church here, the tiny, spare chapel of Santa Maria degli Angeli, just off the central courtyard. To the credit of the Franciscans at La Verna, no one has tarted up the primitive stone chapel. The only addition, inserted into the altar, is an old stone protected by glass.

A legend recounted in the excellent English-language guide to La Verna holds that Francis used the stone as a table for his paltry meals until the day Jesus miraculously appeared to him—"while he was eating lunch," says Father Roy—and sat on the stone. When Jesus withdrew, Francis summoned Leo and said: "Wash this stone first with water and then with wine, oil and milk and last of all with balsam . . . because Jesus Christ was seated upon it." Not surprisingly, the sacred rock has been venerated ever since and was inserted into the altar in 1719.

La Verna has a plethora of Franciscan historical memorabilia, including the cells of St. Bonaventure and St. Anthony of Padua. But we remain focused on Francis and his legend, which is bringing us closer and closer to the actual spot where he received the stigmata.

We pass quickly through the fourteenth-century basilica, pausing only in the seventeenth-century Chapel of the Relics, where there are some real treasures: the tablecloth, eating bowl, and drinking cup used by Francis when he visited Count Orlando in nearby Chiusi, and the count's belt, which Francis is said to have blessed when he girted the count upon his entrance into the Third Order. The belt, described as leather in the thirteenth-century deed awarding these treasures to the Franciscans, is actually made of gold cloth. But no matter.

Another treasure contained in a bronze-and-glass urn is a small piece of linen, which is said to be stained with Francis's blood, having been used to cover the weeping wound in his side. But the relic Father Roy is most excited by is in another glass case: the tattered, ragged habit Francis was wearing when he received the stigmata.

The story of the habit, recounted by Father Roy, involves a rich man who somehow knew that Francis did not have long to live when he prepared to leave La Verna and managed to trade Francis a new habit hastily made by his tailor for the old one. Trades like this were not uncommon. Many people sought Francis's clothes as relics and were eager to pay the cost of a new habit. But after what transpired at La Verna became known, this particular habit was deemed such a treasure that it ended up in Florence for close to eight hundred years. It was only in 2000 that the habit was returned to the Franciscans at La Verna.

My heart begins to race with anticipation as we near the climax of Francis's spiritual experience at La Verna—the Chapel of the Stigmata. I imagine approaching his isolated cell, as he did, on a modern version of the medieval log over the precipitous chasm. I plan to stand on the edge of the cliff, as he did, look heavenward, and imagine the bright light in the sky bearing down on me. But my imagination has run away with me.

The approach to the sacred site is enclosed, and has been since 1582. The Corridor of the Stigmata, as it is called, was constructed after a sixteenth-century blizzard prevented the friars from making their twice-daily pilgrimage to the site. Legend has it that the animals of the forest made the pilgrimage for them, attested to by the tracks the friars found in the snow the next morning.

The corridor, frescoed on the cliff side with scenes from Francis's life and enclosed on the other by leaded windows, gives a glimpse of what medieval La Verna must have been like: Halfway down the corridor and behind a nail-studded door is a precarious cave where Francis often slept. In the center of the cave's supporting rocks is the horizontal stone he used as a bed, protected now from relics seekers by an iron grate.

We pass two more chapels at the end of the corridor, including the Chapel of the Cross, which we had seen from below and which is said to be the site Francis chose for his cell in 1224. And suddenly, there we are, in the small anteroom to the Chapel of the Stigmata. I imagine we'll round the corner to emerge onto the wild outcropping of rock that Francis's medieval biographers and thousands of subsequent paintings have imprinted on my mind. But no.

The Chapel of the Stigmata turns out to be exactly that: a chapel. In front of the altar, over which hangs the enormous and beautiful Andrea Della Robbia *Crucifixion,* is a small, six-sided hole in the floor, framed in red marble and covered with glass. This, then, is the ultimate destination at La Verna. I feel somewhat let down, but then again, what else could the Franciscans have done with the press of pilgrims to La Verna? Brother Leo had marked the spot with a wooden cross, but as more and more people were drawn here, the tiny chapel had begun to rise around it way back in 1263.

I retrace my steps and join my husband and a friend outside in the waning afternoon sun. Father Roy has to leave us, and we heap thanks on him and exchange e-mail addresses. But I still feel sort of down until I suddenly hear the sound of singing. Two lines of friars appear, flanking a friar in the middle carrying a wooden cross. An older friar wearing a green shawl is singing a Laud, to which the others sing responses as they move along the corridor. I follow them and their beautiful, simple sound, in what I learn later is called the Procession of the Stigmata and has occurred every day since 1431.

The procession, made up of twelve friars, a few nuns, and a visiting delegation from Africa, pauses in the anteroom to the Chapel of the Stigmata, where the older friar rings the chapel bell. The procession then enters the chapel, so narrow that there is room only for single carved wooden choir seats on either side of the nave. After a few prayers, the procession moves out of the chapel and back down the corridor, their voices calling back and forth in song. At that moment I realize that it doesn't matter a bit if the stigmata site is merely a hole in the ground. The spirit of Francis continues to burn brightly at La Verna.

Francis would live another two years after receiving the stigmata, but the painful wounds added an almost unbearable burden to his already ravaged body. Having not achieved the traditional martyrdom of death, he became a living martyr for Christ.

How he kept going is beyond reckoning, but he did, albeit slowly. Because of the wounds in his feet, he could barely walk, and when he prepared to leave La Verna with Leo at the end of September, his friars had to borrow a horse from Count Orlando. Francis knew he would never again see La Verna and the friars he was leaving behind at the sanctuary, and according to one account, which may or may not be authentic, he gathered them in the little chapel of Santa Maria degli Angeli to say good-bye.

" 'Farewell, farewell, Brother Masseo. Farewell, farewell, Brother Angelo,' " Masseo quotes Francis in the description he wrote of the leave-taking. "And in the same way he took leave of Brother Sylvester and of Brother Illuminato, adding, 'live in peace, my dear children. Farewell. For I return to the Porziuncola with Brother God's Little Sheep [Leo], never to return again. My body goes away, but I leave you my heart.' "

Francis was just as emotional about leaving the mountain itself. " 'Farewell, Mount La Verna! Farewell, Mount of the angels, beloved mountain!' " Masseo quotes. " 'Farewell, Brother Falcon: once more I thank you for your kindness to me. Farewell, great rock. I shall see you no more.'

"We all broke into sobs," Masseo concludes. "He went away, weeping, bearing our hearts with him."

Francis and Leo made the journey to Assisi in short stages, stopping to rest at various hermitages along the way. So weakened was Francis by the loss of blood from the wound in his side as well as all his other infirmities that the journey, which normally took a week, this time would take him a month.

22 The Painful Road
Back to Assisi

MONTE CASALE *and* BUON REPOSO, *the hermitages where Francis rests ·*
SAN DAMIANO, *where, very ill, he writes the famous Canticle of Brother Sun*

Sansepolcro is nestled in the mountains on the border of Tuscany and Umbria. The town is best known as the birthplace of the fifteenth-century artist Piero della Francesca, but it played a haunting role in Francis's trip home from La Verna. Crowds turned out to welcome him, but Francis was so ill that he did not even acknowledge them. He did not register, in fact, that he had reached Sansepolcro. After passing through the town, he is said to have asked Leo: "When will we reach Sansepolcro?"

⁂ Francis seems to have revived when he reached the nearby hermitage of Monte Casale, where he immediately cured a friar of seizures. He performed another miracle the next day, albeit in absentia. A woman in labor was lying near death in one of the villages Francis had passed through on his way to Monte Casale, but he was long gone by the time the villagers realized that the holy man had come their way. Their hopes soared when his friars reappeared from Monte Casale on their way to return Count Orlando's horse but were dashed when they realized Francis was not with them. It fell to an enterprising friar, realizing Francis had touched the horse's bridle, to place it on the woman's stomach, whereupon she immediately, and painlessly, gave birth.

In happier, healthier days, Francis had taught his friars at Monte Casale an essential lesson in Franciscan morality. According to his medieval biographers, a notorious band of robbers was living in the woods and terrorizing travelers. When the brigands came to the hermitage begging for food, the indignant friars turned them away. Francis chastised the friars when he arrived, reminding them of the Rule he had written governing just such circumstances: "And whoever comes to them, friend or foe, thief or robber, should be received with kindness."

As penance—and a lesson in strategy—Francis ordered the friars to take good bread and wine to the forest and to call out: "Come, Brother Robbers, come to us because we are brothers." Not only were the friars to lay out the food on a tablecloth but they were also to serve the robbers. Francis's strategy was to convert the robbers in stages—to extract their promise after the first meal not to "strike anyone" and, after a second free meal, of eggs and cheese, the next day, to suggest that it would be better for them to serve the Lord than to hide in the forest "dying of hunger" and doing "many evil things for which you will lose your souls." Needless to say, the robbers saw the light, gave up their wicked ways, and promised "to live by the work of their hands."

The aura of Francis's kindness and charity seems to live on at little Monte Casale. We don't see a soul around the stone buildings or the well-tended terraced gardens, so we let ourselves into the small stone chapel to find the altar covered with fresh flowers. A flight of stone steps leads we know not where, so we climb it with some trepidation, imagining our uninvited entry into the living space of this Capuchin sanctuary.

Instead we emerge into a dimly lit rough stone cave, with yet another set of steep stone steps leading to a sort of rock loft. A crude wooden cross on the wall of the loft, the stone slab bed, and wooden "pillow" log define the space as Francis's cell, as do the offerings scattered about—candles, wilted roses, a snapshot of an older couple, another of a young boy eating toast, an old thousand-lire note, a smattering of current euros. We are all alone in this wonderfully intimate space, which easily evokes Francis, especially the darkness he sought in his waning days to protect his light-sensitive eyes.

We blink ourselves in the bright sunlight when we leave the cave and wander around Monte Casale's tiny cloister. A cat is prowling the tiled roof. There are pots of geraniums and a papyrus plant. We can smell woodsmoke and hear a rushing stream but still don't see a soul—save the whimsical, life-size sculpture of a young Francis perched on a stone wall overlooking the valley. On the way back to the car, we look down on a collection of goats and chickens and something white flashing in the air. The white turns out to be a wheeling formation of white doves around their dovecote, a perfect symbol of Francis to carry with us as we leave.

The wounded Francis went on slowly with Leo to Città di Castello, Umbria's most northern town. His health was such that he had to stay a month in this walled town in the Tiber Valley and above, in the hills, at the hermitage of the Buon Reposo. He often passed through Città di Castello on his way to and from La Verna and, on one such visit, miraculously drove the devil out of a possessed woman.

We experience a small miracle of our own in the city. We want to visit Buon Reposo, the hermitage so named because Francis had an especially good night's sleep there on his way back from La Verna, but we don't know where it is. Our hopes are dashed when the Franciscan friar we meet outside the San Francesco church tells us that the hermitage is closed, but they lift when a door suddenly opens in a house along the street and the miraculous Francesca emerges.

Francesca turns out to be the cousin of Buon Reposo's caretaker, Bruno. She whips out her cell phone and has an animated conversation with Bruno, but when she announces that he will receive us the next morning, our spirits droop again because we won't be in Città di Castello the next morning. With a lot of shrugs and "too bads" in various languages, we set out with Francesca's directions to try to see Buon Reposo anyway, if only from a distance. "Maybe St. Francis will work a miracle for you," the friar half-jests in parting. He does.

Somehow, at the end of one of the gravel roads crisscrossing the hills above the town, we arrive at a big house with a cross on the driveway posts. We decide it must be the Eremo di Buon Reposo, but when we knock on the front door, there is no response. We are on our moody way back down the hill when we meet a car heading up. It is Bruno returning from an afternoon out with his wife. "Ah! Americano," he says—and leads us back to Buon Reposo.

Perhaps it is the series of miracles that led us here that makes Buon Reposo seem so magical. Or it might be the fading light, which adds a patina of mystery to everything we see—the old chapel, whose frescoed walls were stuccoed over by austere friars in the seventeenth century; the grille in the old stone floor, under which the bones of a dozen friars were found. But the centerpiece of Buon Reposo is the cave, just off the crumbling cloister, where Francis had such a good night's rest. In a seeming contradiction, the cave is known as the Grotta del Diavolo to mark yet another struggle Francis had with the devil, which would not seem to lend itself to a peaceful sleep.

We contribute to the chapel's restoration fund, which earns my husband a blessing and a kiss on the forehead from Bruno, and we leave, feeling as refreshed as Francis did, or could, in his perilous state of health.

The Francis who finally arrived back at the Porziuncola in November 1224 was a shadow of the man he had been before he went to the Middle East and to La Verna. Yet he soon departed on a donkey for a preaching tour through Umbria, accompanied at times by an increasingly anxious Brother Elias. Leo kept his hands and side bandaged and made sure Francis wore the slippers Clare had made for him, but it was obvious that Francis was very ill. He had migraines, could barely eat, and his eyes had become so painful that his friars had fashioned an oversize hood to keep his face in perpetual shade.

Elias relayed his concerns about Francis to Cardinal Ugolino and the Pope, who collectively summoned the ailing friar to the city of Rieti, some forty miles north of Rome, to be treated by the Pope's physicians. (Rieti had become the temporary refuge for Pope Honorius III and his pontifical court following an insurrection in Rome in April 1225.) Bowing to the combined edicts of the Pope, the protector of his order, and the order's minister general, the ever-obedient Francis reluctantly agreed to go to Rieti—but only after he said good-bye to Clare at San Damiano. That good-bye would stretch out for three months while Francis lay close to death.

. . .

The reed and mud hut the friars built for the ailing Francis in the garden at San Damiano is long gone, but its significance is as strong today as it was in the cold spring of 1225. Night turned into day and back into night to the unknowing Francis, who was undergoing a bout of complete blindness. Sightless and ill, he was also plagued by an infestation of mice. "There were so many mice running around here and there, around him and even on him, that they prevented him from taking a rest," recounts the *Legend of Perugia*. "They even hindered him greatly in his prayer."

In the midst of his suffering, Francis nonetheless composed in that reed hut his most joyous, and famous, poem: the Canticle of Brother Sun.

> *Most High, all-powerful, good Lord*
> *Yours are the praises, the glory, the honor, and all blessing.*
> *To You alone, Most High, do they belong,*
> *and no man is worthy to mention Your name.*
> *Praised be You, my Lord, with all your creatures,*
> *Especially Sir Brother Sun,*
> *Who is the day and through whom You give us light.*
> *And he is beautiful and radiant with great splendor;*
> *And bears a likeness of You, Most High One.*
> *Praised be You, my Lord, through Sister Moon and the stars,*
> *In heaven You formed them clear and precious and beautiful.*
> *Praised be You, my Lord, through Brother Wind,*
> *And through the air, cloudy and serene, and every kind of weather*
> *Through which You give sustenance to Your creatures.*
> *Praised be You, my Lord, through Sister Water,*
> *Which is very useful and humble and precious and chaste.*
> *Praised be You, my Lord, through Brother Fire,*
> *Through whom You light the night*
> *And he is beautiful and playful and robust and strong.*
> *Praised be You, my Lord, through our Sister Mother Earth.*
> *Who sustains and governs us,*
> *And who produces varied fruits with colored flowers and herbs.*
> *Praised be You, my Lord, through those who give pardon for Your love.*

Francis loved his canticle so much that he had his friars sing it every day, and often sang along with them. "When he was laid low by sickness, he often intoned this canticle and had his companions take it up," the *Legend of Perugia* continues. "In that way he forgot the intensity of his sufferings and pains by considering the glory of the Lord."

The canticle turned out to be a tonic for Francis's health. He improved enough to add a new stanza in June, in the hope of heading off a looming civil war in Assisi between the backers of the bishop and the secular *podesta,* or mayor, over granting asylum to nobles fleeing Perugia. In short order he dispatched Brothers Leo and Angelo to sing the canticle to the bishop and the *podesta* along with the new verse:

> *Praised be You, my Lord, through those who give pardon for Your love*
> *And bear infirmity and tribulation.*
> *Blessed are those who endure in peace*
> *For by You, Most High, they shall be crowned.*

It worked. Evidently moved to tears, the bishop and the *podesta* forgave each other and dropped their bombastic charges. "Francis had stopped a war with a song," writes his biographer Julien Green.

Francis did not forget Clare, who along with her sisters was helping to nurse him in the hut at San Damiano. After composing the famous Canticle of Brother Sun, he composed a second canticle, this one to console Clare and her sisters during his grave illness.

> *Listen, little poor ones called by the Lord,*
> *who have come together from many parts and provinces:*
> *Live always in truth,*
> *that you may die in obedience.*
> *Do not look at the life outside,*
> *for that of the Spirit is better.*
> *I beg you through great love,*
> *to use with discretion*
> *the alms which the Lord gives you.*

Those who are weighed down by sickness
and the others who are wearied because of them,
all of you: bear it in peace.
For you will sell this fatigue at a very high price
and each one [of you] will be crowned queen
in heaven with the Virgin Mary.

Still Francis lingered at San Damiano, resisting Cardinal Ugolino's order to go to Rieti for treatment by the Pope's doctors. At heart, Francis was not looking for a scientific cure; he considered his suffering heaven-sent and a well-deserved trial for his sins. He was finally persuaded to leave San Damiano by a reassurance from the Lord. As recorded in *The Deeds of Blessed Francis and His Companions,* the Lord reportedly told him that his suffering was not a penance but a promise of the "treasure of eternal life." "This infirmity and affliction is the pledge of that blessed treasure," the Lord told him. Francis was ecstatic at the explanation and immediately summoned his companion to say: "Let's go to the Lord Cardinal."

And so, in late June 1225, Francis said a final farewell to Clare and set out for Rieti. It was the last time the two saints of Assisi would see each other.

*Agony in
the Rieti Valley*

RIETI, *where Francis's medical treatment fails* · FONTE COLOMBO, *the
hermitage where hot pokers do not cure his eyes* · LA FORESTA, *the hermitage
where piercing his ears fails as well*

rancis was mobbed by the people of Rieti when he
arrived in July at the walled city in central Italy.
Many people, including members of the Papal court
ensconced there, already considered him a saint, and they
pushed and shoved to get near him, pluck at his habit,
and kiss the tips of his fingers protruding from his
protective sleeves. It could not have been an easy time for
the ailing Francis.

⁂ Our hotel, the Quattro Stagioni, miraculously turns
out to be just down the piazza from Rieti's massive
thirteenth-century cathedral and the adjoining Bishop's
Palace, where Francis stayed along with the Papal court.
The old stone building is testament to the turmoil of the
times: One Pope after another had to flee to Rieti to
escape the violent uprisings in Rome. Pope Boniface
VIII, who would escape to Rieti in 1298, added the
Arco del Vescovo (Bishop's Arch) to the thirteenth-
century palace as extra insurance; the still-existing arched
bridge known locally as the Arch of Boniface allowed
him to flee across the street from one part of the building
to another should predators be at his heels.

⁂ Francis was besieged not by predators but by
supplicants during his stay at the Bishop's Palace. One, a
cleric named Gideon, begged the holy man to relieve his
back pain so intense that he "could no longer stand

upright." Though the cleric was a well-known philanderer who lived "according to the desires of the flesh," Francis took pity on his suffering and struck a deal: He would bless Gideon and leave it up to the Lord to cure him or not, for which, in return, the cleric would never return to his sinful ways. Gideon agreed, of course, and Francis made the sign of the cross over him—with instant results. "He immediately stood up and got up, completely healed," recounts the *Assisi Compilation*. "When he stood up, you could hear the bones in his back cracking like dry wood in your hands."

But the cleric did not heed Francis's warning that he would "incur a very harsh judgment" if he returned to his "vomit." Gideon succumbed again to the lure of the flesh a few years later and died shortly thereafter while spending the night in the home of a fellow canon. The roof of the house inexplicably collapsed in the middle of the night, sparing the lives of all the occupants save "only that wretch who was trapped and killed."

One of the Papal physicians treating Francis also looked to him for a miracle. To the eye doctor's great dismay, a large crack suddenly opened in the wall of his new house, threatening the structure with collapse. In desperation, according to St. Bonaventure, the doctor asked Francis's companions to give him something the "man of God had touched" to try to stave off the disaster. The something turned out be a bit of Francis's hair, which the doctor placed in the crack before he went to bed. And voilà. "When he rose in the morning, he found that the crack had been so firmly closed that he could not pull out the hairs he had placed there nor could he find any trace of the crack."

The miracle of the doctor's house has seemingly kept on giving. The Palazzo Piccadori now stands on the exact site of the medieval doctor's house, at the intersection of the Via dei Crispoliti and the Via Garibaldi. According to Stefano, a young architect we chance upon in the palazzo's courtyard, it is one of only two structures in Rieti to have escaped any damage from the major earthquakes of 1800 and 1997.

Francis was the recipient of various miracles himself during his treatment in Rieti. For all the close care Leo was taking of him, the seeping wound in his side evidently saturated its dressing and so fouled his tunic that he asked one of his friars to try to find him material for a new one. The friar was on his way out of the Bishop's Palace to beg for cloth the next morning when he was stopped by a man sitting on the doorstep. "For the love of the Lord, brother, please accept this cloth enough for six tunics," the man said. "Keep one for yourself and distribute the rest as you please for the good of my soul." So Francis, and some lucky other friars, got miraculous new tunics.

Curiously, there is nothing in the medieval biographies about the medical treatment Francis received in Rieti. We do know that one of the Pope's doctors was an Arab named Tebaldo Saraceni, whose house Francis evidently stayed in for a while during his attempt at a cure. The house, now privately owned and identified by a stone cross on the outside wall, is on the Via San Rufo. Its stark exterior gives no indication, however, of the charming miracle that occurred within.

Francis loved music but, according to the *Assisi Compilation,* was harshly critical of those who played instruments "for the sake of vanity and sin" rather than "by holy people to praise God." During his agony, however, he bent his own rule and decided to try to "change that pain of my body to joy and consolation of spirit" by having one of his companions, a former musician, secretly play the lute (some say a zither) for him. But the friar resisted. If the people of Rieti heard him play, he protested, they would think he had reverted to his former, unholy ways. Francis immediately rescinded his request. "Then, brother, let's let it go," he said.

But a higher spirit had evidently heard his entreaty. The next night, around midnight, Francis heard the "sound of a lute playing a melody more beautiful and delightful than he had ever heard in his life." The music came from here, from there, from far away and near, for over an hour. In the morning, an "overjoyed" and "exulted" Francis deemed the music to have been played by an angel. His friars agreed it was a great miracle, confirmed by the fact that the city had a midnight curfew and no one would have dared leave home at that time.

However ill Francis felt in Rieti, his charity and generosity were not diminished. When his eye doctor told him about a destitute woman he was treating for free, Francis determined to give her his mantle. But how? Elias, the order's minister general and the friar appointed as his brother guardian, had ordered Francis not to give any of his clothing away without their permission. So Francis devised a clever ruse, recorded in the *Assisi Compilation,* to secure permission to give the woman his mantle.

"Brother Guardian, we have to give back what belongs to someone else," he said to him. "And what is that, brother?" the guardian asked. "That mantle," Francis replied, "which we received as a loan from that poor woman with eye trouble." When it was posed that way, what could the guardian do but agree, and the mantle, plus a dozen loaves of bread, was quickly dispatched to the woman. She was evidently so startled by her good fortune and fearful of it being taken away that she left Rieti with her bounty in the middle of the night to return to her home.

It is rainy and cold during our last visit to Rieti in February 2004, and as we did during the stolen moments the weather afforded us at the Caffè Meletti in Ascoli, we take time to eat. Dinner is especially memorable at the Palazzo Sinizi. There is no menu. The four-course meal simply unfolds, starting with a delicious antipasto of local sausages, prosciutto, various beans, baked tomatoes, and eggplant. A choice of pasta—red or white—follows. We choose the white, a cream sauce laced with rabbit and juniper berries, and move on to the next choice: filet mignon, pork, wild boar, lamb, or sausage, which is butchered to order and grilled right in front of us in a blazing fire.

We are mesmerized watching the chefs rub the meat with lemon, then expertly grill the meat, accompanied by large, flung handfuls of coarse salt. The thought of dessert leaves us limp, but on it comes, a fluffy, light cream "Mimosa" cake, a specialty of the restaurant. All of this washed down by a delicious local red wine, Colli della Sabina.

We walk it off on a leg of Rieti's recently completed eighty-mile-long walking, biking, and/or horse trail called the Cammino di Francesco, the "walk of Francis." The trail links Rieti with all the Franciscan hermitages in the Rieti Valley: Poggio Bustone, Greccio, Fonte Colombo, and La Foresta, which will soon figure in Francis's medical treatment. The *cammino* winds through forests and up the sides of mountains with a spur to a treasured relic—some of Francis's remains in the National Votive Temple on Mount Terminillo—and another to the Faggio di San Francesco, a miraculous and tortured beech tree near Poggio Bustone that bowed its branches during a storm to shelter Francis. (The latter, which we find just below a sun-drenched pasture on a hill close to heaven, should not be missed.)

Perhaps Francis followed the *cammino* himself when he left Rieti in the late summer of 1225 and went, once again, to the hermitage of Fonte Colombo. For all the good intentions of the Papal physicians, they had not managed to cure his eye disease or alleviate its painful symptoms. But the doctors were not through trying. Francis, by horseback, and we, by car, head back to the nearby sanctuary where he would undergo an experimental and brutal new treatment—the cauterization of his temples with a red-hot poker.

The old stone friary at Fonte Colombo sits diagonally across from the oak tree under which Francis received the Rule of 1223 and directly across from the tiny Chapel of the Magdalene. Though the day is warm, I shiver when we enter the friary's stone anteroom with its now dormant fireplace, where the procedure would take place. The "operation" has been written about so vividly by all of Francis's medieval biographers that it is painfully easy to imagine.

Here is Francis, his eyes so light-sensitive that his friars have sewed a linen band to his hood to cover them. Around him are a few of his friars, worried and exhausted by their worry. They are waiting for Brother Elias, the head of the order, to arrive and order Francis to have the procedure. "The saint hesitated to let himself be treated," says the *Legend of Perugia*. "He found it bitterly repugnant to be so concerned about himself; that is why he wanted the decision to come from his minister."

But the minister does not come. Francis becomes increasingly concerned about the time and attention his friars are paying to his infirmity and promises them that the Lord "will credit you with the good works that you have to neglect in order to take care of me." It seems doubtful that the friars, seeing Francis in such poor health, feel reassured.

While Francis waits for Elias to arrive, he dictates several letters, probably to Leo. Some of the letters are to Clare, though they have never been found. Others, which have survived, indicate that Francis knew he was nearing the end of his days. One, in which he mentions his "sickness," is addressed to the "Entire Order" and firmly instructs his friars to observe the discipline of the Rule or risk being seen by him as neither "Catholics nor my brothers."

Another, addressed to the "Rulers of the Peoples," exhorts "all the mayors and counsels, magistrates and rulers throughout the world" to remember that the "day of death is coming" and not to turn away from the Lord but to embrace him. Francis also suggests that the authorities send a town crier through their respective streets every evening to announce to all the people that "praise and thanks may be given to the all-powerful Lord God," a clear reference to the Islamic call to prayer five times a day, which Francis had heard—and admired—in Egypt.

But Elias still does not come to Fonte Colombo. The most frequent visitor is the Arab doctor who becomes the catalyst for yet another miracle recorded in the *Legend of Perugia*. Just as he is leaving one day, Francis suddenly directs the friars to invite the doctor to join them for a "good meal." The ashamed friars "blushingly admit" there is very little to eat, but Francis insists. "O men of little faith, do not make me repeat myself," he says.

So the rich doctor, who says he is honored to eat with the poor brothers, sits down with them to share a crust or two of bread and a few vegetables when there is an unexpected knock on the door and in comes a woman with a basket full of "white bread, fish, lobster-pie, some honey and some grapes that seemed to have been freshly picked." To the doctor and the friars, the timing of the miracle meal, which has been sent to Fonte Colombo by "the lady of a castle about seven miles away," is yet another irrefutable example of Francis's sanctity.

A visit from another doctor does not end so happily. Elias evidently never arrives, but the obedient Francis finally bows to the insistence of Cardinal Ugolino and consents to the cauterization. The friars build up the fire. The doctor takes out his "cautery" and heats the metal until it is crimson. The friars feel faint with dread, but Francis, facing the reality of what he is about to endure, speaks directly to the flames.

"Brother Fire," he says, "the Lord created you as something noble and useful among all creatures. Be courteous to me in this hour." As Francis makes the sign of the cross over the fire and the doctor advances with the crimson steel, the friars flee.

The doctor lays the hissing steel on Francis's temple, burning the flesh from the ear to the eyebrow. He then reheats the steel and repeats the sear-ing on the other side. Francis does not cry out or give any indication of what must have been excruciating. Instead he chastises his brothers when they cautiously reenter the room, calling them "cowards," and "men of lit-tle faith" because they did not believe he would feel no pain.

Francis presumably recuperated in one of the two tiny cells just off the anteroom, the door openings so low that even I, at five foot two, have to stoop to enter. I need some time to recuperate myself, having imagined per-haps too vividly the medieval and useless torture Francis must have suffered in that cold, stone anteroom. Whether or not he felt his pain, I did. And the doctors were still not through with him.

The small hermitage of La Foresta, known then as San Fabiano, is also in the Rieti Valley, some five miles from Fonte Colombo. Francis's friars brought him to this charming sanctuary, nestled in a sun-drenched clear-ing in a forest of chestnuts and oaks, in the fall of 1225. Somewhere at La Foresta, either in the still-smoke-blackened interior of the stone *domus,* or guesthouse, or in the nearby Grotta di San Francesco, the rock fissure to which Francis moved to spare his eyes from the smoke, the doctors tried an-other and equally futile procedure: They heated a poker once again—and pierced both his ears.

La Foresta is such a cheerful place now that it is more difficult to imag-ine Francis's suffering here. Like those of several other Franciscan her-mitages we've visited, La Foresta's immaculate gardens and vineyards are tended by a Mondo X community. There is no television allowed, no newspapers, no distractions from the outside world. It is very Franciscan. "Our life here is based on manual work and dialogue, so that those suffer-ing from alcoholism, drug addiction, depression, the Mafia, existential cri-sis, can develop a better inner life," says Daniele, the community's leader, whom we meet arranging carnations and daisies in the medieval church of San Fabian.

La Foresta's vineyards played a central role in Francis's protracted stay here, some say for twenty days, others, fifty. La Foresta is only three miles from Rieti, and Francis's arrival at the hermitage caused an enormous stir. The cardinals and clerics from the refugee Papal court in Rieti visited him daily. The people of Rieti and its neighboring villages also flocked to see the living saint, with the obvious consequences. Because the guesthouse had only one door and because the sole approach to the door was through the vineyard, many of the priest's grapevines were either ravaged or tram-pled.

The priest, naturally, was upset. According to the *Legend of Perugia,* he complained to anyone who would listen that the vintage he was counting on for his year's needs was lost. When Francis was informed of the priest's distress, he summoned him. "How many loads of wine does your vineyard produce every year?" Francis asked him. "Thirteen," the priest answered. "Have confidence in the Lord, and in my words," Francis counseled him. "If you harvest less than twenty loads, I promise to make up the differ-ence." There was no need, of course. The priest harvested a bumper crop of twenty loads from his ragged vines, which was considered by all "a great miracle due to the merits of blessed Francis."

The remains of the old stone winepress with the original rock in it are still in the priest's guesthouse. The stone slab altar in the charming church of San Fabian is the original one used by the poor priest, and the church's original stone floor is clearly visible through glass panels in the newish floor. It takes little imagination to see Francis here, under the church's primitive peaked wooden roof with red tau crosses painted in every panel, or in the Grotta di San Francesco, the cave little bigger than a narrow crevice in a rock.

Some historians, especially those in Rieti, believe that Francis wrote the famous Canticle of Brother Sun, or at least some of the verses, in this stone crevice. He had the time, they point out. He was surrounded by the very el-ements of nature he extols in the canticle—Brother Sun, Sister Moon and Stars, Brothers Wind and Air, Mother Earth. And it is possible that they are right.

What remains indisputable is that Francis's health did not improve. Wasted by tuberculosis, recurring malaria, liver disease, his eye infection, and possibly leprosy, he barely survived the winter of 1225 in the various hermitages in the Rieti Valley. But the doctors still had not finished with him.

In April 1226, just as the sun was warming the winter earth, the ever-obedient Francis acquiesced to the orders of Cardinal Ugolino and Brother Elias to be treated by yet more doctors. His loyal friars took him, on horseback, to Siena. Francis would never return to his beloved Rieti Valley.

24 Hearing the Larks Sing

SIENA, *where Francis vomits blood* · the CELLE DI CORTONA, *where his body bloats* · BAGNARA, *where he can breathe the cool air* · THE PORZIUNCOLA, *where Francis dies*

The medieval sanctuary of Alberino, where Francis spent two months during the last and futile attempt at a medical cure, sits on a hill a few blocks outside the walls of Siena.

When Francis was brought here in April 1226 by his friars and a doctor from Rieti, Alberino was in the wilderness; now it is a tiny hilltop oasis in the built-up Siena suburb of Ravacciano. A lull in the traffic, however, affords a glimpse of medieval Siena as Francis knew it: clearly visible in the nearby city walls is the twelfth-century, arched Porta Ovile, through which Francis first walked to Alberino in 1212 and, finally, fourteen years later, was carried on horseback.

The little chapel at Alberino is a stone diary of Francis in Siena, the pages inscribed on plaques on the wall. One plaque tells the charming story, recounted in the *Little Flowers,* of the boy and the turtledoves he was taking to market in Siena—until he ran into Francis. Francis somehow convinced the boy to give him the doves so they would not "fall into the hands of cruel men who will kill them." Francis then took the doves on with him, presumably to Alberino, where he made nests for them so the doves could "fulfill the Creator's commandment to multiply." And multiply they did until Francis blessed the doves and gave them permission to leave.

Other Francis artifacts in the chapel are familiar ones: a replica of the San Damiano cross hanging over the altar; his stone pillow behind a grille on the wall; the representations of yet another miraculous tree, which grew here from the staff he planted in the ground on his first visit in 1212. (This tree lived for four hundred years and survived being cut down in the 1600s to reemerge one hundred years later.) There are other familiar themes, like the plaque commemorating Francis's gift of his cloak to a poor man on the road between Rieti and Siena. And there is a plaque commemorating a more mysterious exchange that took place on that same road on this his last visit to Siena.

Three poor and identical women appeared on the road as Francis and his doctor approached on horseback. "Welcome, Lady Poverty," Celano quotes the women as saying to Francis, an unlikely salutation from strangers, which "filled him with unspeakable joy." Francis asked the doc-tor to give something to the women; he gave them coins. But as suddenly as the women had appeared, they vanished, leaving Francis and the doctor with the conclusion that they had been the heaven-sent Franciscan virtues of Chastity, Poverty, and Obedience.

We experience a taste of that obedience ourselves in Siena. We are being shown around the city by Father Paolo, a sturdy, sixty-seven-year-old Fran-ciscan friar who had come to Siena's thirteenth-century church of San Francesco via postings in Naples and the Philippines. Because we had arranged to meet Father Paolo at the cavernous brick church on the north-eastern ridge of Siena, we have booked a hotel outside the city walls near the millennium escalators installed for Jubilee, which carry us up the ridge almost to San Francesco's front door. Alberino turns out to be a short walk from the church. It is the next leg with Father Paolo that almost does us in.

We accept the priest's generous offer to show us all the places in Siena that Francis is known, or is thought, to have gone, and without further ado, we set out. Even now I can visualize Father Paolo in his gray habit and black watch cap as he strides ahead of us around the outside of the northern perimeter walls of Siena in the midst of late afternoon traffic to fetch up finally at the beginning of Francis in Siena: the northwestern gate of Porta Camollia. It was through this arched portal in 1212 that Francis

made his first and triumphant entry into Siena on the shoulders of the ex‐
cited Sienese. According to Father Paolo's steady stride, Francis either
walked or was carried along the Via Camollia to Siena's distinctive white
and gray striped cathedral, where he preached in the Piazza del Duomo.

That sermon, Father Paolo says, brought peace to the warring people of
the city and won Francis their hearts. Mounting the steps of the duomo and
keeping a firm grip on his umbrella, the otherwise taciturn friar reenacts the
gist of the personalized sermon Francis delivered with such effect. "You
['put in Christian name,' he says], do the work of the devil. You have the
chance to convert and do penance. Before you is either salvation or damna‐
tion." After hearing Francis, the Sienese evidently chose salvation.

Directly across the splendid medieval piazza—indeed, all of Siena is
splendid—is a tantalizing possibility for Francis: the enormous, eleventh‐
century Ospedale di Santa Maria della Scala. Originally a rest stop for
travelers and pilgrims along the heavily traveled Via Francigena, the *os‐
pedale* grew to offer medical treatment as well. Though there is no record of
Francis being treated here for his eyes, many believe he must have been. In
the process now of being converted to a museum to display Siena's over‐
flow art treasures—a stunning Duccio exhibit is under way while we are
here—the "hospital" seems such a natural location for the ailing Francis
that I sense his presence up and down the marble corridors, especially out‐
side the Clinica Oculistica.

But Father Paolo is off again. We leave the piazza and its Bishop's
Palace, where Francis is thought to have stayed on occasion, and stride past
a view of St. Catherine of Siena's house, where Francis might also have
stayed because of its proximity to therapeutic mineral springs. Somewhere
else in this university city, the "unlettered" Francis had a legendary ex‐
change with a Dominican doctor of sacred theology. The intellectual
Order of Preachers and the humble Order of the Friars Minor had a
tremendous rivalry at the time, and this exchange clearly casts Francis as
the winner.

According to Celano, the learned preacher was querying the biblical
directive from Ezekiel—"If you do not warn the wicked man about his
wickedness, I will hold you responsible for his soul." He was both relieved
and enlightened when the poorly educated Francis offered him his inter‐

pretation—that simply by example, the brilliance and reputation of the pure soul would expose the wickedness of others. "My brothers," the Do-minican professor reported to his order, "the theology of this man, held aloft by purity and contemplation, is a soaring eagle, while our learning crawls on its belly on the ground."

The Lord had reminded Francis of the importance of example in a rev-elation at Alberino. Francis had prayed to the Lord to tell him when he was pleasing him as his "servant" and when he was not. Francis woke up his brothers to report to them the Lord's answer. " 'Know that you are in truth my servant when you think, speak, or do things that are holy,' " Fran-cis recounted. "And so I have called you, brothers, because I want to be shamed in front of you if ever I am not doing any of those three."

Still we walk on in the wake of Father Paolo, not knowing the signifi-cance, if any, of the various palazzos and churches we are passing. It finally dawns on us that we are simply following the long, semicircular route Francis took through Siena from the Porta Camollia to the duomo, then on to the Porta Ovile, from which he first saw the tiny chapel on the hill that would become Alberino. And so we return to where we started, hav-ing followed Father Paolo in Francis's footsteps for a good two hours.

Francis's last stay at Alberino was not a happy one. Whatever medical treatment he received in Siena did not improve his condition. His spirits were raised, however, by the gift of a pheasant from a Sienese nobleman. "Brother Pheasant" took such an immediate liking to Francis that every time the friars released it back into the wild, it returned to Francis's cell. The doctor finally took the pheasant home with him, but the bird's heart was broken and it refused to eat. Frightened it would die, the doctor took the pheasant back to Francis, whereupon "it threw off its sadness and began to eat with joy."

Francis was not as fortunate. One anguishing night at Alberino, he came close to death. He began to vomit, the *Assisi Compilation* tells us, "be-cause of the disease of his stomach." Francis was often nauseated, but this time the strain of his retching led to a life-and-death crisis: According to his medieval biographers, "he vomited up blood all night until morning."

Various modern explanations are offered for the hemorrhaging. A gastric ulcer might have been the cause according to a 1999 study, "The Ill-nesses of Francis During the Last Years of His Life." But there is also the possibility of stomach cancer or Francis's ongoing and recurring bouts with malaria with its attendant parasites. To the friars in 1226, however, the nightlong vomiting of blood that left Francis "almost dying from weakness and the pain of his illness" simply signaled the end.

Gathered around him in his cell at Alberino, the friars begged Francis to bless them and to leave a remembrance so all could say: "Our father left these words to his sons and brothers at his death." And so Francis hastily summoned a friar priest and told him: "Write that I bless all my brothers, those who are and who will be in the religion until the end of the world.

"Since I cannot speak much because of my weakness and the pain of my illness," Francis continued in what has become known as the Siena Testament, "I am showing my will to my brothers in these three words: may they always love each other, as a sign of remembrance of my blessing and my testament; may they always love and observe our Lady Holy Poverty; and may they always remain faithful and subject to the prelates and all the clerics of holy Mother Church."

But Francis did not die. In fact, he rallied a bit. Brother Elias, the order's minister general, rushed to his side and decided to take Francis, before the heat of the summer, to the mountain hermitage just outside Cortona, where he might improve. And briefly, he did.

Perhaps it was the sound of the water rushing by the Celle di Cortona or the sweet mountain air or the call of the birds, but Francis gained enough strength there to dictate a more thorough and ultimately provoca-tive document, known as the Last Testament.

Francis began the forty-one-sentence testament with a history of his con-version twenty years before: "The Lord granted me, Brother Francis, to begin to do penance in this way: While I was in sin, it seemed very bitter to me to see lepers. And the Lord Himself led me among them and I had mercy upon them. And when I left them that which seemed bitter to me was changed into sweetness of soul and body; and afterward I lingered a little and left the world."

Francis went on to reminisce about his first converts in Assisi and the doubts that ensued—"And after the Lord gave me brothers, no one told me what I should do"—and the simple Rule he adopted from the Gospels to lead them "that the Lord Pope confirmed for me." He extolled the virtues of his earliest companions, who "were content with one tunic, patched inside and out, with a cord and short trousers," then added wistfully, in light of the more hedonistic friars to come: "And we had no desire for anything more."

But then the tone turns stern and authoritative, as if he were still the order's minister general. He "firmly" wishes the friars to do "honest work" with their hands and to "beware" receiving any "churches or poor dwellings or anything that is built for them" that is not in keeping with Holy Poverty. Other directives begin with the words "I firmly command," "I firmly wish," "I strictly forbid," "I strictly command." However ill he was, Francis was obviously not going to go quietly into that good night.

But what makes the Testament so controversial is the seeming contradiction it contains. On the one hand, Francis stated clearly that the "brothers" should not say, "This is another Rule," but should take the Testament rather as "a reminder, admonition, exhortation, and my testament, which I, Brother Francis, worthless as I am, leave to you, my brothers." On the other hand, Francis instructed the leadership of the order to read "these words" every time they read the Rule; to "not add or subtract" from the words, and to understand these words from the Lord "simply and without gloss and observe them with holy manner of working until the end."

The early friars and later like-minded friars would take literally and "without gloss" Francis's dictates in the Testament against owning or accepting any property that did not conform to Holy Poverty, prompting a bitter division in the order. The struggle between the Spirituals, as the sometimes fanatic purists were known, and the Conventuals, the more progressive friars, who studied or taught at universities and eschewed remote hermitages to live in houses and worship at their own churches, would go on for years. Pope after Pope would have to address the schism, starting with the order's guardian, Cardinal Ugolino, who became Pope Gregory IX in 1227. To the fury of some of the fanatical Spirituals, Pope Gregory decreed in 1230 that Francis's Testament was not legally binding, a decree that led a group of Spirituals in Tuscany to accuse him publicly of heresy.

It is tempting to think that Francis, close to death, was deliberately am-
biguous in his Testament. His early Rule had been rejected, after all, and
the later Rule he had written at Fonte Colombo had been greatly modified
by Ugolino and Pope Honorius III. This Testament is pure Francis,
unabridged, unedited—and unyielding.

What is equally memorable about the Testament is that Francis summoned the energy to write it. After a brief rally, his health had begun to de-
teriorate dramatically during his brief interlude at the *celle.* "The swelling
began in his abdomen, his legs and his feet," Celano writes, "and his stomach became so weak that he could hardly eat any food at all."

Francis wanted to return to the Porziuncola in Assisi, but Elias hesitated. The direct route from the *celle* to Assisi went right by Perugia, and
the fear was that the Perugians might try to kidnap the dying Francis, bury
him in Perugia, and thus establish the city as a profitable pilgrimage destination. If Francis were to die en route, the fear was even greater of losing
possession of his body to any number of hill towns, especially Perugia. A
further reward would be the division of his body into valuable relics for
profit or for future distribution in return for favors. So Elias decided to
bring Francis home on a long and circuitous route through the hills around
Gubbio.

The cortege finally set out from the Celle di Cortona and, in June 1226,
returned Francis safely to the Porziuncola. However grateful Francis must
have been to be home, he lasted there for only two weeks. The summer heat
was stifling in the wooded valley, making it hard for Francis to breathe. So
once more Elias and Francis's closest friars packed him up and moved him,
to a new hermitage, eighteen miles away, high in the mountains above Bagnara.

The scenery changes radically as we approach Bagnara along the old
Via Flaminia. The valley narrows, the wooded hills are craggier, and there
are very few open fields. We stop briefly, as did Francis, at the walled medieval hill town of Nocera Umbra. The town seems gloomy, but there is
good reason. Nocera Umbra was hit very hard by the 1997 earthquake; 80
percent of its old stone houses were damaged, if not destroyed, and its civic
symbol, a tall rock tower, was leveled. So we press on, after an artichoke

sandwich in a rather desultory coffee bar, to follow Francis to the tiny community of Bagnara.

In its Roman heyday, Bagnara was a spa town, and evidently it still is, though its population of fewer than two thousand does not speak of a thriving spa economy. But the air is definitely cooler in Bagnara's hills, which would have eased Francis's breathing. And perhaps the healing powers of Bagnara's water brought him some relief, though by now Francis was beyond any medicinal cure.

Virtually blind, his spleen and liver enlarged by malarial parasites, his abdomen and legs hideously bloated by the fluid retention of dropsy, the rest of his body emaciated, and his pallor gray from anemia, Francis was obviously not long for this world.

Messengers raced back and forth between Bagnara and Assisi, and plans were formalized for Francis's final return to the city of his birth in August 1226. Bishop Guido was away, but Francis would stay, under guard, in the Bishop's Palace. To make sure no one could kidnap him en route, knights were dispatched to bring him safely home. What a poignant scene it must have been. Francis was too weak to ride a horse on his own, so the knights, some of whom were his childhood friends, took turns carrying him in their arms.

Francis was not too weak, however, to give the knights a final lesson in humility. As the procession wound its way through the hills northeast of Assisi, Francis and his escorts stopped in the poor village, now vanished, of Satriano. The hungry knights went door to door trying to buy food and drink but came back empty-handed.

"You didn't find anything because you trust more in those flies [coins] of yours than in God," St. Bonaventure quotes Francis. Francis sent the knights back out, advising them this time to "humbly ask for alms" after offering the villagers the "love of God as a reward." To the knights' amazement, according to Celano, they "bought more with the love of God than with money."

Francis and his military escort entered Assisi through the Porta Perlici, which still stands on the northeastern edge of the hill town and bears an 1199 inscription designating it the gateway to the Marches. The knights ensconced Francis in the Bishop's Palace on the Piazza del Vescovado, then took up guard duty outside. Francis had come full circle, from his childhood nearby in his family's house; his rudimentary schooling at San Giorgio, now St. Clare's basilica, just around the corner; his nude renunciation of his father in the palace's courtyard; and now, his approaching death.

"Brother, what is your prognosis?" Francis asked Buongiovanni, a friend and doctor from Arezzo who came to visit him in the palace. When the doctor replied that, with the grace of God, all would be well, Francis pressed him for the truth. "I am not a coward who fears death," the *Legend of Perugia* quotes him as saying. "The Lord by his grace and in his goodness, has so closely united me to himself that I am as happy to live as I am to die." The doctor then told him straight out that his disease was incurable and that he would die either at the end of September or on the fourth day of October. Instead of despairing, Francis exulted at the news and cried out—"Welcome, Sister Death!"

Without further ado, Francis summoned Brother Leo and Brother Angelo to praise Sister Death with him. And together, with the friars fighting tears, Francis added a new and final verse to the Canticle of the Sun:

All praise be yours, my Lord, through Sister Death,
From whose embrace no mortal can escape.
Woe to those who die in mortal sin!
Happy those She finds doing your will!
The second death can do no harm to them.

Francis loved the new verse and had his friars sing the entire canticle to him at all hours of the day and night to lift his spirits as well as the morale of the knights guarding the palace. In a clear indication of the irreconcilable differences between the old and new guards of the Franciscan Order, Brother Elias reportedly objected to the singing on the grounds that the joyous sound wafting out of the palace windows was sending the wrong message to the people of Assisi.

"How can he display such great joy when he is going to die?" Elias asked, voicing what he believed to be the people's confusion. "Would it not be better to think of death?" But Francis had always chosen joy. "Brother,

let me rejoice in the Lord and sing his praises in the midst of my infirmities," he answered his minister general. And the singing continued.

There were other joyous moments at the Bishop's Palace. Francis, who
had virtually stopped eating, had a craving one day for fish. And instantly
and miraculously, a brother arrived unannounced from Rieti with a gift
"basket containing three well-cooked pike and a quantity of lobster." Another night he craved parsley, and when an anguished friar told him there
was none in the garden, Francis directed him to go out into the darkness
and bring him "the first herbs your hand touches." The handful of wild
herbs, Celano reports, turned out to have "a tender stock of parsley in the
middle of them," which Francis ate a bit of and "felt much better."

But time was running out for Francis, and toward the end of September,
heeding the doctor's timetable for his death, Francis asked to be taken to the
Porziuncola. Again, it must have been an amazing scene. His loyal friars
carried him down the hill from Assisi on a litter. When they reached a
crossroad, which is still there, by an old *lazzaretto,* which is now thought to
be the Casa Gualdi, Francis asked his friars to turn the litter around and
prop him up so he could "see" Assisi for the last time. Perhaps his vision
cleared for an instant so he could take in what is still a stunning view of
Assisi from below. And then he blessed the city of his birth.

Francis lingered for a week or so in the infirmary at the Porziuncola. At
one point he struggled out of his habit and lay naked on the floor in order
to die on the earth in absolute poverty, without even a tunic to his name.
Elias could not bear the sight and came up with a brilliant ruse. He commanded Francis, under holy obedience, to accept the tunic, underwear,
and hood that he was "lending" him. "And so that you know that they in
no way belong to you, I take away all your authority to give them to anyone," Elias told him. Francis then consented to wear the borrowed clothes.

It was his wish for a specific gray cloth for a burial tunic that brought
about one of Francis's last living miracles. At his request, a brother was
just about to depart for Rome with a letter to Lady Jacopa di Settesoli, asking her to send not only the "gray-colored monastic material" but some of
his favorite almond-honey cake, when suddenly there was a knock on the
door. It was "Brother" Jacopa.

The miracle of her spontaneous arrival multiplied with what she had brought: the exact shroud cloth, the ingredients for his favorite cake, plus incense and wax candles to burn "before the holy body after his death." She had been told to come to the Porziuncola, she explained to the friars, by a "voice" that had interrupted her prayers in Rome. "Go and visit your father, blessed Francis," the voice had instructed her, according to the *Legend of Perugia*. "But hurry . . . for if you delay, you will not find him alive." The voice had also told her what to take.

Francis's friars busied themselves by having the gray tunic hastily made for his shroud, with sackcloth, at his direction, sewed over it as a "sign of most holy humility and poverty." Francis was so ill, however, he could eat only a crumb or two of the almond cake Lady Jacopa made for him.

With his last strength, he dictated a letter to the ailing Clare, known as "The Blessing Sent to St. Clare and Her Sisters." The letter was prompted less by his illness than by the severe bout of illness Clare was suffering at the time and her fear that she would die without seeing him again. "She wept in bitterness of spirit and could not be comforted because she would not be able before her death to see her only father after God, that is blessed Francis," reports the *Assisi Compilation*. But any meeting was impossible, of course, "since they were both seriously ill." So he wrote her a note.

The text of the letter Francis sent Clare has never been found, but all the medieval biographies report that it contained his blessing of Clare and his absolution of her for any failings she might have committed. Francis also promised her what she so desperately craved, though, ironically, it would be after his death, not hers. "Let her know, in truth, that before she dies she and all her sisters will see me again and will receive great consolation from me," Francis instructed the friar bearing the letter to her at San Damiano.

Finally, there were only Francis and his friars in the little infirmary at the Porziuncola. As we stand inside the Cappella del Transito, a restoration of that simple cell inside the massive Santa Maria degli Angeli, it is difficult to sense the intimacy and the anguish that must have filled this space eight hundred years ago. Somewhere, under the acres of marble in this, the seventh largest Christian church in the world, the friars were sitting on the earth around Francis, crying.

Brother Elias was in the cell with Francis. So were Brother Leo and several others among the first companions: Brother Rufino, Brother Giles, Brother Angelo, and Brother Bernard of Quintavalle. Eighteen years had passed since Francis spent the entire night in prayer at the Quintavalle home and converted Bernard, his first friar.

"Write this just as I tell you," Francis said to Leo. "Brother Bernard was the first brother whom the Lord gave me, as well as the first to put into practice and fulfill most completely the perfection of the Holy Gospel by distributing all his goods to the poor. Because of this and many other prerogatives, I am bound to love him more than any other brother of the entire Order. Therefore, as much as I can, I desire and command that, whoever the Minister General is, he should cherish and honor him as he would me."

Then it was the other friars' turn for their blessings. And the call from Francis for bread, which he blessed before giving a piece to each of his brothers. And the reading he asked his friars for, from the Gospel According to St. John. And then Francis, faltering, began to recite Psalm 142. "Lead me out of my prison, that I may give thanks to your name," he whispered. "Then the just shall gather around me because you have been good to me."

Francis died just after sunset on October 3, 1226, at the age of forty-five. It is said that the bells of the twelfth-century church of San Stefano in Assisi began tolling spontaneously. His friars, however far-flung, also sensed his passing. One saw his "blessed soul under the appearance of a radiant star carried up on a shining cloud." Another, many miles away, who was himself at death's door and unable to speak, suddenly cried out: "Wait for me, Father. Wait! Look, I am coming with you"—and he did. Bishop Guido, too, saw a vision of Francis that night while he was on a pilgrimage to Monte Gargano. "Behold, I am leaving the world and am going to heaven," Francis said to his old friend. And all the legends began.

We leave the reconstructed chapel where Francis died and exit the cavernous Santa Maria degli Angeli, only to be met by the jarring sound of music, albeit sacred, being broadcast over loudspeakers. After all the hundreds of miles we have traveled with Francis, however, I have learned to blot out intrusions into the simple spaces we have shared with this extraordinary man and his legend. And so I don't hear the canned music. I hear the sound of larks.

Francis was particularly fond of larks. He admired their dark heads, which he saw as "capuches" or hoods worn by his friars, and their "earth-colored plumage," because it gave a good example to "religious who ought not to wear garish and choice garments." He also admired Sister Lark, according to the *Legend of Perugia,* because she is a "humble bird" who eats little and "praises the Lord" in flight.

So it is not surprising that larks marked the moment of his death at the Porziuncola. It is said that an exaltation of larks, which had assembled on the roof of Francis's hut, suddenly—and inexplicably—took to the air just after sunset, wheeling and singing.

ACKNOWLEDGMENTS

Many thanks to my editor, Bob Loomis, for his patience and support; my agent, Lynn Nesbit, for the idea; my friends and colleagues, Fred Smith, Sarah Meacham, Tony Sifton, Alice Mayhew, Cheryl Merser, Liz Meryman, Missy McHugh, Canio Pavone, Leonard Mayhew, Linda Purrazzella, Jan Moran, Mary Lenore Blair, Ed Kern, Peter Sutro, Jane Nissen, and Julian Stein for their participation; and my son, Andrew Mackenzie, for quiet office space. A special thank-you to our Egyptian host, Ambassador Abdel Raouf el-Reedy, and Dr. Abdel Azim Wazir, governor of Damietta; to my Italian colleagues and friends Angela Seracchioli, Rita Giovannelli, Andrea Mercanti, and Anna Licori; to my U.S. Franciscan contacts: Father Murray Bodo, O.F.M.; Father John Abela; Sister Daria Mitchell; Brother Rex Anthony Norris, S.S.F.; Domenick Morda, S.F.O.; and, in Italy, to all the friars who generously gave us so much of their time. But thanks, most of all, to my husband, Harvey Loomis, driver, navigator, photographer, and fellow adventurer, who made this book a reality.

TRAVEL NOTES

We found the various Rough Guides to Italy and Egypt to be most informative and helpful (see bibliography). We prebooked most of our hotels over the Internet and booked our "villa" near Perugia through www.italianvillas.com, phone 800-700-9549.

We rented a series of excellent cars and Italian cell phones from Auto Europe through a referral at www.italianvillas.com. The cell phones, programmed in English and delivered to us in the United States before our departure for Italy, proved invaluable.

We found the following road maps most helpful:

Umbria e Marche, Grande carte stradale (scale of 1:200,000), published by Touring Club Italiano and available on the Internet or at any good map store, is an excellent map that covers the heart of St. Francis country.

A handy booklet of road maps for Italy, at a scale of 1:300,000, is *Euro-Travel Atlas, Italy,* published by the American Map Corporation of Maspeth, New York, and available through www.italianvillas.com.

An extensive series of first-rate city and provincial maps covering all of Italy (at scales ranging from 1:5,000 to 1:150,000) is produced by Litografia Artistica Cartographic of Florence; individual maps are available on the Internet at www.initaly.com/ads/maps.htm.

SOURCE NOTES

Brother Thomas of Celano wrote four works on St. Francis, three of which I use in the book. The first, *The Life of St. Francis,* is abbreviated in the notes as 1C; the second, *The Remembrance of the Desire of a Soul,* is abbreviated as 2C; the third, *The Treatise on the Miracles,* is abbreviated as 3C.

I use three sources for Celano: *Saint Francis of Assisi by Thomas of Celano,* translated from the Latin by Placid Hermann, O.F.M., and published in 1963 by the Franciscan Herald Press; Marion A. Habig, O.F.M., ed., *St. Francis of Assisi, Writings and Early Biographies: English Omnibus of the Sources for the Life of St. Francis,* also published by the Franciscan Herald Press, in 1973; and its successor, *Francis of Assisi: Early Documents,* a stunning three-volume, 2,362-page anthology of Franciscan documents—vol. 1, *The Saint;* vol. 2, *The Founder;* and vol. 3, *The Prophet*—published by New City Press between 1999 and 2001.

The thirteenth- and fourteenth-century recollections of Francis—the *Legend of the Three Companions,* the *Legend of Perugia,* the *Anonymous of Perugia,* the *Assisi Compilation,* the *Kinship of St. Francis,* and *A Mirror of the Perfection*—all appear in the *English Omnibus* and/or *Early Documents.*

The Little Flowers of St. Francis is cited in the 1958 book by the same name and in *Early Documents,* vol. 3, as the Deeds of Blessed Francis and His Companions. Similarly, the book *The Life of St. Francis* by St. Bonaventure, edited by Cardinal Henry Edward Manning, appears in *Early Documents,* vol. 2, as the Major and Minor Legends of St. Francis by Bonaventure of Bagnoregio.

1. Mozart Among the Giottos

p. 4 A stern German bishop . . . : Buckley et al., *Tuscany and Umbria: The Rough Guide,* p. 498.

p. 4 "of a decoration . . .": Desbonnets, *Assisi,* p. 104.

p. 6 "medium height, closer to shortness": 1C-83, *St. Francis of Assisi by Thomas of Celano,* p. 74.

p. 7 her biography: *The Life of St. Clare Virgin,* p. 18.

p. 7 "cheerful countenance": 1C-83, *St. Francis of Assisi by Thomas of Celano,* p. 74.

p. 9 born here—in a stable: Desbonnets, *Assisi,* p. 24.

p. 10 "dark cellar": Legend of the Three Companions, no. 17, p. 907.

p. 11 "He would use only . . .": Legend of the Three Companions, no. 2, *English Omnibus*, p. 891.

p. 11 "He was the admiration . . .": 1C-2, *St. Francis of Assisi by Thomas of Celano*, p. 6.

p. 11 "while I was in sin": Testament, *Francis and Clare: The Complete Works*, p. 154.

p. 12 "And what is no less to be admired . . .": 1C-82, *St. Francis of Assisi by Thomas of Celano*, p. 73.

p. 12 "strong, sweet . . .": 1C-83, ibid., p. 74.

p. 15 The cathedral's piazza was ablaze . . . : Green: *God's Fool*, p. 46.

2. Lost in Perugia

p. 19 "interfered with his words," et cetera: 2C-37, *St. Francis of Assisi by Thomas of Celano*, p. 169.

p. 20 "I shall send them all . . .": Green, *God's Fool*, p. 178.

p. 21 "His grieving companions resented . . ." et cetera: 2C-4, ibid., p. 138.

p. 21 "he went outside one day . . .": 1C-3, ibid., pp. 7, 8.

p. 21 "freed from his chains" et cetera: 2C-5, ibid., p. 139.

p. 22 "Upon hearing this . . .": 1C-4, ibid., p. 8.

p. 22 "raised his spirits . . ." et cetera: 1C-5, ibid., p. 9.

3. The Missing Letter in Spoleto

p. 23 "The Lord," et cetera: 2C-6, *St. Francis of Assisi by Thomas of Celano*, p. 140.

p. 25 Letter to Brother Leo: *Francis and Clare: The Complete Works*, p. 47.

p. 26 "The world was tasteless . . .": 2C-94, *St. Francis of Assisi by Thomas of Celano*, p. 215.

p. 28 "He was chosen . . . ," et cetera: 2C-7, ibid., p. 141.

p. 28 "Francis, do you wish to get married?" et cetera: 1C-7, ibid., pp. 11, 12.

p. 29 "in a certain grotto," et cetera: 1C-6, ibid., p. 10.

p. 29 a "humpbacked and deformed woman . . .": Legend of the Three Companions, no. 12, *English Omnibus*, p. 901.

p. 29 "inopportune ideas": Ibid., p. 902.

p. 29 "Consequently, when he came out again . . .": 1C-6, *St. Francis of Assisi by Thomas of Celano*, p. 11.

p. 31 "his heart was aglow . . .": Legend of the Three Companions, no. 12, *English Omnibus*, p. 902.

p. 31 "He was already a benefactor . . .": Ibid., no. 8, p. 897.

p. 31 "He would give his belt . . .": Ibid.

p. 31 "new ardor which was taking possession . . .": No. 12, p. 902.

4. THE OLD ROME

p. 33 "Astounded when he came . . .": 2C⁄8, *St. Francis of Assisi by Thomas of Celano*, p. 142.

p. 34 "He put off his fine garments . . .": Ibid.

p. 34 "Many times he would have done . . .": Ibid.

p. 34 begging for alms himself: Legend of the Three Companions, no. 10, *English Omnibus*, p. 899.

p. 34 "Considering himself one of them . . .": 2C⁄8, *St. Francis of Assisi by Thomas of Celano*, p. 142.

p. 35 "if, by chance, he happened . . .": Legend of the Three Companions, no. 11, *English Omnibus*, p. 901.

p. 36 "O, Francis, if you want to know . . .": Ibid., p. 900.

p. 36 "Though the leper caused him . . .": 2C⁄9, *St. Francis of Assisi by Thomas of Celano*, p. 143.

p. 36 "He washed all the filth off them . . .": Celano, 1C⁄7, *Early Documents*, vol. 1, p. 195.

p. 36 "When I was yet in sin . . .": Ibid.

p. 36 "When postulants presented themselves . . .": Legend of Perugia, no. 102, *English Omnibus*, p. 1079.

p. 37 "Strengthened by God's grace . . .": Legend of the Three Companions, no. 11, *English Omnibus*, p. 901.

p. 37 "Francis, go, repair my house . . .": 2C⁄10, *St. Francis of Assisi by Thomas of Celano*, p. 144.

p. 37 "After fortifying himself . . .": Celano, 1C⁄4, *Early Documents*, vol. 1, p. 188.

p. 39 "It seemed to him that Francis . . . ," et cetera: Ibid., pp. 189, 190.

p. 39 "Calling together his friends . . . ," et cetera: Legend of the Three Companions, no. 16, *English Omnibus*, pp. 906, 907.

p. 39 "prayed continually . . . ," et cetera: Ibid.

p. 40 "When his friends and relatives saw him . . . ," et cetera: Ibid.

p. 40 "sprang on his son . . . ," et cetera: Ibid.

p. 40 "When she saw that his mind . . . ,": Ibid., no. 18, p. 908.

p. 40 "When the authorities saw . . . ," et cetera: no. 19, p. 908.

p. 41 "repeated his accusation," et cetera: Ibid.

5. Showdown in Assisi

p. 43 "Your father is highly incensed . . .": Legend of the Three Companions, no. 19, *English Omnibus,* p. 908.

p. 43 "My Lord Bishop, not only will I . . .": Ibid., no. 20, p. 909.

p. 43 "Listen all of you . . .": Ibid.

p. 44 "His father rose up . . .": Ibid., no 19, p. 909.

p. 44 "prompted by divine counsel . . . ," et cetera: Legend of the Three Companions, no. 20, *Early Documents,* vol. 2, p. 80.

p. 45 "singing praises to the Lord . . . ," et cetera: Celano, 1C-7, *Early Documents,* vol. 1, pp. 194, 195.

p. 46 "graciously" host Francis "quite often": Passion of San Verecondo, in *Early Documents,* vol. 2, p. 806.

p. 47 "ravenous bite" of a "cruel sow," et cetera: Bonaventure, Major Legend, no. 8, ibid., pp. 590–591.

p. 47 "ferocious wolves": Passion of San Verecondo, ibid., p. 806.

p. 48 "No mercy was shown to him . . . ," et cetera: Celano, 1C-VI, *Early Documents,* vol. 1, p. 195.

p. 49 "Brother Wolf," et cetera: *Little Flowers,* ch. 21, pp. 89, 90, 91.

p. 51 "see what kind of man this Francis is": Celano, 2C-48, *Early Documents,* vol. 2, p. 299.

p. 52 seven-year-old capons: Ibid., p. 298, n. b.

p. 52 "so crippled that she could do no work . . . ," et cetera: 1C-24, *St. Francis of Assisi by Thomas of Celano,* p. 60.

p. 53 "When he saw his bowl . . .": 2C-1X, ibid., p. 148.

p. 53 "bashfulness and retraced his steps," et cetera: 2C-8, ibid., p. 147.

p. 54 "Tell Francis to sell you a pennysworth": 2C-7, ibid., p. 146.

p. 54 "would lash out at him . . .": Celano, 1C-7, *Early Documents,* vol. 2, p. 251.

p. 54 "the holy virgins of Christ": Celano, 2C-43, *St. Francis of Assisi by Thomas of Celano,* p. 147.

6. Clare's "Prison"

p. 56 "And they shall take care . . .": Rule of Saint Clare, *Francis and Clare: The Complete Works,* p. 214.

p. 56 "how to form words as they should": 1C-20, *St. Francis of Assisi by Thomas of Celano,* p. 21.

p. 57 "not to let a day go by . . .": Celano, *Life of Saint Clare Virgin by Fra' Tommaso da Celano*, no. 18, p. 40.

p. 57 "a stiff hair shirt . . . ," et cetera: Ibid., no. 17, p. 38.

p. 58 "rivers of tears," et cetera: Ibid., no. 19, p. 42.

p. 59 "possession or ownership . . . ," et cetera: Rule of Saint Clare, *Francis and Clare: The Complete Works*, p. 219.

p. 59 Agnes of Prague forswore marriage: Celano, *Life of Saint Clare Virgin*, p. 29.

p. 60 "For this reason, she gazed lovingly . . . ," et cetera: Bargellini, *Little Flowers of Saint Clare*, p. 163.

p. 60 "No one is permitted . . .": Rule of Saint Clare, *Francis and Clare: The Complete Works*, p. 225.

p. 61 "What you do, may you always do . . .": Second Letter to Blessed Agnes of Prague, ibid., p. 196.

p. 61 "But our flesh is not bronze . . .": Third Letter to Blessed Agnes of Prague, ibid., p. 202.

7. Peace March in Santa Maria degli Angeli

p. 64 "church of the Blessed Virgin Mother . . .": 1C-21, *St. Francis of Assisi by Thomas of Celano*, p. 22.

p. 65 "He decided to stay there . . .": Bonaventure, Major Legend, no. 8, *English Omnibus*, p. 645.

p. 67 "Come, Sister Cricket . . . ," et cetera: Legend of Perugia, no. 84, *English Omnibus*, pp. 1059, 1060.

8. Francis Gets His Marching Orders

p. 70 "inconceivable joy," et cetera: Bonaventure, Life of St. Francis, no. 111, *Early Documents*, vol. 2, p. 26.

p. 71 "wishing peace to the congregation . . .": Quoted in Englebert, *St. Francis of Assisi*, p. 44.

p. 72 "praying all night long . . .": 1C-24, *St. Francis of Assisi by Thomas of Celano*, p. 203.

p. 72 "If you wish to be perfect . . . ," et cetera: Legend of the Three Companions, no. 29, *English Omnibus*, p. 917.

p. 72 "Having sold everything . . .": Ibid., p. 918.

p. 73 Francis had to scold Brother Giovanni: *Little Flowers*, p. 328.

p. 73 "Blessed Francis betook himself . . .": 1C-42, *St. Francis of Assisi by Thomas of Celano,* p. 40.

p. 74 "The place was so cramped . . . ," et cetera: Legend of the Three Companions, no. 55, *English Omnibus,* p. 939.

p. 74 "Very often for lack of bread . . .": Ibid.

p. 74 "I'm dying . . . ," et cetera: Legend of Perugia, no. 1, *English Omnibus,* p. 977.

p. 74 "Go your way, Brother Fly . . .": Ibid., no. 64, p. 1040.

p. 75 "he either mixed them with ashes . . .": 1C-51, *St. Francis of Assisi by Thomas of Celano,* p. 48.

p. 75 "temptation of the flesh . . .": 1C-42, ibid., p. 40.

p. 75 "And when that brother . . .": 1C-53, ibid., p. 49.

p. 75 "These were the teachings . . .": 1C-41, ibid., p. 39.

p. 75 "a little farther from the city": Bonaventure, *Life of St. Francis of Assisi,* no. 2, p. 24.

p. 76 "chariot of fire . . .": Bonaventure, ibid., no. 4, p. 36.

p. 76 "next to the very parade route": Celano, 1C-43, p. 41.

p. 77 "his glory would last . . .": Ibid.

p. 77 "I know that God has not called me . . .": Legend of the Three Companions, no. 55, *English Omnibus,* p. 939.

9. The First Tour to the Marches

p. 79 by 1282: *Little Flowers,* p. 18.

p. 79 "mad," "fools," or "drunkards," et cetera: Anonymous of Perugia, no. 3, *Early Documents,* vol. 2, p. 40.

p. 79 "Love and fear of God . . .": Legend of the Three Companions, no. 9, *Early Documents,* vol. 2, p. 88.

p. 79 "Believe him": Anonymous of Perugia, no. 3, *Early Documents,* vol. 2, p. 40.

p. 79 "faithful people, meek and kind . . .": Legend of the Three Companions, nos. 10–36, *Early Documents,* vol. 2, p. 90.

p. 80 "to bear . . . ," et cetera: Ibid.

p. 82 "with a trade they have learned," et cetera: Earlier Rule, *Early Documents,* vol. 1, pp. 68, 69.

p. 82 "Let them be careful . . .": Ibid., p. 69.

p. 84 "He persevered there . . .": 1C-26, *St. Francis of Assisi by Thomas of Celano,* p. 26.

p. 85 "Little by little . . . ," et cetera: Ibid.

p. 86 "In this way, he often ascribed . . .": 2C⁄131, ibid., p. 245.

p. 87 "He rejoiced in all the works . . .": 2C⁄165, ibid., pp. 269, 270.

p. 87 "You have worn the belt . . .": Quoted in Englebert, *St. Francis of Assisi,* p. 54.

p. 88 "Chaste embraces, gentle feelings . . .": 1C⁄38, *St. Francis of Assisi by Thomas of Celano,* p. 37.

p. 88 "They were therefore, everywhere secure . . .": 1C⁄39, ibid., p. 37.

p. 89 murdering the Papal legate: House, *Francis of Assisi,* p. 87.

10. THE POPE HAS A DREAM

p. 91 "Go find your pigs . . .": Quoted in Englebert, *St. Francis of Assisi,* p. 63.

p. 91 "Fearful that the holy man . . .": Celano, 1C⁄33, *Early Documents,* vol. 1, p. 212.

p. 91 "Their greatest joy . . .": Englebert, *St. Francis of Assisi,* p. 65.

p. 92 "My dear young sons . . .": Legend of the Three Companions, no. 49, *Early Documents,* vol. 2, p. 96.

p. 92 "When he awoke, stunned and shaken . . .": Ibid., no. 51, p. 97.

p. 96 "nudged her with its horns . . .": Bonaventure, Major Legend, no. 8⁄7, *Early Documents,* vol. 2, p. 591.

p. 96 "the green things of the gardens": 1C⁄81, *St. Francis of Assisi by Thomas of Celano,* p. 73.

11. DESPERATELY SEEKING FRANCIS AND THE BIRDS

p. 97 "a great multitude of birds . . .": Celano, 1C⁄58, *Early Documents,* vol. 1, p. 234.

p. 98 "He gave you feathers to wear . . .": Ibid.

p. 98 "he carefully exhorted all birds . . .": Ibid.

p. 98 "place near the city of Orte": Celano, 1C⁄14, *Early Documents,* vol. 1, p. 213.

p. 98 forty days there: Julian of Speyer, *Life of St. Francis,* vol. 1, p. 384.

p. 99 "with gratitude and joyful hearts": Celano, 1C⁄14, *Early Documents,* vol. 1, p. 214.

p. 99 "the size of a large loaf of bread": Celano, 3C⁄179, *Early Documents,* vol. 2, p. 462.

p. 100 "only move his tongue . . .": 3C⁄176, ibid., p. 461.

p. 100 "The blessed Francis preferred . . .": Celano, 1C⁄25, *Early Documents,* vol. 1, p. 241.

p. 100 "twisting miserably and screaming . . .": Ibid., p. 242.

p. 103 "At the taste of it . . .": Bonaventure, Minor Legend, 2nd lesson, *Early Documents,* vol. 2, p. 704.

p. 104 one of his modern biographers suggests: Green, *God's Fool,* p. 103.

p. 105 "might have hope of sprouting again," et cetera: *St. Francis of Assisi by Thomas of Celano,* p. 270.

p. 106 "He spoke as compelled . . . ," et cetera: Sabatier, *Road to Assisi,* p. 58.

p. 106 The *Little Flowers of St. Francis*: *Little Flowers,* ch. 12, p. 66.

p. 106 "so absorbed in God . . . ," et cetera: *Little Flowers,* ch. 30, p. 115.

12. CLARE FLEES TO FRANCIS

p. 108 "brothers, who were holding . . .": Celano, *Life of Saint Clare Virgin,* no. 8, p. 22.

p. 109 "tonsured" et cetera: Ibid., p. 23.

p. 109 "united to Christ": Celano, *Life of Saint Clare Virgin,* no.8, p. 23.

p. 109 in his biography *Francis of Assisi*: Englebert, p. 110.

p. 111 "with violence, venomous counsel": Celano, *Life of Saint Clare Virgin,* no. 2C⁄284, p. 24.

p. 111 Celano reports that: Ibid.

p. 112 "It seems as if . . .": Bargellini, *Little Flowers of St. Clare,* pp. 39–41.

p. 112 "little flower" or his "little plant": Bonaventure, Major Legend, ch. 4, vol. 2, p. 554.

p. 113 "I do not want anyone to offer . . .": 2C⁄205, *St. Francis of Assisi by Thomas of Celano,* p. 301.

p. 113 "rebuke him very severely . . .": 2C⁄206, ibid., p. 301.

p. 113 "walk several miles naked . . .": Ibid., p. 302.

p. 114 "honeyed poison": Celano, 2C⁄112, *Early Documents,* vol. 2, p. 321.

p. 114 "All of us must keep close watch . . .": Rule of 1221, ch. 12, "Impure Glances and Frequent Association with Women," *Francis and Clare: The Complete Works,* p. 120.

p. 114 "He declared that all conversation . . .": Celano, 2C⁄114, *Early Documents,* vol. 2, p. 322.

p. 114 "in a loud voice . . . ," et cetera: 2C⁄112, ibid., p. 321.

p. 114 "inappropriate chattering": Ibid., p. 322.

p. 114 "God has taken away . . .": Quoted in Erikson, *Saint Francis and His Four Ladies*, p. 84.

p. 115 "Brother Leo, what do you think . . .": Ibid., p. 85.

p. 115 "Blessed Francis," et cetera: Celano, *Life of Saint Clare Virgin*, no. 10, p. 26.

p. 115 "daughters and servants . . .": *Francis and Clare: The Complete Works*, p. 44.

p. 115 "the riches and pomp . . . ," et cetera: *Little Flowers*, ch. 15, pp. 72, 73.

p. 116 "in such a sweet and holy . . .": Ibid., p. 73.

p. 116 "a heavenly and not material fire," et cetera: Ibid.

p. 116 "Francis, when will we see . . .": Bodo, *Clare: A Light in the Garden*, p. 47.

p. 118 "agony of doubt," et cetera: *Little Flowers*, ch. 16, p. 74.

13. Eating Well and Tuscany's First Hermitages

p. 119 "during the night before . . .": Deeds of Blessed Francis and His Companions, 6⁄3, *Early Documents*, vol. 3, p. 448.

p. 120 "Since there was no shelter . . . ," et cetera: 6⁄6, ibid.

p. 122 "It is believed . . .": 6⁄9, ibid.

p. 122 "even when he was burning . . .": 1C⁄51, *St. Francis of Assisi by Thomas of Celano*, p. 227.

p. 124 "hand it over to anyone . . . ," et cetera: Assisi Compilation [33], *Early Documents*, vol. 2, p. 140.

p. 124 "offer to others things . . .": [89], ibid., p. 193.

p. 125 "promoted study . . .": Englebert, *St. Francis of Assisi*, p. 188.

p. 128 "Hurry, and clothe them all . . .": 2C⁄117, *St. Francis of Assisi by Thomas of Celano*, p. 234.

p. 129 "He often chose solitary places . . .": 1C⁄28, *St. Francis of Assisi by Thomas of Celano*, p. 243.

p. 129 Rule for Hermitages: *Francis and Clare: The Complete Works*, p. 146.

14. Shrieking Swallows in Alviano

p. 132 "My sister swallows . . .": Celano, 3C⁄4, *Early Documents*, vol. 2, p. 412.

p. 132 "they wanted to follow him . . . ," et cetera: *Little Flowers*, ch. 16, *English Omnibus*, p. 1335.

p. 132 "Many of the people . . .": 1C⁄37, *St. Francis of Assisi by Thomas of Celano*, p. 36.

p. 132 "Thus through Blessed Francis's perfect devotion . . .": Legend of the Three Companions, no. 60, *English Omnibus,* p. 944.

p. 132 "It is an historical fact . . .": G. G. Messerman, quoted in Pazzelli, *St. Francis and the Third Order,* p. 102.

p. 133 "Oh, how happy and blessed . . . ," et cetera: First Version of the Letter to the Faithful or Exhortation to Brothers and Sisters of Penance, *Francis and Clare: The Complete Works,* p. 63.

p. 133 Approved orally by Pope Honorius II: Secular Franciscan Q and A, www.members.cox.net/sfobro/page.

p. 136 "He sometimes feared . . .": Legend of Perugia, no. 93, *English Omnibus,* p. 1070.

15. THE MARCHES AGAIN—GREEN FIELDS, BLUE ADRIATIC

p. 137 "to preach the Christian faith . . . ," et cetera: Bonaventure, Major Legend, ch. 9, 5, *Early Documents,* vol. 2, p. 600.

p. 139 "to take him with them . . . ," et cetera: Ibid.

p. 140 "great storm," et cetera: Celano, 1C-55, *Early Documents,* vol. 1, p. 230.

p. 140 "multiplied so much . . . ," et cetera: Bonaventure, Major Legend, ch. 9, 5, *Early Documents,* vol. 2, p. 601.

p. 140 "began to walk the earth . . . ," et cetera: Ch. 9, 6, ibid.

p. 140 "many good and suitable men . . .": Celano, 1C-56, *Early Documents,* vol. 1, p. 230.

p. 141 "would run as if drunk . . .": *Little Flowers,* ch. 49, *Early Documents,* vol. 3, p. 649.

p. 142 "Do you see that sheep . . .": Celano, 1C-77, *Early Documents,* vol. 1, p. 248.

p. 142 "touched in his heart . . . ," et cetera: 1C-78, ibid., p. 249.

p. 143 "as a great gift from God," et cetera: Ibid.

p. 143 "very vain youth," et cetera: *Deeds of Blessed Francis and His Companions,* vol. 3, p. 539.

p. 144 "Stunned at once . . .": Bonaventure, Major Legend, ch. 4, 9, *Early Documents,* vol. 2, p. 556.

p. 145 "He is entering the city . . .": Versified Life of St. Francis by Henri d'Avranches, bk. 9, ll. 74–81, *Early Documents,* vol. 1, p. 493.

p. 146 "There he spoke the word . . .": Celano, 1C-62, *Early Documents,* vol. 1, p. 236.

p. 148 "Let's go up to that festival . . .": Pt. 2, Considerations on the Holy Stig, mata, First Consideration, *Little Flowers,* p. 172.

p. 148 "And in fervor of spirit . . . ," et cetera: Ibid.

p. 149 "great and wealthy Count . . .": Ibid.

p. 149 "Brother Francis, . . . I have a mountain . . .": Ibid., p. 173.

p. 150 "as though they were angels of God": Ibid.

p. 150 Deed of La Verna, related documents: *Early Documents,* vol. 3, pp. 801–803.

16. FINDING FRANCIS ALONG THE NILE

p. 156 "pseudo-prophet," et cetera: Hoeberichts, *Francis and Islam,* p. 10.

p. 156 "suitable" men: Ibid., p. 12.

p. 156 "Innocent no longer insisted . . .": Ibid.

p. 158 "Granada as we know it . . .": Green, *God's Fool,* p. 200.

p. 159 with blackened skin: Runciman, *History of the Crusades,* vol. 3, p. 156.

p. 159 as many as ten thousand Christians: House, *Francis of Assisi,* p. 207.

p. 160 "The Lord has showed me . . . ," et cetera: 2C-30, *St. Francis of Assisi by Thomas of Celano,* p. 163.

p. 160 "And behold . . .": Ibid.

p. 161 "especially over the Spaniards . . .": Ibid., p. 164.

p. 161 beheading fifty knights: House, *Francis of Assisi,* p. 209.

p. 162 "there was no way of passing . . . ," et cetera: Bonaventure, Major Legend, ch. 9, 7, *Early Documents,* vol. 2, p. 602.

p. 163 "like wolves": Ibid.

p. 163 "When that ruler inquired . . .": 8, ibid.

p. 165 "enormous fire," et cetera: Ibid., p. 603.

p. 165 "When, during his stay among the Muslims . . .": Hoeberichts, *Francis and Islam,* p. 196.

p. 165 "many precious gifts": Bonaventure, Major Legend, ch. 9, vol. 2, p. 603.

p. 167 "The Saracens gladly listened . . .": Jacques de Vitry, History of the Ori, ent, *English Omnibus,* p. 1612.

p. 167 The annual Nile flood: Maalouf, *Crusades Through Arab Eyes,* p. 226.

p. 168 "He had also observed . . .": House, *Francis of Assisi,* p. 218.

p. 169 "life of the primitive church": Jacques de Vitry, Letter 1, *English Omnibus,* p. 1688.

17. Cruising the Venice Lagoon

p. 171 "maintaining he was a most holy man . . .": Kinship of St. Francis, ch. 1, 4a, *Early Documents,* vol. 3, p. 681.

p. 171 very sick on the voyage home: Spoto, *Reluctant Saint,* p. 166.

p. 172 "marshes of Venice . . . ," et cetera: Bonaventure, Major Legend, ch. 8, 9, *Early Documents,* vol. 2, p. 592.

p. 173 "I, little Brother Francis . . .": Quoted in Green, *God's Fool,* p. 210.

p. 173 "the house of the brothers": Celano, 2C-58, *Early Documents,* vol. 2, p. 286.

p. 174 "They pulled his capuche . . . ," et cetera: Little Flowers, ch. 5, *Early Documents,* vol. 3, p. 575.

p. 174 "After you have a psalter . . .": Mirror of the Perfection, vol. 3, ch. 4, ibid., p. 258.

p. 175 "a fiery drop of sulfur . . .": Kinship of St. Francis, vol. 3 11:21, ibid., p. 706.

p. 175 "plain man . . . ," et cetera: Thomas of Spalato, quoted in Sabatier, *Road to Assisi,* p. 108.

p. 176 "The era of sweet evangelical anarchy . . .": Green, *God's Fool,* p. 211.

p. 177 "From now on . . .": Ibid., p. 212.

18. Poor Francis

p. 178 One of his biographers: Green, *God's Fool,* p. 215.

p. 178 "desiring by divine inspiration . . .": Earlier Rule, *Francis and Clare: The Complete Works,* p. 110.

p. 178 "only the books necessary . . .": Ibid., p. 111.

p. 179 "whatever is placed before them": Ibid.

p. 179 "content with one tunic . . .": 1C-39, *St. Francis of Assisi by Thomas of Celano,* p. 37.

p. 179 "carry nothing with you . . .": Earlier Rule, *Francis and Clare: The Complete Works,* p. 120.

p. 179 "The brothers should beware . . .": Ibid., p. 115.

p. 179 "In his whole life . . .": Green, *God's Fool,* p. 215.

19. Following Francis to Italy's Boot

p. 181 "near Bari," et cetera: Celano, 2C-68, *Early Documents,* vol. 2, p. 292.

p. 183 "rushed upon him . . .": Bonaventure, Major Legend, 12:6, ibid., p. 625.

p. 184 "By you, most holy Lord . . .": Celano, 2C⸗156, ibid., p. 348.

p. 184 "construction of the church . . .": 3C⸗59, ibid., p. 429.

20. THE BEAUTIFUL RIETI VALLEY

p. 187 "Who are these brothers? . . . ," et cetera: Mirror of the Perfection, Introduction The Sabatier Edition, *Early Documents,* vol. 3, p. 254.

p. 188 "forced by necessity . . . ," et cetera: Rule of 1223, *English Omnibus,* pp. 57–64.

p. 189 "to relax or tarry": Legend of Perugia, no. 34, *English Omnibus,* p. 1011.

p. 189 "Now, it seems to me . . .": Assisi Compilation [74], *Early Documents,* vol. 2, p. 176.

p. 190 "From that moment . . .": Celano, 3C⸗18, *Early Documents,* vol. 2, p. 411.

p. 190 "I believe there's a devil . . . ," et cetera: Assisi Compilation, [119], ibid., p. 227.

p. 191 "will recall to memory . . .": 1C⸗84, *St. Francis of Assisi by Thomas of Celano,* p. 76.

p. 191 "The woods rang . . .": 1C⸗85, ibid.

p. 191 "so that our sister larks . . .": Sabatier Edition, ch. 114, *Early Documents,* vol. 3, p. 363.

21. TOUCHED BY AN ANGEL AT LA VERNA

p. 193 "that rock 'twixt Tiber and Arno": Dante Alighieri, *Paradiso, The Divine Comedy,* canto 11.

p. 194 "From now on . . .": Assisi Compilation, [87], *Early Documents,* vol. 2, p. 192.

p. 194 "If the brothers knew . . .": [118], ibid., p. 227.

p. 194 "Whenever he had to walk . . .": [88], ibid., p. 192.

p. 194 "I place all the words . . .": Letter to Brother Leo, *Francis and Clare: The Complete Works,* p. 47.

p. 195 "to ride on . . . ," et cetera: 2C⸗46, *St. Francis of Assisi by Thomas of Celano,* p. 178.

p. 195 "a great number of different kinds . . . ," et cetera: Deeds of Blessed Francis and His Companions, ch. 9:23, *Early Documents,* vol. 3, p. 454.

p. 195 "separated from the others": Ibid.

p. 195 dates of the fast of St. Michael: Ibid., note a.

p. 195 "None of his companions . . .": Ibid., p. 454.

p. 195 "approach him saying nothing . . .": Ibid.

p. 196 "elevated in the air . . . ," et cetera: Ibid., p. 455.

p. 196 "it anticipated him . . . ," et cetera: Bonaventure, Major Legend, ch. 8:10, *Early Documents,* vol. 2, p. 594.

p. 196 "Who are you . . . ," et cetera: Deeds of Blessed Francis and His Companions, ch. 9:37, *Early Documents,* vol. 3, p. 455.

p. 196 "afraid and retreating . . . ," et cetera: 9:43, ibid., p. 456.

p. 196 "a tunic, a cord and trousers," et cetera: 9:52, ibid., p. 457.

p. 197 "man standing above him . . . ," et cetera: 1C-94, *St. Francis of Assisi by Thomas of Celano,* p. 85.

p. 197 "round on the inner side . . .": 1C-95, ibid., p. 85.

p. 197 "The heads of the nails . . .": Bonaventure, Major Legend, ch. 13, *Early Documents,* vol. 2, p. 633.

p. 198 "overexcited neural activity": House, *Francis of Assisi,* pp. 261–265.

p. 198 "He did not seek . . .": Celano, 2C-95, *Early Documents,* vol. 1, p. 265.

p. 198 "from which . . . his sacred blood . . .": Bonaventure, Major Legend, ch. 13, *Early Documents,* vol. 2, p. 633.

p. 198 "the crucified servant . . .": Celano, 2C, *Early Documents,* vol. 1, p. 264.

p. 200 "suddenly by a miracle . . . ," et cetera: Considerations on the Holy Stigmata, Second Consideration, *Little Flowers,* p. 184.

p. 203 " 'Farewell, farewell, Brother Masseo . . . ,' " et cetera: Quoted in Englebert, *St. Francis of Assisi,* p. 246.

22. The Painful Road Back to Assisi

p. 205 "And whoever comes to them . . .": Earlier Rule, *Francis and Clare: The Complete Works,* p. 115.

p. 205 "Come, Brother Robbers . . . ," et cetera: Assisi Compilation, [115], *Early Documents,* vol. 2, pp. 221, 222.

p. 208 "There were so many mice . . .": Legend of Perugia, no. 43, *English Omnibus,* p. 1020.

p. 208 Canticle of Brother Sun: *Francis and Clare: The Complete Works,* pp. 38–39.

p. 209 "When he was laid low . . .": Legend of Perugia, no. 43, *English Omnibus,* p. 1022.

p. 209 "Francis had stopped a war . . .": Green, *God's Fool,* p. 259.

p. 209 "Listen, little poor ones . . .": Canticle of Exhortation to Saint Clare and Her Sisters, *Francis and Clare: The Complete Works*, pp. 40–41.

p. 210 "treasure of eternal life," et cetera: Deeds of Blessed Francis and His Companions, 31:7, *Early Documents*, vol. 3, p. 479.

23. AGONY IN THE RIETI VALLEY

p. 211 "could no longer stand upright," et cetera: Assisi Compilation, [95], *Early Documents*, vol. 2, pp. 197, 198.

p. 212 "man of God had touched," et cetera: Bonaventure, Major Legend, ibid., p. 584.

p. 213 "For the love of the Lord . . .": Celano, 3C/35, ibid., p. 416.

p. 213 "for the sake of vanity and sin," et cetera: Assisi Compilation, [66], ibid., p. 169.

p. 214 "Brother Guardian, we have to give back . . .": [89], ibid., p. 193.

p. 215 "The saint hesitated . . . ," et cetera: Legend of Perugia, no. 46, *English Omnibus*, p. 1026.

p. 216 A Letter to the Entire Order: *Francis and Clare: The Complete Works*, pp. 55–61.

p. 216 A Letter to the Rulers of the Peoples: Ibid., pp. 77, 78.

p. 216 "good meal," et cetera: Legend of Perugia, no. 26, *English Omnibus*, p. 1004.

p. 216 "Brother Fire . . .": No. 48, ibid., p. 1026.

p. 218 "How many loads of wine . . . ," et cetera: No. 25, ibid., p. 1003.

24. HEARING THE LARKS SING

p. 220 "fall into the hands . . . ," et cetera: *Little Flowers*, ch. 22, p. 92.

p. 221 "Welcome, Lady Poverty," et cetera: Celano, 2C/93, *Early Documents*, vol. 2, p. 307.

p. 222 "If you do not warn . . . ," et cetera: 2C/103, ibid., p. 315.

p. 223 " 'Know that you are in truth . . .' ": 2C/159, ibid., p. 350.

p. 223 "Brother Pheasant . . . threw off": 2C/170, ibid., p. 356.

p. 223 "because of the disease . . . ," et cetera: Assisi Compilation, [59], ibid., p. 161.

p. 224 Octavian Schmucki, "The Illnesses of Francis During the Last Years of His Life,": *Gray Friar* 13 (1999): 42–46; note, ibid., p. 161.

p. 224 "Our father left these words . . . ," et cetera: Assisi Compilation [59], *Early Documents,* vol. 2, p. 162.

p. 224 The Testament: *Francis and Clare: The Complete Works,* pp. 154–156.

p. 225 accuse him publicly of heresy: "Ubertino of Casale," *Catholic Encyclopedia,* www.newadvent.org.

p. 226 "The swelling began . . .": Celano, 2C⁄105, *Early Documents,* vol. 1, p. 274.

p. 227 "You didn't find anything . . . ," et cetera: Bonaventure, Major Legend, ch. 7, 10, *Early Documents,* vol. 2, p. 583.

p. 228 "Brother, what is your prognosis?" et cetera: Legend of Perugia, no. 65, *English Omnibus,* p. 1042.

p. 228 "All praise be yours . . .": No. 100, ibid., pp. 1076, 1077.

p. 228 "How can he display . . . ," et cetera: No. 64, ibid., p. 1041.

p. 229 "basket containing three well⁄cooked pike . . .": No. 29, ibid., p. 1007.

p. 229 "the first herbs . . . ," et cetera: Celano, 2C⁄31, *Early Documents,* vol. 2, p. 281.

p. 229 "And so that you know . . .": 2C⁄215, ibid., p. 386.

p. 229 "gray⁄colored monastic material": Legend of Perugia, no. 101, *English Omnibus,* p. 1077.

p. 230 "Go and visit your father . . . ," et cetera: Ibid., pp. 1077–78.

p. 230 "Blessing Sent to St. Clare and Her Sisters": *Francis and Clare: The Complete Works,* p. 160.

p. 230 "She wept in bitterness . . . ," et cetera: Assisi Compilation, [13], *Early Documents,* vol. 2, p. 128.

p. 230 "Let her know . . .": Legend of Perugia, no. 109, *English Omnibus,* p. 1085.

p. 231 "Write this just as I tell you . . .": Blessing Given to Brother Bernard, *Francis and Clare: The Complete Works,* p. 159.

p. 231 "blessed soul under the appearance . . . ," et cetera: Bonaventure, Major Legend, ch. 14⁄6, *Early Documents,* vol. 2, p. 644.

p. 232 "earth⁄colored plumage," et cetera: Legend of Perugia, no. 110, *English Omnibus,* p. 1087.

BIBLIOGRAPHY

Armstrong, Regis J., O.F.M. Cap., and Ignatius C. Brady, O.F.M., trans. *Francis and Clare: The Complete Works*. Ramsey, N.J.: Paulist Press, 1982.

Armstrong, Regis J., O.F.M. Cap.; J. A. Wayne Hellmann, O.F.M. Conv.; and William J. Short, O.F.M., eds. *Francis of Assisi: Early Documents*, vol. 1, *The Saint;* vol. 2, *The Founder;* vol. 3, *The Prophet*. New York, London, and Manila: New City Press, 1999–2001.

Bargellini, Piero. *The Little Flowers of Saint Clare*. Assisi: Edizioni Porziuncola. English trans., Edmund O'Gorman, O.F.M. Conv. Padua: Messaggero Editions, 2002.

Belford, Ros, Martin Dunford, and Celia Woolfrey. *The Rough Guide to Italy*, 6th ed. London: Rough Guides, 2003.

Bodo, Murray. *Clare: A Light in the Garden*. Cincinnati, Ohio: St. Anthony Messenger Press, 1992.

———. *Francis: The Journey and the Dream*. Cincinnati, Ohio: St. Anthony Messenger Press, 1988.

Brown, Raphael, trans. *The Little Flowers of St. Francis*. New York: Image Books, 1958.

Buckley, Jonathan, Mark Ellingham, and Tim Jepson. *Tuscany and Umbria: The Rough Guide*. London: Rough Guides, 2000.

Cure, Karen, ed. *Rome*, Fodor's Pocket, 5th ed. 2002.

Dante Alighieri. *The Divine Comedy*, trans. Lawrence Grant White. New York: Pantheon Books, 1948.

Desbonnets, P. Theophile. *Assisi: In the Footsteps of Saint Francis*. Assisi: Edizioni Porziuncola, 2000.

Dozzini, Bruno. *Giotto: The "Legend of St. Francis" in the Assisi Basilica*. Assisi: Editrice Minerva, 1994.

Duncan, Fiona, and Peter Greene. *Central Italy Trip Planner and Guide*. Lincolnwood, Ill.: Passport Books, 1999.

Englebert, Omer. *St. Francis of Assisi, A Biography*, trans. Eve Marie Cooper; 2nd English ed. revised and augmented by Ignatius Brady, O.F.M., and Raphael Brown. Chicago: Franciscan Herald Press, 1965.

Erikson, Joan Mowat. *Saint Francis and His Four Ladies*. New York: W. W. Norton, 1970.

Green, Julien. *God's Fool: The Life and Times of Francis of Assisi.* New York: Harper & Row, 1985.

Habig, Marion A., O.F.M., ed. *St. Francis of Assisi, Writings and Early Biographies: English Omnibus of the Sources for the Life of St. Francis,* 3rd rev. ed. Chicago: Franciscan Herald Press, 1973.

Hermann, Placid, O.F.M., trans. *Saint Francis of Assisi by Thomas of Celano.* Chicago: Franciscan Herald Press, 1963.

Hoeberichts, J. *Francis and Islam.* Quincy, Ill.: Franciscan Press, 1997.

House, Adrian. *Francis of Assisi: A Revolutionary Life.* Mahwah, N.J.: HidenSpring (an imprint of Paulist Press), 2001.

Maalouf, Amin. *The Crusades Through Arab Eyes,* trans. Jon Rothschild. London: Al Saqi Books, 1984.

Magrini, Catherine Bolton, trans. *The Life of Saint Clare Virgin by Fra' Tommaso da Celano.* Assisi: Editrice Minerva, 2000.

Manning, Cardinal Henry Edward, ed. *The Life of St. Francis of Assisi by St. Bonaventure.* London: Burns, Oates & Washbourne, 1925; Rockford, Ill.: Tan Books, 1988.

Martin, Valerie. *Salvation: Scenes from the Life of St. Francis.* New York: Vintage Books, 2002.

Pagnani, Giacinto. *I Viaggi di S. Francesco Nelle Marche.* Milano: Dott. A. Giuffre Editore, 1962.

Pazzelli, Raffaele, T.O.R. *St. Francis and the Third Order.* Chicago: Franciscan Herald Press, 1989.

Richardson, Dan, with Daniel Jacobs and Jessica Jacobs. *The Rough Guide to Egypt,* 5th ed. London: Rough Guides, 2003.

Runciman, Steven. *A History of the Crusades,* vol. 3, *The Kingdom of Acre and the Later Crusades.* Cambridge and New York: Cambridge University Press, 1951.

Sabatier, Paul. *The Road to Assisi: The Essential Biography of St. Francis,* ed. Jon M. Sweeney. Published originally in 1894 as *La Vie de Saint François D'Assise.* Brewster, Mass.: Paraclete Press, 2003.

Seracchioli, Angela Maria. *Di qui passo Francesco.* Milano: Terre di Mezzo, 2004.

Spoto, Donald. *Reluctant Saint: The Life of Francis of Assisi.* New York: Viking Compass, 2002.

Uribe, Fernando. *Itinerari Francescani: Visita al Luoghi Dove Visse San Francesco.* Padua: Messaggero di S. Antonio Editrice, 1997.

Williams, Roger, ed. *Southern Italy.* London: Insight Guides, 2003.

INDEX

ABOUT THE AUTHOR

LINDA BIRD FRANCKE, an award-winning author and
a former editor at *Newsweek,* has written *Ground Zero:
The Gender Wars in the Military; Growing Up Divorced;*
and *The Ambivalence of Abortion.* She has also worked with a
number of prominent women on their memoirs, including
Rosalynn Carter, Geraldine Ferraro, Jehan Sadat,
Benazir Bhutto, Diane von Furstenberg, and Queen Noor
of Jordan. She lives in Sagaponack, New York,
with her husband, Harvey Loomis, who accompanied
her on the trail of Saint Francis.